Series Editors:
Robert C. Pianta
Carollee Howes

ncrece
national center for research on early childhood education
SERIES

Dual Language Learners in the Early Childhood Classroom

Also in the *National Center for*
Research on Early Childhood Education Series:

Foundations for Teaching Excellence:
Connecting Early Childhood Quality Rating,
Professional Development, and Competency Systems in States
edited by Carollee Howes, Ph.D., and Robert C. Pianta, Ph.D.

The Promise of Pre-K
edited by Robert C. Pianta, Ph.D., and Carollee Howes, Ph.D.

Dual Language Learners in the Early Childhood Classroom

edited by

Carollee Howes, Ph.D.
University of California, Los Angeles

Jason T. Downer, Ph.D.
University of Virginia
Charlottesville

and

Robert C. Pianta, Ph.D.
University of Virginia
Charlottesville

·P A U L·H·
BROOKES
PUBLISHING CO.®

Baltimore • London • Sydney

·P A U L·H·
BROOKES
PUBLISHING C̣O.®

Paul H. Brookes Publishing Co.
Post Office Box 10624
Baltimore, Maryland 21285-0624
USA

www.brookespublishing.com

Book design by Erin Geoghegan.
Typeset by Aptara, Inc., Falls Church, Virginia.
Manufactured in the United States of America by
Versa Press, Inc., East Peoria, Illinois.

Supported in part by the Institute of Education Sciences, U.S. Department of Education,
through Grant R305A060021 to the University of Virginia. However, the content does
not necessarily reflect the position of the U.S. Department of Education, and no official
endorsement should be inferred.

Library of Congress Cataloging-in-Publication Data
Dual language learners in the early childhood classroom / edited by Carollee Howes, Jason
T. Downer, and Robert C. Pianta.
    p.   cm.—(National Center for Research on Early Childhood Education series; 3)
   Includes bibliographical references and index.
   ISBN-13: 978-1-59857-182-0
   ISBN-10: 1-59857-182-6
   1. Bilingualism in children—United States.   2. Language acquisition.   3. Early childhood
education—United States.   I. Howes, Carollee.   II. Downer, Jason.   III. Pianta, Robert C.
   P115.2.H68 2011
   372.65'1—dc22   2010054614

British Library Cataloguing in Publication data are available from the British Library.

2015   2014   2013   2012   2011

10   9   8   7   6   5   4   3   2   1

Contents

II Describing the Language and Literacy Practices in Classrooms with Dual Language Learners

Series Preface

The National Center for Research on Early Childhood Education (NCRECE) series on the future of early childhood education addresses key topics related to improving the quality of early childhood education in the United States. Each volume is a culmination of presentations and discussions taking place during the annual NCRECE Leadership Symposium, which brings together leaders and stakeholders in the field to discuss and synthesize the current knowledge about prominent issues that affect the educational experiences and outcomes of young children. Most important, it is the aim of these symposia, and the related series volumes, to be forward looking, identifying nascent topics that have the potential for improving the quality of early childhood education and then defining, analyzing, and charting conceptual, policy, practice, and research aims for the future. Topics to be addressed in subsequent volumes include the nature and quality of publicly funded preschool programs and the integration of quality rating systems, early childhood competencies, and models of professional development.

The series is designed to stimulate critical thinking around these key topics and to help inform future research agendas. The series should be of interest to a broad range of researchers, policy makers, teacher educators, and practitioners.

Robert C. Pianta, Ph.D.
Carollee Howes, Ph.D.

About the Editors

Carollee Howes, Ph.D., is the director of the Center for Improving Child Care Quality, Department of Education, and a professor of the Applied Developmental Psychology doctorate program at the University of California, Los Angeles. Dr. Howes is an internationally recognized developmental psychologist focusing on children's social and emotional development. She has served as a principal investigator on a number of seminal studies in early child care and preschool education, including the National Child Care Staffing Study; the Family and Relative Care Study; the Cost, Quality, and Outcomes Study; and the National Study of Child Care in Low Income Families. Dr. Howes has been active in public policy for children and families in California as well as across the United States. Her research focuses on children's experiences in child care, their concurrent and long-term outcomes from child care experiences, and child care quality and efforts to improve child care quality. Dr. Howes is the editor of *Teaching 4- to 8-Year-Olds: Literacy, Math, Multiculturalism, and Classroom Community* (Paul H. Brookes Publishing Co., 2003) and the coeditor of *The Promise of Pre-K* (Paul H. Brookes Publishing Co., 2009) and *Foundations for Teaching Excellence: Connecting Early Childhood Quality Rating, Professional Development, and Competency Systems in States* (Paul H. Brookes Publishing Co., 2011).

Jason T. Downer, Ph.D., is a senior research scientist at the University of Virginia's Center for Advanced Study of Teaching and Learning in Charlottesville. He is a clinical–community psychologist whose work focuses on the identification and understanding of contextual and relational contributors to young at-risk children's early achievement and social competence. Specifically, Dr. Downer is interested in the role of fathers in children's early learning, as well as the development of observational methods to capture valid, reliable estimates of teacher–child interactions in prekindergarten through elementary classrooms. Dr. Downer also has a keen interest in translating research-to-practice through school-based, classroom-focused interventions.

Robert C. Pianta, Ph.D., is the dean of the Curry School of Education, Novartis US Foundation Professor of Education, the director of the National Center for Research on Early Childhood Education, and the director of the Center for Advanced Study of Teaching and Learning at the University of Virginia in Charlottesville. A former special education teacher, Dr. Pianta is particularly interested in how relationships with teachers and parents, as well as classroom experiences, can help improve outcomes for at-risk children and youth. Dr. Pianta is a principal investigator on several major grants, including MyTeaching Partner, the Institute of Education Sciences Interdisciplinary Doctoral Training Program in Risk and Prevention, and the National Institute of Child Health and Human Development Study of Early Child Care and Youth Development. He was also a senior investigator for the National Center for Early Development and Learning and served as Editor of the *Journal of School Psychology.* He is the author of more than 300 journal articles, chapters, and books in the areas of early childhood development, transition to school, school readiness, and parent–child and teacher–child relationships, including *School Readiness and the Transition to Kindergarten in the Era of Accountability* (with Martha J. Cox & Kyle L. Snow, Paul H. Brookes Publishing Co., 2007) and *Classroom Assessment Scoring System™* (CLASS™; with Karen M. La Paro & Bridget K. Hamre, Paul H. Brookes Publishing Co., 2008), and the coeditor of *The Promise of Pre-K* (Paul H. Brookes Publishing Co., 2009) and *Foundations for Teaching Excellence: Connecting Early Childhood Quality Rating, Professional Development, and Competency Systems in States* (Paul H. Brookes Publishing Co., 2011). Dr. Pianta consults regularly with federal agencies, foundations, and universities.

About the Contributors

Sally Atkins-Burnett, Ph.D., M.Ed., is a senior researcher at Mathematica Policy Research. In her work on the Early Childhood Longitudinal Study–Kindergarten Class of 1998–99 and other longitudinal studies and program evaluations in diverse settings, Dr. Atkins-Burnett has developed many different measures of child outcomes and classroom processes and quality.

Margaret Caspe, Ph.D., Ed.M., is the associate director of Early Childhood Curriculum and Applied Research at the Children's Aid Society. She oversees teaching and learning in various early childhood programs throughout New York City and leads private-sector research and evaluation projects focused on how families and schools influence young children's language, literacy, and social-emotional development.

April D. Crawford, Ph.D., is a program manager with the Children's Learning Institute, part of the Department of Pediatrics at the University of Texas Health Science Center at Houston. Her research interests include understanding the extent to which institutional settings shape children's early learning experiences, whether programs aimed at quality improvement are differentially effective in a mixed-delivery early care system, and the development of observational systems for research and performance measurement. Dr. Crawford currently serves on projects examining the role of mentors in early childhood professional development, implementation of the Texas School Ready! program, and the development of the Texas School Readiness Certification System.

Katie Fallin, Ph.D., is the assistant director of research and evaluation at First 5 LA, a child advocacy organization funded through California tobacco tax revenues to improve the lives of young children in Los Angeles County. After earning her bachelor's degree in psychology from Scripps College, she received her master's and doctoral degrees in applied developmental psychology from Claremont Graduate University. In her current position, she oversees more than 40 research and evaluation projects on a range of topics, including preschool, transitional kindergarten, child abuse prevention, low birth weight prevention, and community strengthening.

Alexandra E. Figueras-Daniel, M.A., a research project coordinator at the National Institute for Early Education Research (NIEER), has overseen the collection of information and data on six major studies at NIEER, including one in Colombia, South America. She has also provided professional development to early childhood teachers and administrators regarding practices supportive of dual language acquisition. Previously, she worked as a teacher in a dual language early childhood education center in New Jersey's Abbott Preschool Program. She holds a bachelor's degree in American studies from Rutgers University and a master's degree in early childhood education from the Steinhardt School of Education at New York University. She is pursuing doctoral studies in early childhood education policy at Rutgers University.

Ellen Frede, Ph.D., is the co-director and a research professor at the National Institute for Early Education Research at Rutgers University. A developmental psychologist specializing in early childhood education, Dr. Frede is a researcher and teacher with experience in early childhood program implementation and state prekindergarten administration. Her research has primarily investigated the relationship of program quality to child outcomes. *Young English Language Learners: Current Research and Emerging Directions for Practice and Poilcy,* co-edited with Eugene García, is among her recent publications (Teachers College Press, 2010).

Margaret Freedson, Ed.D., is an assistant professor of early childhood, elementary, and literacy education at Montclair State University and a research fellow at the National Institute for Early Education Research at Rutgers University. Her research and publications examine bilingualism, early literacy development, and effective preschool practices for Spanish-speaking dual language learners and the preparation of early childhood teachers to serve multilingual, multicultural student populations. She is coauthor of the Classroom Assessment of Supports for Emergent Bilingual Acquisition—an observational rating scale that assesses preschool classroom supports for emergent bilingual acquisition—and it is the focus of her current research. She received her Ed.D. in language and literacy from the Harvard Graduate School of Education.

Allison Sidle Fuligni, Ph.D., is an assistant professor in the Department of Child and Family Studies at California State University, Los Angeles. Dr. Fuligni is a developmental psychologist with interests in understanding and improving the contextual influences on young children's development. Her research has focused on many topics, including poverty, child care, parenting, and early education interventions. She is a member of the Early Head Start Research Consortium and the study director of the LA ExCELS (Los Angeles: Exploring Children's Early Learning Settings) Study.

Eugene E. García, Ph.D., is a professor of education and the vice president for education partnerships at Arizona State University. He has published extensively in the areas of bilingual development of Hispanics and on the education of English language learning students in the United States.

Alison Hauser, M.A., earned her master's degree in child development from Tufts University and is a research analyst at the American Institutes for Research. Ms. Hauser currently serves as deputy project director for the evaluation of the First 5 LA School Readiness Initiative.

Kwanghee Jung, Ph.D., is an assistant research professor at the National Institute for Early Education Research (NIEER) at Rutgers University. Her research interests include program evaluation of prekindergarten, early childhood social and emotional development, young children of immigrant families, and program evaluation methodology. Recently, she and colleagues at NIEER have conducted evaluation studies of state-run prekindergarten programs in Arkanas, California, Michigan, New Jersey, New Mexico, Oklahoma, South Carolina, and West Virginia.

Youngok Jung, M.Ed., M.A., is a doctoral candidate at the University of California, Los Angeles.

Susan H. Landry, Ph.D., is a developmental psychologist and the Albert & Margaret Alkek Chair in Early Childhood in the Department of Pediatrics at the University of Texas Health Science Center at Houston. She is the director and founder of the Children's Learning Institute at the University of Texas as well as the director of the State Center for Early Childhood Development.

Carolyn Layzer, Ph.D., is a senior associate at Abt Associates, Inc. Dr. Layzer coauthored the Observation Measures of Language and Literacy Instruction—a state-of-the-art observation system for evaluating the quality of instructional practices in literacy and language development in early childhood programs. She has been responsible for the training and use of these observation measures in studies of language and literacy instruction (formal and informal) in preschool through early school years, in settings that include home, center, and public school. Dr. Layzer is an expert in the areas of literacy, curriculum, and instruction, with particular emphasis in reading, second language acquisition, and bilingual education.

Michael López, Ph.D, is the executive director of the National Center for Latino Child & Family Research, which is dedicated to research on issues relevant to practices and policies affecting the lives of Latino children and families. Previously, Dr. López directed the Child Outcomes Research and Evaluation team in the Administration for Children and Families, where he managed a number of large-scale national research projects, including the National Head Start Impact Study, a randomized study examining the impact of Head Start on children's school readiness. Dr. López's current work is focused on applied policy research and programmatic activities on such topics as language and literacy development, early childhood care and education, bilingual education, early childhood prevention and intervention programs, and young children's mental health, with an emphasis on at-risk, low-income, and/or culturally and linguistically diverse populations.

Karen Manship, M.A., is a research analyst in the Education, Human Development and the Workforce division at American Institutes for Research. Her work focuses on early childhood and K–12 education program evaluation, finance, and policy. She serves as the deputy project director for the evaluation of the First 5 LA Family Literacy Initiative Evaluation.

Kenyon R. Maree, M.Ed., spent 4 years working with many young dual language learners as a kindergarten paraprofessional. After completing a master's program in education policy, he began working for Abt Associates, Inc., where he focuses on K–12 education policy analysis and program evaluation as a senior analyst.

Deborah Parrish, M.A., is a vice president for the Education, Human Development and the Workforce division at the American Institutes for Research, with more than 25 years of combined research, evaluation, technical assistance, and early childhood and parent education teaching experience. Recently, she served as principal investigator for the 8-year Family Literacy Initiative Evaluation in Los Angeles County, a study of the implementation and child and family outcomes of four-component family literacy programs offering adult education, parent education, early childhood education, and parent and child interactive literacy activities. Ms. Parrish is a former preschool teacher and parent educator in a state-subsidized developmental preschool and parent education program.

Heather Quick, Ph.D., is a principal research scientist in the American Institutes for Research's Education, Human Development and the Workforce program focusing on family literacy, early childhood education programs, and school readiness. She serves as project director for the 8-year evaluation of the First 5 LA Family Literacy Initiative.

John Sideris, Ph.D., is a statistician at the FPG Child Development Institute. He has extensive experience in measurement analysis and longitudinal and mixed models. As an FPG statistician, he has been involved in many early childhood projects, including current projects developing new measures for child care quality and autism sensory experiences.

Emily J. Solari, Ph.D., is an assistant professor at the Children's Learning Institute at the University of Texas Health Science Center at Houston. Dr. Solari's research is focused on early interventions with at-risk populations, language and literacy development of English language learners, early identification and remediation of reading disabilities, text-level interventions for Spanish-speaking English language learners, cognitive development, and individual differences in children.

Susan Sprachman, M.A., is or has been the senior survey director on a number of early childhood projects conducted by Mathematica Policy Research, where she is a senior fellow. She specializes in taking complex early childhood projects and making it possible for field interviewers to collect the data—whether it is child assessments or classroom observations. She was part of the team that developed the Desired Results Developmental Profiles for the state of California and is the co-developer of the Language Interaction Snapshot (LISn). Ms. Sprachman has been at Mathematica Policy Research for 24 years, and before that she was at National Opinion Research Center, where she designed the training protocol for the first large-scale research study that included child assessments.

Virginia E. Vitiello, Ph.D., earned her doctoral degree in developmental psychology at the University of Miami. She spent a year at the Center for Advanced Study of Teaching and Learning at the University of Virginia as a research associate and is now the research and evaluation director at Teachstone, a nonprofit organization dedicated to measuring and improving classroom experiences in early childhood and elementary school classrooms.

Amanda P. Williford, Ph.D., is a senior research scientist at the Center for Advanced Study of Teaching and Learning at the University of Virginia. She is a licensed clinical psychologist specializing in young children's mental health. Her research interests focus on the developmental trajectories of children's disruptive behavior problems and early intervention strategies that promote children's readiness to enter kindergarten.

Tricia A. Zucker, Ph.D., is an assistant professor in the Children's Learning Institute, part of the Department of Pediatrics at the University of Texas Health Science Center at Houston. Her research interests include early identification and prevention of reading disabilities, early childhood curriculum and instruction, literacy and technology, family- and school-based interventions, and early childhood assessment. Dr. Zucker currently serves on research projects examining language and literacy development of dual language learners, the role of mentors in early childhood professional development, and implementing response to intervention frameworks in preschool.

Acknowledgments

We recognize that this book would not be possible without the dedication and hard work of the very wide and diverse range of people working in the field of early childhood education to support the development of young children. Scholars, child care professionals, teachers, parents, and administrators have all contributed to the "promise of pre-K" and should be remembered and appreciated daily for their work.

We also acknowledge the support of the Institute of Education Sciences, U.S. Department of Education, through Grant R305A060021 to the University of Virginia. We have been fortunate to have received support for the work involved in putting this volume together, and we especially recognize our program officer, Caroline Ebanks, for her help and advice.

Classroom Experiences and Learning Outcomes for Dual Language Learning Children

An Early Childhood Agenda for Educators and Policy Makers

Eugene E. García

Some 2–3 million children birth through age 8 in the United States are learning English as a second language (García & Jensen, 2009). The definitions and labels ascribed to these children can be confusing. Several terms are used in the literature to describe school children in the United States whose native language is other than English, the mainstream societal language in the United States (García, 2005). *Linguistic minority, limited English proficient*, and *English language learner* are common. In this volume and in this chapter, a variant of these terms is utilized—*dual language learner (DLL)*—as a way of emphasizing students' learning and progress in two languages at early ages of language development. Specifically, a recent analysis of young children identified as speaking a language other than English in the United States indicates that most children (85%) living in predominantly non-English environments are also exposed in a substantial manner to English (Hernández, Macartney, & Denton, 2010). These children are in dual language environments. The term acknowledges, emphasizes, and strategically recognizes that integrating children's knowledge, skills, and abilities related to two languages is central to the educational practices needed in early learning settings aimed at improving educational opportunities for DLLs.

This chapter provides a brief overview of the demography of English learners in U.S. schools, the educational circumstances of DLLs, and the challenges related to assessing the experiences and outcomes of early education for DLLs. In addition, an effort is made, in concert with all of the contributors in this volume, to address a practice and policy that would generate the types of data that would assist in determining the implementation and effects of early learning opportunities for young DLLs.

YOUNG DUAL LANGUAGE LEARNERS: WHO ARE THEY?

Young DLLs have been the fastest growing student population in the country over the past few decades, due primarily to increased rates in immigration. As of 2005, one in five children ages 5–17 in the United States had a foreign-born parent (Capps et al., 2005), and many of these children learn English as a second language, though not all. Whereas the overall child population speaking a non-English native language in the United States rose from 6% in 1979 to 14% in 1999 (National Clearinghouse for English Language Acquisition, 2006), and the number of language minority students in K–12 schools has been recently estimated to be more than 14 million (August 2006), the representation of DLLs in U.S. schools has its highest concentration in early education. This is because most DLL children attending U.S. public school since entry develop oral and academic English proficiency by Grade 3. The DLL share of students from prekindergarten (pre-K) to Grade 5, for example, rose from 4.7% to 7.4% from 1980 to 2000, whereas the DLL share of students in Grades 6–12 rose from 3.1% to 5.5% over this same time span (Capps et al., 2005).

Assessing the development of young DLLs demands an understanding of who these children are in terms of their linguistic and cognitive development, as well as the social and cultural contexts in which they are raised. The key distinguishing feature of these children is their non–English-language background. In addition to linguistic background, other important attributes of DLL children include their ethnic, immigrant, and socioeconomic histories (Abedi, Hofstetter, & Lord, 2004; Capps et al., 2005; Figueroa & Hernández, 2000; Hernández et al., 2010). Though diverse in their origins, DLL students, on average, are more likely than their native English-speaking peers to have an immigrant parent, to live in low-income families, and to be raised in cultural contexts that do not reflect mainstream norms in the United States (Capps et al., 2005; Hernández et al., 2010).

Young DLLs represent diverse ethnic backgrounds. In the most recent census, approximately four in five DLLs were from Spanish-speaking homes, followed by Vietnamese (2%), Hmong (1.6%), Cantonese (1%), Korean (1%), and many more native and foreign languages. Although a majority of Hispanic DLLs are of Mexican origin (approximately 7 in 10), substantial proportions have origins in Puerto Rico, Central America, South America, Cuba, and the Dominican Republic (Hernández, 2006). Within and among these groups, DLL children represent diverse social and cultural customs and histories, which are essential to consider thoroughly when assessing the child's linguistic, cognitive, social, and emotional development within home and school contexts.

Finally, it is important to consider the socioeconomic status of English language learners, including family income as well as the amount of educational capital (i.e., parental education) in the home. In 2000, 68% of DLLs in pre-K to Grade 5 were in low-income families (defined as family income below 185% of the federal poverty level), compared with 36% of English-proficient children in the same grades (Capps et al., 2005; Hernández et al., 2010). Moreover, nearly half of DLL children in elementary school had parents with less than high school educations in 2000, compared with 9% of parents of English-proficient children. A quarter of DLL elementary school students had parents with less than ninth-grade educations, compared with 2% of parents of English-proficient students (Hernández et al., 2010). Parent education levels are important indices, as they influence language and educational practices in the home and therefore the development of skills valued in U.S. schools.

EDUCATIONAL CIRCUMSTANCES

The academic performance patterns of DLL students as a whole cannot be adequately understood without considering their social and economic characteristics in comparison with native English speakers, in addition to the institutional history of U.S. schools (Jensen, 2008). Although a great deal of socioeconomic variation exists among DLLs, they are more likely than native English-speaking children, on average, to live in poverty and to have parents with limited formal education (García & Cuellar, 2006). In addition, DLL students are more likely to be an ethnic/racial minority (Capps et al., 2005). Each of these factors—low income, low parent education, and ethnic/racial minority status—decreases group achievement averages across academic areas, leading to the relatively low performance of DLL students.

In their analyses of a national dataset of elementary academic performance in early elementary school, Reardon and Galindo (2006) found reading and mathematics achievement patterns from kindergarten through third grade to vary by home language environments among Hispanic students. Those living in homes categorized as "primarily Spanish" or "Spanish only" lagged further behind Caucasian children than did Hispanics who lived in homes in which primarily English or English only was spoken. Given the associations among educational risk factors for DLL students, the impact of language background on achievement outcomes should be contextualized. The interrelationship of risk variables has been documented in several reports (Collier, 1987; Jensen, 2007). In a separate analysis of the same national dataset, Jensen (2007) compared Spanish-speaking kindergarteners with their general education peers on a number of outcomes, including socioeconomic status (SES), parent education, and mathematics achievement. He found that Spanish-speaking kindergarteners, on average, scored four fifths of a standard deviation lower than the general body of kindergarteners in mathematics. They also fared an entire standard deviation below their peers in terms of SES and maternal educational attainment. Nearly half of the kindergarteners from Spanish-speaking homes had mothers who had not completed high school.

Thus, rather than pointing to one or two student background factors that account for the low achievement of DLL students, it should be understood that educational risk, in general, is attributable to a myriad of interrelated out-of-school factors, including parent education levels, family income, parent English language proficiency, mother's marital status at the time of birth, and single- versus dual-parent homes (National Center for Education Statistics, 1995). The more risk factors the child is subject to, the lower the probability the child will do well in school in terms of learning and attainment in the standard educational environment. Because DLL children, on average, exhibit three of the five risk factors at higher rates than native English speakers, they are generally at greater risk for academic underachievement (Hernández, Denton, & Macartney, 2008). Using Census 2000 data, Capps and colleagues (2005) found that 68% of DLL students in pre-K through fifth grade lived in low-income families, compared to 36% of English-proficient children. The percentages changed to 60% and 32%, respectively, for 6th- to 12th-grade students. Moreover, 48% of DLL children in pre-K through fifth grade and 35% of English language learners in the higher grades had a parent with less than a high school education, compared with 11% and 9% of English-proficient children in the same grades (Capps et al., 2005).

LANGUAGE, SCHOOLING, AND BEST PRACTICES

Available Programs

There are many possible program options for young bilingual students and children learning English as a second language—these carry various titles, including *transitional bilingual education, maintenance bilingual education, 90–10 bilingual education, 50–50 bilingual education, developmental bilingual education, dual-language, two-way immersion, English-as-a-second-language, English immersion, sheltered English, structured English, submersion,* and so forth. These programs differ in the ways in which they use the native language and English during instruction (Ovando, Collier, & Combs, 2006). They also differ in terms of theoretical rationale, language goals, cultural goals, academic goals, student characteristics, ages served, entry grades, length of student participation, participation of mainstream teachers, teacher qualifications, and instructional materials (García, 2005; Genesee, 2010). The extent to which a program is successful depends on local conditions, choices, and innovations.

Because sociodemographic conditions differ—and local and state policies demand assorted objectives from their schools and teachers—no single program works best in every situation. When selecting a program, one of the most fundamental decisions should be whether bilingual proficiency is an objective. Clearly, given the cognitive and economic advantages of bilingual proficiency in a world that is becoming increasingly globalized, promoting bilingualism is an intuitive ambition (García & Jensen, 2009). However, the development of balanced bilingualism depends on state and local policies as well as the availability of teachers and course curricula to meet the need. Indeed, the feasibility of bilingual promotion varies between schools.

A second feature that should be considered when selecting a program designed for DLLs is optimizing individual achievement and literacy development. Academic performance continues to be the driving force behind educational policy reform and practice in the United States, and programs developed for young DLLs should strive to reduce achievement gaps. It is additionally important, however, that programs support the development of the whole child, simultaneously sustaining the cognitive, social, emotional, and psychological development of children—a holistic approach is especially important during the early years (i.e., pre-K–3) of schooling (Zigler, Gilliam, & Jones, 2006).

Decades of research support the notion that children can competently acquire two or more languages (Espinosa, 2010). The acquisition of these languages can be parallel but need not be. That is, the qualitative character of one language may lag behind, surge ahead of, or develop equally with the other language. Moreover, the relationship of linguistic properties between languages is quite complex. Several theories have been put forward to explain how language and literacy develop for young children managing two or more linguistic systems. Currently, among the available theoretical approaches, transfer theory is the most widely accepted to explain the language development of young bilingual and emergent bilingual Hispanics. This theoretical position asserts that language skills from the first language transfer to the second. In like manner, errors or interference in second-language production occur when grammatical differences between the two languages are present. However, not all aspects of second-language development are affected by the first language. Language that is contextually embedded and cognitively undemanding—or automatic, overlearned interaction—does not lend itself well to transfer (García & Jensen, 2009). This is the language involved in day-to-day interpersonal communication. Research shows that contextually reduced and cognitively demanding linguistic skills, on the other hand, transfer between languages (August & Shanahan, 2006; Genesee, 1999). Higher order cognitive skills relevant to academic content are more developmentally interdependent and therefore amenable to transfer.

Bringing together the disciplines of psychology, semiotics, education, sociology, and anthropology, sociocultural theory has become an important way of understanding issues of language, cognition, culture, human development, and teaching and learning (García, 2005). This approach posits that children's linguistic, cognitive, and social character are fundamentally connected and interrelated. A child's basic cognitive framework is shaped by his or her native language, early linguistic experiences, and cultural context. Children from non–English-speaking homes often must adjust their cognitive and linguistic representations to negotiate social exchanges within the school environment. Though research in this area is limited, extant best practices (Goldenberg, Rueda, & August, 2006) suggest that bridging home–school sociocultural differences can enhance students' engagement and level of participation in classroom instruction. As home linguistic interactions (which vary by SES indicators—e.g., parent education) and teacher practices, perspectives, and expectations influence the development of literacy skills, children whose teachers recognize and take full advantage of home resources (including child's home language and cultural practices) and parental supports tend to experience more optimal outcomes.

Given the demographic circumstances of young DLL children in the United States, the development of school programs and practices that recognize the conditions and strengths of DLL children and families is crucial. Because three in four young Hispanic children are exposed to Spanish in the home, and even more are exposed to Spanish through relatives, neighbors, or both, ways in which these programs integrate language in teaching and learning are important. Young Hispanic children, on average, lag substantially behind their Asian American and Caucasian peers in terms of academic achievement; differences are quite large at the beginning of kindergarten, and the gap closes very little thereafter. Within the Hispanic population, first- and second-generation children and those of Mexican and Central American origins demonstrate the lowest achievement levels—influenced by multiple out-of-school factors, including SES, low parent education, limited English proficiency of parents, and other home circumstances (National Task Force on the Early Education for Hispanics, 2007).

Educational practices in the home are important to evaluate because they have a bearing on children's early cognitive development and therefore influence school readiness and sustained academic performance. The amount of language (regardless of the particular linguistic system) used in the home has been found to be strongly associated with early literacy and cognitive development. More specifically, research indicates that the amount of "extra" talk between caregivers and their children, book reading, and parent–child interactions (e.g., reading, telling stories, singing) influence early development. This is an important consideration, because low-income families are less likely, on average, to engage in these activities—DLL parents are less likely than non-DLL parents to read, tell stories, and sing to their children (National Task Force on the Early Education for Hispanics, 2007).

Schooling program options for young DLLs differ in terms of their goals, requirements for staff competency, and the student populations they are meant to serve. The effectiveness of a given program depends on local conditions, choices, and innovations. In terms of student achievement outcomes, meta-analyses and best evidence syntheses suggest that programs supporting bilingual approaches to curriculum and instruction are favorable to English-only or English immersion programs. These programs provide sound instruction in both Spanish and English.

Driven by sociocultural notions of language and learning, dual language (DL), or two-way immersion programs—a particular approach to bilingual education—include language minority and language majority students in the same classroom. Educators in DL programs use English-plus-Spanish (EPS) approaches to teach both languages through course content. Studies suggest that students (from multiple language backgrounds) in DL programs perform at equal levels as their peers and, in many cases, outperform those in other programs. More research is needed to assess the effectiveness of programs that incorporate EPS strategies for the various segments of the Hispanic child population.

Preliminary evidence suggests that prekindergarten programs (for students 3 and 4 years old) can increase early learning for young DLL children. High-quality pre-K programs can improve school readiness for young Hispanic children and decrease achievement differences between racial/ethnic groups at kindergarten entry. Further research evaluating the longitudinal benefits and curricular and instructional strategies of preschool programs serving young Hispanic populations is needed.

THE CHALLENGE OF ASSESSING DUAL LANGUAGE LEARNERS IN EARLY EDUCATION SETTINGS

The increasing demand for evaluation, assessment, and accountability in early education, including preschool through Grade 3, comes at a time when the fastest growing student population in the country is children whose home language is not English. This presents several challenges to practitioners and school systems generally who may be unfamiliar with important concepts such as second language acquisition, acculturation, and the role of socioeconomic background as they relate to test development, administration, and interpretation. Because assessment is key in developing and implementing effective curricular and instructional strategies that promote child development and learning, young DLLs children should be included in all assessments in an appropriate manner. Through such assessments, teachers can personalize instruction, make adjustments to classroom activities, assign children to appropriate program placements, and have more informed communication with parents. Also, systems need to know how young DLLs are performing in order to make proper adjustments and policy changes. However, there is a lack of adequate instruments to use with young DLLs, especially considering the hundreds of languages represented in the United States. Some assessments exist in Spanish, but most lack the technical qualities of high-quality assessment tools. In addition, there is a shortage of bilingual professionals with the skills necessary to evaluate these children and conceptual and empirical work systematically linking context with student learning.

ASSESSMENT ISSUES

Young DLLs have the right to benefit from the potential advantages of assessment. The current empirical knowledge base and the legal and ethical standards are limited yet sufficient to improve ways in which young DLLs are assessed. Improvements will require commitments from policy makers and practitioners to implement appropriate assessment tools and procedures, to link assessment results to improved practices, and to utilize trained staff capable of carrying out these tasks. Researchers and scholars can facilitate the improvement of assessment practices by continuing to evaluate implementation strategies in schools and by developing systematic assessments of contextual factors relevant to linguistic and cognitive development. Assessments of contextual processes will be necessary if current assessment strategies, which largely focus on the individual, are to improve classroom instruction, curricular content, and therefore student learning (Rueda, 2007; Rueda & Yaden, 2006; Snow & Van Hemel, 2009).

Why Assess

Several skills and developmental abilities of young children are assessed in early education programs, including in preschool and the first few elementary school years. Sensing an increase in demand for greater accountability and enhanced educational performance of young children, the National Education Goals Panel developed a list of principles to guide early educators through appropriate and scientifically sound assessment practices (Shepard, Kagan, & Wurtz, 1998). Moreover, the National Research

Council Panel (Snow & Van Hemel, 2009) presented four purposes for assessing young children: 1) to promote children's learning and development; 2) to identify children for health and special services; 3) to monitor trends and evaluate programs and services; and 4) to assess academic achievement to hold individual students, teachers, and schools accountable (i.e., high-stakes testing).

Ethical Issues

The impetus for appropriate and responsive assessment practices of young DLLs is supported by a number of ethical standards and guidelines. These include standards written jointly by the American Psychological Association (APA), the American Educational Research Association (AERA), and the National Council on Measurement in Education (NCME) titled *Standards for Educational and Psychological Testing* (1999). This professional document includes a specific discussion of the assessment parameters relevant to children from diverse linguistic backgrounds, addressing the irrelevance of many psychoeducational tests developed for and normed with monolingual, English-speaking children.

The standards presented by APA, AERA, and NCME have outpaced present policy, practice, research, and assessment tool development (Figueroa & Hernández, 2000). However, in a notable exception, the federal Individuals with Disabilities Education Improvement Act of 2004 (PL 108-446) does provide particular requirements related to the assessment of DLLs. It requires, for example, the involvement of parents/guardians in the assessment process as well as a consideration of the child's native language in assessment. Unlike ethical guidelines, which often represent professional aspirations and are not necessarily enforceable, public law requires compliance. The Office of Civil Rights is given the charge of evaluating compliance with federal law and, where necessary, auditing public programs engaged in assessment practices and interpretations of DLLs and other minority children.

Use and Misuse

Several domains of development are assessed during the early childhood years. These include cognitive (or intellectual), linguistic, socioemotional (or behavioral), motor, and adaptive (or daily living) skills, as well as hearing, vision, and health factors. Educational settings are primarily concerned, however, with the cognitive, academic, and linguistic development of children. In addition to the concerns that afflict the assessment of all young children, there are central issues inherent in the assessment of young children from non–English-language backgrounds. Implementation research suggests that assessment practices with young DLLs continue to lag behind established legal requirements and ethical standards set forth by the federal government and the APA, AERA, and NCME. In part, this lapse is due to 1) a lack of available instruments normed on representative samples of English language learners, 2) inadequate professional development and training, and 3) insufficient research to inform best practice. Such is the case for the assessment of language, cognitive skills, academic achievement, and other areas of educational "classroom" intervention.

In the early learning enterprise, DLLs need to be exposed to multiple developmental opportunities related to language, cognition, and social and physical enhancement in unstructured and structured environments. These should allow children to utilize and develop language(s) that serve to promote academic achievement, as well as overall student development. To do so, it is imperative that teachers optimize students' opportunities in the classroom to practice meaningful academic language. "An interactive classroom ensures that English Language Learners will use the language, experiment with it, and gain confidence in their ability to communicate as time progresses" (García, 2005, p. 92). Instruments like those provided in this volume address in a significant way two types of interaction within the classroom: student–student interaction and student–teacher interaction. It is imperative that interactions are within optimal conditions for second-language acquisition. These optimal conditions include access for DLLs to native and proficient English speakers (Peregoy & Boyle, 2008).

Student–student interaction can be accomplished through group work such as working in pairs, literature circles, think-pair-share, cooperative learning, and related inquiry-based opportunities. Group work for DLLs increases their language practice, improves the quality of student talk, benefits individualized instruction, promotes positive affective climate, and motivates the classroom learners (National Task Force on the Early Education of Hispanics, 2007). Students interacting with other students in the classroom will be able to monitor and adjust their speech to mirror native speakers to be understood in addition to getting their ideas across in a conversation. This process is called negotiation of meaning, which is the "trial-and-error process of give-and-take in communication as people try to understand and be understood" (Perogoy & Boyle, 2008, p. 26). When students are provided opportunities to work with one another on academic tasks, this can motivate students because they are "asking and answering questions, negotiating meaning, clarifying ideas, giving and justifying opinions, and more" (Echevarria, Vogt, & Short, 2008, p. 21). DLLs benefit from student interaction that will allow them to work in a nonthreatening environment to improve their oral development through language practice.

Classrooms that utilize language-rich environments allow English language learners to accelerate their oral and academic language through meaningful learning experiences. Teachers can also encourage students to elaborate on their responses by using a variety of techniques. Some of the techniques include having teachers ask students to expand on their thoughts, encouraging more language use by asking direct questions, providing restatements, and allowing pause time for students to process the information (Echevarria et al., 2008). Teachers also need to take into consideration second-language acquisition strategies that promote language teaching practices: "(1) focus on communication, not grammatical form; (2) allow students a silent period, rather than forcing immediate speech production; and (3) create a low-anxiety environment" (Perogoy & Boyle, 2008, p. 55). The classroom assessments empirically tested and described in this volume are making new and important advances specific to the assessment of the educational circumstances of young DLLs.

PRINCIPLES IN THE ASSESSMENT OF DUAL LANGUAGE LEARNERS IN EARLY EDUCATION SETTINGS

The gap between current *practice* in the assessment of young English language learners in the United States and the *standards* set forth through research, policy, and ethics is largely a function of the gap between practical and optimal realities. Due to the many demands and constraints placed on teachers and schools from local, state, and federal governments, including budgeting responsibilities and the many programs implemented each school year, it can be extremely challenging to keep pace with best practices and ethical standards (Snow & Van Hemel, 2009). However, given the large and increasing size of the young DLL child population in the United States, the current focus on testing and accountability, and the documented deficits in current assessment practices, improvements are critical. These improvements are necessary at all phases of the assessment process, including preassessment and assessment planning, conducting the assessment, analyzing interpreting the results, reporting the results (in written and oral format), and determining eligibility and monitoring.

Researchers and organizational bodies have offered principles for practitioners engaged in the assessment of young DLLs. Among the most comprehensive comes a list from the National Association for the Education of Young Children (NAEYC; Clifford & Morgan, 2005). Included as a supplement to the NAEYC position statement on early childhood curriculum, assessment, and program evaluation, Clifford et al. present seven detailed recommendations "to increase the probability that all young English language learners will have the benefit of appropriate, effective assessment of their learning and development" (p. 1). The last of these recommendations concerns further needs (i.e., research and practice) in the field, which is covered here subsequently. Because these recommendations—presented here as *principles*—materialized as a collaborative effort from a committee comprising more than a dozen researchers in the field, they are quite representative of recommendations found in the literature.

First, *assessment instruments and procedures are used for appropriate purposes.* Screening tools should result in needed supports and services and, if necessary, further assessment. Assessments should be used fundamentally to support learning, including language and academic learning. For research, evaluation, and accountability purposes, young DLLs should be included in assessments.

Second, *assessments should be linguistically and culturally appropriate.* This means assessment tools and procedures should be aligned with cultural and linguistic characteristics of the child. When a test is translated from its original language to that of the native language of the DLL child, it should be culturally and linguistically validated to verify the relevance of the content (i.e., content validity) and the construct purported to be measured (i.e., construct validity). Observation protocols and their analysis should be responsive to language and cultural diversity.

Third, *the primary purpose of assessment should be to improve instruction.* The assessment of student outcomes using appropriate tools and procedures should be linked closely to classroom processes. This means relying on multiple methods and measures, evaluating outcomes over time, and using collaborative assessment teams, including the teacher, who is a critical agent for improved learning and development. Assessment that systematically informs improved curriculum and instruction is the most useful.

Fourth, *caution ought to be used when developing and interpreting standardized formal assessments.* It is important that young DLLs are included in large-scale assessments and that these instruments continue to be used to improve educational practices and placements. However, those administering and interpreting these assessments should use caution. Assessment development issues—including equivalence, translation, and validity indicators—must be scrutinized.

Fifth, *those engaged in the assessment process should have cultural and linguistic competence.* This may be the most challenging of the recommendations. Professional development and training of teachers, observers, school psychologists, and unit administrators constitutes a long-term goal that will demand ongoing funding and implementation research. Those assessing young DLLs should be bicultural, bilingual, and be knowledgeable about second-language acquisition. In many cases, consultants and interpreters are used where the supply of school personnel possessing these qualifications is limited. Implementation research is needed to understand best practices in working with consultants and interpreters through the preassessment and assessment planning, conducting the assessment, analyzing the results, reporting the results (in written and oral format), and determining eligibility and monitoring.

Finally, *families should play critical roles in the assessment development, implementation, and interpretation.* Ethically and in some cases legally, parents should be included in the decision-making process regarding many aspects of their children's educational experiences. Moreover, the educational benefit of a quality assessment process for a given child is optimal when parents' wishes are voiced and considered throughout. Particularly for DLLs, given the linguistic and cultural diversity of the population, families should be encouraged to be involved in development/selection, implementation, and interpretation of all forms of assessments. The process and results of assessment should be explained to parents in a way that is meaningful and easily understandable.

FUTURE DIRECTIONS FOR RESEARCH, PRACTICE, AND POLICY

As mentioned, there is a gap between current assessment practice of young DLLs and what the research and the legal and ethical standards suggest is best practice. It is important, therefore, that research and practice continue an ongoing dialogue to improve this scenario. There are three ways in which researchers and scholars will be able to engage assessment scholarship to this end, and support and necessary funding should be provided by policy makers, institutions of higher education, and other research programs to pursue this course.

First, the field needs more assessment developed especially for young DLLs. Many of the contributions to this volume provide important foundational efforts that support this type of development. This effort will continue to require a bottom-up approach, meaning assessment tools, procedures, and factor analytic structures are aligned with cultural and linguistic characteristics of DLL children, as opposed to top-down approaches, where, for example, test items are simply translated from their original language to the native languages of young DLLs.

Second, it is time that conceptual and empirical work on student assessment move beyond the individual level. Again, this volume is a testament to this effort. It has become clear that processes outside the individual—including within the classroom (e.g., teacher–student interactions, peer–peer interactions), within the home (e.g., frequency of words spoken, amount of books), and within the school (e.g., language instruction policies)—affect learning, and the field currently lacks conceptual frameworks and the measures necessary to move this research forward to systematically improve student learning. Preliminary research on the role of context in learning suggests that various environmental factors can increase student engagement and participation (Christenson, 2004; Goldenberg et al., 2006), which in turn can lead to increased learning, and that the influence of contextual contingencies on learning outcomes is mediated by children's motivation to learn (Rueda, 2007; Rueda, MacGillivray, Monzó & Arzubiaga, 2001; Rueda & Yaden, 2006). Conceptual frameworks should account for the multilevel nature of contexts, including the nesting of individuals within classrooms and families, classrooms within schools, and schools within school districts, communities, and institutions. Moreover, the role of culture and the feasibility of cultural congruence across within- and out-of-school contexts will be important to this work. Meaningful empirical work in this area will require the convergence of research methods (e.g., multilevel statistics and the mixing of qualitative approaches with quasi-experimental designs) and social science disciplines (e.g., cognitive psychology, educational anthropology, sociology of education).

Finally, more research documenting the current scenario of the assessment of young DLLs across the country is needed. As the population of young DLLs continues to grow and disperse to states with historically low representations of DLL students, more work is needed to evaluate assessment practices in their localities. Research and observational approaches will be needed to document practices in preassessment and assessment planning, conducting the assessment itself, analyzing the results, and reporting the results (in written and oral format). This work will aid the development of strategies to train professionals with the skills necessary to serve young DLL children and will help move the overall field of DLL early education forward.

STUDY QUESTIONS

1. What key features of language and culture need to be considered in assessments related to DLLs?

2. How is the "transitional" (moving from native language to English) nature of native language development and English acquisition addressed in assessing DLLs?

3. What local, state, and federal policies come into play with regard to the assessment of quality services to DLLs?

REFERENCES

Abedi, J., Hofstetter, C.H., & Lord, C. (2004). Assessment accommodations for English-language learners: Implications for policy-based empirical research. *Review of Educational Research, 74*(1), 1–28.

American Educational Research Association, American Psychological Association, & National Council on Measurement in Education. (1999). *Testing and assessment:*

The standards for educational and psychological testing. Washington, DC: American Educational Research Association. Retrieved from http://www.apa.org/science/standards.html.

August, D. (2006). Demographic overview. In D. August & T. Shanahan (Eds.), *Report of the National Literacy Panel on language minority youth and children.* Mahwah, NJ: Lawrence Erlbaum Associates.

August, D., & Shanahan, T. (Eds.). (2006). *Report of the National Literacy Panel on language minority youth and children.* Mahwah, NJ: Lawrence Erlbaum Associates.

Capps, R., Fix, M., Murray, J., Ost, J., Passel, J.S., & Herwantoro, S. (2005). *The new demography of America's schools: Immigration and the No Child Left Behind Act.* Washington, DC: The Urban Institute.

Christenson, S.L. (2004). The family-school partnership: An opportunity to promote learning and competence of all students. *School Psychology Review, 33*(1), 83–104.

Clifford, D., & Morgan, J. (2005). *Screening and assessment of young English-language learners.* Washington, DC: National Association for the Education of Young Children. Retrieved from http://www.naeyc.org/about/positions/ELL_Supplement.asp.

Collier, V.P. (1987). Age and rate of acquisition of second language for academic purposes. *TESOL Quarterly, 21*(4), 617–641.

Echevarria, J., Vogt, M., & Short, D.J. (2004). *Making content comprehensible for English language learners: The SIOP model* (2nd ed.). Boston: Allyn & Bacon.

Espinosa, L.M. (2010). Assessment of English language learners. In E.E. García & E.C. Frede (Eds.), *Young English language learners* (pp. 119–143). New York: Teachers College Press.

Figueroa, R.A., & Hernández, S. (2000). *Testing Hispanic students in the United States: Technical and policy issues.* Washington, DC: President's Advisory Commission on Educational Excellence for Hispanic Americans.

García, E.E. (2005). *Teaching and learning in two languages: Bilingualism and schooling in the United States.* New York: Teachers College Press.

García, E.E., & Cuellar, D. (2006). Who are these linguistically and culturally diverse students? *Teachers College Record, 108*(11), 2220–2246.

García, E.E., & Jensen, B.T. (2009). *Language development and early education of young Hispanic children in the United States.*

Genesee, F. (Ed.). (1999). *Program alternatives for linguistically diverse students.* Berkeley: University of California, Center for Research on Education, Diversity & Excellence.

Genesee, F. (2010). Dual language development in preschool children. In E.E. García & E.C. Frede (Eds.), *Young English language learners* (pp. 59–79). New York: Teachers College Press.

Goldenberg, C., Rueda, R., & August, D. (2006). Synthesis: Sociocultural contexts and literacy development. In D. August & T. Shanahan (Eds.), *Report of the National Literacy Panel on language minority youth and children.* Mahwah, NJ: Lawrence Erlbaum Associates.

Hernández, D. (2006). *Young Hispanic children in the U.S.: A demographics portrait based on Census 2000. Report to the National Task Force on Early Childhood Education for Hispanics.* Tempe: Arizona State University.

Hernández, D.J., Denton, N.A., & Macartney, S.E. (2008). Children in immigrant families: Looking to America's future. *Social Policy Report: A Publication of the Society for Research in Child Development, 22*(3), 1–24.

Hernández, D., Macartney, S., & Denton, N.A. (2010). A demographic portrait of young English language learners. In E.E. García & E.C. Frede (Eds.), *Young English language learners* (pp. 10–41). New York: Teachers College Press.

Individuals with Disabilities Education Improvement Act (IDEA) of 2004, PL 108-446, 20 U.S.C. §§ 1400 *et seq.*

Jensen, B.T. (2007). The relationship between Spanish use in the classroom and the mathematics achievement of Spanish-speaking kindergarteners. *Journal of Latinos and Education, 6*(3), 267–280.

Jensen, B.T. (2008, April). *Understanding differences in binational reading development: Comparing Mexican and U.S. Hispanic students.* Paper presented at the annual meeting for the American Educational Research Association, New York City.

National Center for Education Statistics. (1995). *Approaching kindergarten: A look at preschoolers in the United States. National household survey.* Washington, DC: U.S. Department of Education, Office of Educational Research and Improvement.

National Clearinghouse for English Language Acquisition. (2006). *The growing numbers of limited English proficient students: 1993/94–2003/04.* Washington, DC: U.S. Department of Education, Office of English Language Acquisition.

National Task Force on Early Childhood Education for Hispanics. (2007). *Para nuestros niños: Expanding and improving early childhood education for Hispanics—Main report.* Tempe, AZ. Retrieved September 15, 2008, from http://www.ecehispanic.org/work/expand_MainReport.pdf.

Ovando, C.J., Collier, V.P., & Combs, M.C. (2006). *Bilingual and ESL classrooms: Teaching in multicultural contexts* (4th ed.). Boston: McGraw-Hill.

Peregoy, S., & Boyle, O. (2008). *Reading, writing, and learning in ESL* (5th ed.). Boston: Allyn & Bacon.

Reardon, S., & Galindo, C. (2006, April 11). *K–3 academic achievement patterns and trajectories of Hispanics and other racial/ethnic groups.* Paper presented at the Annual AERA Conference, San Francisco.

Rueda, R. (2007, April). *Motivation, learning, and assessment of English learners.* Paper presented at the California State University, Northridge School of Education.

Rueda, R., MacGillivray, L., Monzó, L., & Arzubiaga, A. (2001). Engaged reading: A multi-level approach to considering sociocultural features with diverse learners. In D. McInerny & S. Van Etten (Eds.), *Research on sociocultural influences on motivation and learning* (pp. 233–264). Greenwich, CT: Information Age.

Rueda, R., & Yaden, D. (2006). The literacy education of linguistically and culturally diverse young children: An overview of outcomes, assessment, and large-scale interventions. In B. Spodek & O.N. Saracho (Eds.), *Handbook of research on the education of young children* (2nd ed., pp. 167–186). Mahwah, NJ: Lawrence Erlbaum Associates.

Shepard, L., Kagan, S.L., & Wurtz, L. (Eds.). (1998). *Principles and recommendations for early childhood assessments.* Washington, DC: National Education Goals Panel, Goal 1 Early Childhood Assessments Resource Group. Retrieved March 10, 2010, from http://eric.ed.gov/ERICDocs/data/ericdocs2/content_storage_01/0000000b/80/24/51/e6.pdf

Snow, C.E. & Van Hemel, S.B. (Eds.). (2009). *Early childhood assessment: Why, what, and how.* Washington, DC: National Academies Press.

Zigler, E., Gilliam, W.S., & Jones, S.M. (2006). *A vision for universal preschool education.* New York: Cambridge University Press.

I

Describing the Classroom Experiences of Dual Language Learners

1

Experiences of Low-Income Dual Language Learning Preschoolers in Diverse Early Learning Settings

Allison Sidle Fuligni and Carollee Howes

Children from low-income families and those whose home language is not English face multiple challenges when entering formal schooling in kindergarten. Numerous early education programs have been developed to help increase these children's school readiness, and an extensive body of research suggests that the most high quality and intentionally delivered of these programs can have lasting positive effects on the school achievement and later outcomes for at-risk children (e.g., Howes et al., 2008; Loeb, Fuller, Kagan, & Carrol, 2004; Love et al., 2002; NICHD Early Child Care Research Network, 2000; Schweinhart, Barnes, Weikart, Barnett, & Epstein, 1993; Votruba-Drzal, Coley, & Chase-Lansdale, 2004).

Note: Information in this chapter was presented at the National Center for Research on Early Childhood Education Third Annual Leadership Symposium: Investigating the Classroom Experiences of Young Dual-Language Learners, November 3, 2009, Arlington, Virginia.

The research reported in this chapter was supported through the Interagency School Readiness Consortium (NICHD, ACF, ASPE; Grant Number: 5-R01-HD046063). The authors wish to acknowledge the other senior members of the study team: Dr. Sandraluz Lara-Cinisomo, University of North Carolina, Charlotte, and Dr. Lynn Karoly, RAND Corporation.

This chapter was prepared with partial support from the National Center for Research on Early Childhood Education (NCRECE). It was supported by Grant R305A060021, administered by the Institute of Education Sciences, U.S. Department of Education. However, the contents do not necessarily represent the positions or policies of the U.S. Department of Education or NCRECE, and endorsement by the federal government or NCRECE should not be assumed.

In Southern California, the concern of educators about the school readiness of language-minority children is particularly strong. School districts must address the learning needs of large numbers of children from immigrant families. In Los Angeles, the predominant language of minority families is Spanish, but there are numerous students attending Los Angeles schools with other non-English home languages. Language census reports conducted by the Los Angeles Unified School District (2006) indicated that in 2006 there were 250,575 English language learners (ELLs) in the school district, 94% of whom were Spanish speaking. Knowing Spanish rather than English has implications for school readiness and achievement, especially for children who attend English monolingual schools, the mandated norm in California. Children who do not speak English must learn English vocabulary, grammar, and literacy skills while they learn the constructs and content of other academic subjects. In doing so, ELLs may fall behind in learning more complex conceptual skills that they will need in later academics, causing them further difficulties (Droop & Verhoeven, 2003; Suarez-Orozco & Suarez-Orozco, 2001).

Low-income language-minority children therefore face multiple challenges when entering the formal education system. As with monolingual low-income children, they are likely to experience less language-rich environments in their home language while needing to participate in learning opportunities provided in English in school. Children's vocabulary size is strongly related to their development of reading comprehension skills, and this presents a challenge to children learning to read in English while having only a small functional English vocabulary (Droop & Verhoeven, 2003). In addition to the challenge of learning a second language, ELL children may find many of the expected activities and desired behaviors in the classroom to be less familiar due to cultural variation in home practices between nonimmigrant English-speaking families and Spanish-speaking families with immigrant backgrounds. For instance, children from low-income families of Latin American descent (Latino children) may have literacy experiences in the home that are more skill based (e.g., focusing on learning letters and decoding text) and less holistic or decontextualized (e.g., having a story read to them and predicting how it will end). There is evidence that Latino families' cultural beliefs about early learning and literacy prevent them from engaging in literacy practices before children enter schooling but that when home literacy activities are promoted by schools or preschools as important, parents will engage in reading with their young children (Reese, Garnier, Gallimore, & Goldenberg, 2000).

Opportunities for early child care and education in Southern California are quite varied. Low-income families often decide to enroll their children in early education programs based on multiple needs, including a need for child care while parents are working, and beliefs about the needs of children to experience social, academic, or both settings to prepare them for formal schooling. In Los Angeles County, programs serving low-income families are quite diverse and include publicly funded, center-based programs such as Head Start, state-funded preschool, and local school district early education centers; private community-based preschools, including private child care centers and church-based preschools; and licensed home-based family child care programs.

Few studies have observed the variation in actual instructional practices and children's experiences in both center-based and home-based early education settings, with a focus on low-income children who are at risk for school difficulties. The Los Angeles: Exploring Children's Early Learning Settings (LA ExCELS) Study followed children from age 3 years through the end of kindergarten as they experienced a diverse set of early learning experiences, including 0, 1, or 2 years of participation in public and private preschools and family child care homes. The study incorporated in-depth observations of preschool settings, multiple developmental assessments of children, caregiver surveys, and parent interviews.

The study measured children's developing school readiness skills using assessments of their English and Spanish language development from age 3 through the end of kindergarten, as well as measurements of their early literacy and math skills, social and emotional development, and self-regulation skills. Observations of early learning settings measured emotional and instructional support, materials, activities, and interactions between children and their peers and caregivers.

Because of the demographic makeup of Los Angeles, that city represents an ideal setting for considering the experiences and development of Spanish-speaking dual language learners (DLLs) from preschool through kindergarten. This chapter describes the experiences and development of DLLs in a diverse set of observed early education programs by addressing the following questions:

1. What are the early education experiences of children in classrooms or programs serving DLLs? Is the proportion of DLL children in the classroom associated with observable differences in children's experiences of quality of instruction and interaction and the amount of time children spend in various preacademic activities?

2. How do DLL children's school-readiness skills develop over the preschool-age period in the domains of English-language development, Spanish-language development, early numeracy skills, and emergent literacy skills?

3. How are DLL children's experiences in early learning programs associated with their development of school-readiness skills over time?

THE LA ExCELS STUDY: METHODS AND SAMPLE

For this study, 295 children were originally recruited in four early education categories: 69 children in public preschool programs, 77 children in private preschools or community child care, 48 in licensed family child care, and 101 initially in no licensed early education program. The children came from primarily low-income families, with median income-to-needs ratio of 1.15 and 75% of families with family incomes less than twice the federal poverty level. Maternal education levels ranged from second grade through completing graduate a degree, with a high school education being the median. A large portion of the sample (48%) came from Spanish-speaking households.

In the first year of the study, 3-year-old children were recruited in the previously mentioned four categories. First, public, private, and family child care programs were recruited, and teachers or child care providers distributed recruitment materials to the children in their programs. Up to four children were selected from the volunteering families in each preschool classroom or family child care program. The comparison group of children was recruited in multiple ways, including solicitation of families on wait lists for the participating programs, a mass mailing to families on Los Angeles County's centralized eligibility list for subsidized child care, fliers in pediatric offices, and a radio announcement on Spanish-language radio. Children in the comparison group had to be 3 years old (age eligible for kindergarten in 2 years) and not attending a licensed child care or preschool program. In the second year of the study, all study children were followed into whatever early learning program they attended, including new schools entered by the comparison group and new classrooms or programs into which the other children may have moved.

In the initial recruitment, 22 programs were recruited (3 public Head Start programs and a public school district with early learning programs serving 3-year-olds; 10 private, nonprofit preschool/child care programs; and 8 agencies supporting licensed home-based family child care programs). Across these three program types, 58 individual classrooms participated. These included 21 public, 18 private, and 19 individual family child care programs. Throughout this chapter, family child care homes are treated and referred to as "classrooms" along with the center-based classrooms. In each classroom, up to four target children from among volunteers with parent permission were randomly selected to participate in the longitudinal study.

Classroom Characteristics

The classrooms and programs, although all serving children from low-income families, represented a fair amount of variation in several structural characteristics. Most of the programs in this initial sample were full-day programs operating from early morning through lunchtime, a naptime, and some additional program time following the nap. A smaller percentage (approximately 20%) of programs comprised part-day programs operating for 4½ hours or less in the morning or afternoon. Public centers were most likely to offer part-day programs, with 38% of their classrooms offering part-day services. Only two private center-based programs and two family child care programs were part-day (see Table 1.1).

On average, group size was 16.26 children, and the number of paid adults in each classroom was 2.65. Groups ranged from 3 to 41 children, and the number of adults ranged from 1 to 6. Ratios ranged from 3 children per adult to a high of 12 children per adult. Both the lowest and highest child–adult ratios were found in the family child care programs. On average, family child care providers cared for the fewest children (5.7), and teachers in center-based programs had the highest average number of children per adult (6.6–6.7; see Table 1.2).

In the second year of the study, children were tracked into any program they attended. This process involved relocating the child through parent contact, determining the child's current early learning setting (if any), and obtaining permission from that setting to conduct observations. In all, 106 classrooms were observed in Year 2, including 48 in public preschools, 41 in private preschool or child care programs, and 17 family child care homes.

In Year 2, the 4-year-olds were more likely to be found in part-day programs than they were in Year 1 (41% of observed classrooms were part-day classes). Again, public center-based programs were most likely to be part-day, with 55% of the observed programs being part-day. Private center-based and family child care programs were still most likely to be full-day (68% and 73%, respectively).

Table 1.1.   Proportion of full-day, morning-only, and afternoon-only classrooms

	Total	Public	Private	Family child care
Year 1				
Full day	83.3	63.0	86.0	88.0
a.m.	6.3	25.0	14.0	6.0
p.m.	10.4	12.0	0.0	6.0
Year 2				
Full day	59.0	39.6	61.0	64.7
a.m.	22.0	25.0	14.6	17.6
p.m.	19.0	25.0	14.6	5.9

Note: Numbers in table are percentages.

Table 1.2. Numbers of children, adults, and child–adult ratio, Year 1

	Mean	Standard deviation	Minimum	Maximum
Number of children enrolled				
All child care programs	16.3	7.66	3	41
Public	21.5	6.72	15	41
Private	19.1	5.42	11	32
Family	8.9	3.29	3	14
Number of paid adults in classroom				
All child care programs	2.7	1.16	1	6
Public	3.4	1.02	2	6
Private	3.0	1.00	2	5
Family	1.6	0.61	1	3
Child–adult ratio				
All child care programs	6.3	1.85	3.00	12.00
Public	6.6	1.82	3.80	10.00
Private	6.7	1.56	4.25	9.50
Family	5.7	2.02	3.00	12.00

Table 1.3 presents the number of children and paid adults in the Year 2 classrooms, as well as child-to-adult ratios. Group size in the programs for 4-year-olds ranged from 5 to 58 children, with an average of 19.3 children per group, and child-to-adult ratios ranged from 4 to over 19, with an average of 7.7 children per adult. The largest group sizes were found in private centers, which ranged from 11 to 58 children per group; at the low end were the family child care programs, ranging from 5 to 15 children enrolled. It is hard to know, particularly in the private and family child care programs, whether these numbers represent full-time-equivalent students or counts of children who might not attend the program at the same time (e.g., children who attend only part-time or only a few days per week). Child–adult ratios were highest in the private center-based programs (on average 8.3 children per adult). Ratios were somewhat lower in both the public and family child care programs (closer to 7 children per adult; 7.3 and 7.0, respectively).

Dual Language Learner Sample Characteristics

Home language patterns were determined using information from parent interviews that were conducted at four time points throughout the study. At any given time point, there was a sample of parents who did not participate in the interview due to locating or scheduling constraints. Data across the four possible interviews were compiled to create a measure of children's home language. Out of the 295 target children in the study, 282

Table 1.3. Numbers of children, adults, and child–adult ratio, Year 2

	Mean	Standard deviation	Minimum	Maximum
Number of children enrolled				
All child care programs	19.3	8.00	5	58
Public	20.5	7.22	8	49
Private	21.3	8.09	11	58
Family	10.8	3.61	5	15
Number of paid adults in classroom				
All child care programs	2.6	0.98	1	6
Public	2.9	0.96	2	6
Private	2.6	0.89	1	6
Family	1.5	0.52	1	2
Child–adult ratio				
All child care programs	7.7	2.33	4.0	19.3
Public	7.3	1.69	4.0	12.5
Private	8.4	2.88	4.0	19.3
Family	7.2	2.18	5.0	14.0

had at least one parent interview and could be coded into a home language category. The sample included a substantial group of children for whom a non-English language was spoken to the child by at least one individual in the home (57%). The great majority of these children were children with Spanish spoken at home (48% of the full sample). For the purposes of the further child-level analyses in this chapter, the 9% of DLLs with other non-English languages (mostly Armenian and Asian languages) spoken in the home have been dropped from the analyses, leaving two groups for this discussion: monolingual English-language learners ($n = 122$) and Spanish-speaking DLLs ($n = 135$).

The Spanish-speaking DLLs came from families facing more disadvantages than the monolingual English speakers. Their mothers had fewer years of education, and they faced more economic disadvantages, with lower income-to-needs ratios than the monolingual children (see Table 1.4).

In the first year of the study, there were significant differences in the types of programs from which we recruited the Spanish DLL and monolingual English-speaking children. Spanish DLL children were less likely to be attending the family child care programs in our study and more likely to be in our comparison group of children not attending formal licensed preschool or child care than the monolingual English-speaking children (see Table 1.5).

Table 1.4. Maternal education and family income-to-needs ratios by home language

	Mean/median[a]	Standard deviation	Minimum	Maximum
Mother's education: highest grade completed				
Spanish dual language learners	11.1	3.03	2	18
Monolingual English-speaking children	14.0	2.76	8	20
Household income-to-needs ratio				
Spanish dual language learners	0.97	1.40	0	1 over 10
Monolingual English-speaking children	1.76	2.86	0	2 over 10

Key: [a]Median is presented for income-to-needs ratio due to some high outliers.

There were many possible configurations of Year 1 to Year 2 program attendance. Table 1.6 provides the overall number of children who stayed in the same classroom and those who moved into different classrooms, broken down by language group. The largest group of children stayed in the same classroom ($n = 92$), followed by 65 children who remained in the comparison group for both years. Fifty-five children who had been in a program during Year 1 were followed into new classrooms, as were 44 children who entered an early learning program during Year 2 after being in the comparison group in the first year. Finally, 38 children who were in a program during Year 1 could not be observed in their Year 2 early learning setting owing to the new school refusing participation ($n = 4$) or the child moving or not being found in the tracking procedures ($n = 34$).

Study Procedures

The study collected detailed information on children's early learning experiences, family context, and school-readiness development over a 3-year period. The multiple time points of data collection, settings in which data were collected, and data-collection measures and procedures are described next.

Table 1.5. Distribution of English- and Spanish-speaking children in each early learning program category at entry to the study

	Percentage in each language group			
	Public centers	Private centers	Family child care programs	Comparison group
Spanish dual language learners	27.5	27.5	5.9	39.2
Monolingual English-speaking children	29.4	30.4	23.5	16.7

Key: $\chi^2(3)$, 20.30; p, .000.

Table 1.6.   Year 1 (Y1) to Year 2 (Y2) classroom/program patterns (number of children in each category)

	Total	English monolingual	Spanish bilingual	Other bilingual
Same classroom	92	48	31	8
Changed classroom	55	25	25	4
Entered preschool Y2	44	17	20	4
Comparison group, both years	63	16	41	6
In school both years, but Y2 school refused	4	3	1	0
In school Y1, but lost contact or moved Y2	34	13	14	1

Note: Language groups do not equal total because not all cases could be coded into language groups.

Data Collection Timeline   The study was designed to collect observational data on children's early learning settings annually in Year 1 (the 3-year-old year), Year 2 (the prekindergarten year), and Year 3 (kindergarten). In addition, child-level data collection was planned for four time points: the beginning (fall/winter) of Year 1, spring of Year 1, spring of Year 2, and spring of Year 3. This design provided a 3-year-old baseline measurement of child characteristics and longitudinal follow-up across a 3-year period through the end of kindergarten.

Observational Measures of Early Learning Settings   Observation in early learning settings took place over 2 or 3 days during the program year. The intent of the observations was to measure the experiences of children in their early learning programs in order to describe children's experiences across the three program types. The domains of interest focused on program features that might distinguish high-quality programs to promote the school readiness of low-income children and that could be targeted for quality improvement.

The first day of observation focused on timed observations using the Emerging Academics Snapshot (Snapshot; Ritchie, Howes, Kraft-Sayre, & Weiser, 2001), the Early Elementary Classroom Quality Observation System (CLASS, 2001 version; La Paro, Pianta, Hamre, & Stuhlman, 2001), and the Adult Involvement Scale (AIS; Howes & Stewart, 1987). In 30-minute cycles, the following activities took place: a 20-minute cycle of Snapshot observation and coding in 1-minute increments and a 10-minute coding cycle in which CLASS and AIS ratings were recorded. During the 20-minute Snapshot period, a target child was observed for 20 seconds, and then the child's engagement was coded according to several categories during the next 40 seconds. At the end of this minute, the second target child was located and observed for a cycle of observation and coding, followed by a third and fourth target child. After rotating through a maximum of four children, the observations continued with the first child and continued to rotate through until 20 minutes had been observed and coded (i.e., five observations per child). This 20-minute cycle was followed by 10 minutes for coding the CLASS and AIS (described next), and then the full 30-minute set of Snapshot, CLASS, and AIS was repeated several more times to capture at least 3 hours of the program morning. Typically in half-day programs the entire program was observed, and in full-day programs the observations continued through lunch and until naptime.

Domains coded in the Snapshot included Activity Setting, Child Engagement, and Teacher Engagement. Activity Setting was a forced-choice category describing the format in which the child was engaging in classroom activities, including free choice, whole group, small group, meals, basics (transitions between activity settings), and teacher-assigned individual tasks. Child Engagement consisted of a large set of nonmutually exclusive codes to describe the academic content or type of activity in which the child was engaged. These codes included being read to, prewriting activities, prereading activities (talking about books), oral language development, math, science, social studies (including fantasy role-playing), gross motor, aesthetics (art and music), computers, television, and others. Teacher Engagement also consisted of a set of non–mutually exclusive categories of possible ways in which adults may be engaged with the target child, such as Scaffolding, Didactic Instruction, Facilitating Peer Interactions, and Using a Second Language. For each set of Snapshot codes, data were aggregated across the entire observation to create a measure of the proportion of the observed time in which the children experienced each activity or type of interaction.

Teaching quality was also measured observationally using the CLASS (CLASS, 2001 version; La Paro et al.). Two scales were constructed based on averages of individual items: Instructional Climate (Productivity, Concept Development, Instructional Learning Formats, Quality of Feedback, and Children's Engagement), and Emotional Climate (Positive Climate, Negative Climate, Teacher Sensitivity, Over-Control, Behavior Management). Scores on all CLASS items were recorded every 30 minutes during classroom observations and then averaged across the full observation period. During this same scoring cycle, ratings were made on the AIS (Howes & Stewart, 1987), also on a 7-point scale ranging from 1 (*no adult response to child communication*) to 7 (*elaborated adult interaction with child*).

The second day of observation was devoted to observing the global quality of the setting, rather than from the target children's perspective. Items from the Early Childhood Environmental Rating Scale–Revised (Harms, Clifford, & Cryer, 1998) and Early Childhood Environmental Rating Scale–Extended (also known as Extended Early Childhood

Environmental Rating Scale; Silva, Siraj-Blatchford, & Taggart, 2003) were selected to measure the quality of teacher–child interaction and the quality of the educational opportunities available to children. The overall ECERS observation was shortened to include only 13 items from the ECERS-R and 6 items from the ECERS-E. ECERS-R items were selected based on the ECRQ article by Perlman, Zellman, and Le (2004), which identified high redundancy among ECERS-R items and provided evidence that smaller groups of items may be substituted for the whole ECERS-R. The authors tested several different groupings of item subsets and identified a set of 10 items ("expert items") identified by practitioners as most associated with child care quality and tending to be more process oriented than materials oriented.

To capture the preacademic, or curricular, content in the child care setting, items from the ECERS-E and ECERS-R were selected to reflect preacademic content areas of literacy, math/number, science, art, and dramatic play. Literacy curriculum was assessed with five items from ECERS-E, math was assessed with the Counting item from ECERS-E, and the Math/Number item was from ECERS-R. Also included were the individual ECERS-R items of Nature/Science, Blocks, Art, and Dramatic Play. (*Note:* Blocks and Art are included in the expert items subset as well.) A new subscale was created from these items called ECERS Academic, which included the following items from ECERS-E and ECERS-R to capture the curricular/preacademic content of the environment: ECERS-R—Blocks, Dramatic Play, Nature/Science, Math/Number, Art, ECERS-E—Environmental Print Letters and Words, Books and Literacy Areas, Adult Reading with Children, Sounds in Words, Emergent Writing/Mark Making, and Counting. This ECERS Academic Scale has good internal reliability ($\alpha = .73$). In addition, three ECERS-R items together formed a scale representing the quality of teacher–child interaction (Discipline, Encouraging Children to Communicate, and Staff–Child Interactions). This ECERS Interactions Scale also has acceptable reliability ($\alpha = .72$).

Child Assessment Procedures   Children were assessed using an extensive protocol, including standardized tests of language, math, literacy, and self-regulation skills. Three different protocols were used, depending on the child's bilingual status. Children who had no Spanish spoken at home were given the English Only assessment, which included all measures in English only. If children had any Spanish spoken at home, they received one of two bilingual protocols, depending on their apparent level of English proficiency. The Spanish Bilingual assessment included measures of expressive and receptive vocabulary in both Spanish and English, with Spanish-language assessments of math, literacy, and self-regulation skills. The English Bilingual assessment also included both Spanish- and English-language assessments, but measures of math, literacy, and self-regulation were conducted in English. Trained assessors determined the appropriate assessment protocol for children with Spanish-language backgrounds using a decision matrix, taking into account teacher reports of children's home language, the assessor's own experience speaking with the children during a rapport-building interaction, and children's initial scores on the language assessments in both languages. The use of the bilingual assessment procedures for all Spanish-speaking children provides a rich longitudinal data set that tracks DLL children's language development in both English and Spanish. Assessment measures reported in this chapter are the Peabody Picture Vocabulary Test–IIIA (PPVT-IIIA; Dunn & Dunn, 1997), measuring English-language receptive vocabulary; the Test de Vocabulario en Imagenes Peabody (TVIP; Dunn, Padilla, Lugo, & Dunn, 1986), measuring Spanish receptive vocabulary; Woodcock-Johnson and Woodcock-Muñoz Picture Vocabulary tests in both English and Spanish, measuring English and Spanish expressive vocabulary (Woodcock, McGrew, & Mather, 2001; Woodcock & Muñoz-Sandoval, 1996, respectively); the Woodcock-Johnson Applied Problems test (Woodcock, McGrew, & Mather, 2001; Woodcock & Muñoz-Sandoval, 1996) measuring math reasoning skills and administered in Spanish or English; and the Story and Print Concepts task (Mason & Stewart, 1989), measuring emergent literacy and administered in Spanish or English using a storybook in either Spanish or English.

Training and Reliability of Observers   Each of the observational tools required extensive observer training and assessment of reliability. Training for each measure was initially conducted in the weeks prior to the beginning of their administration in the study. Training included initial group introductions and background readings for each measure; video-taped observations for practice purposes; in-the-field practice, including debriefing with a certified trainer; and reliability testing done either in the field or via videotape. The trainers were individuals with master's or doctoral degrees in child development or psychology who had been trained by and established interobserver reliability with the principal investigators and/or the developers of the measure and also had skills in training others on the measure. These trainers were considered to have achieved "gold standard" status on the measures.

Requirements for certification of observers before collecting data included successful completion of the training course as well as achievement of item-level scores of at least kappa (κ) greater than or equal to .60 with gold-standard trainers for the ECERS and Snapshot measures. Requirements for certification on the CLASS were to code five reliability clips independently and score within 1 point on the master-code videotapes on 80% of scores averaged across the segments and within 1 point on each dimension for more than 50% of the dimensions. Retraining and reliability testing were repeated prior to each new year of observation.

RESULTS

Descriptive data for the observed characteristics of the early learning programs are provided in Tables 1.7 and 1.8. These tables illustrate the great diversity in observed quality of materials and interactions and the range of variation in time use captured with the Snapshot measure. Table 1.7 provides the averages for Year 1 and Year 2 from the Snapshot measure. These averages represent the proportion of time that individual children were observed in each category of activity setting, selected child engagement codes (literacy-related activities, math, science, fantasy play, and

Table 1.7. Year 1 and Year 2 Snapshot results: proportion of observed time spent in activity settings, child engagement in academic activities, and teacher engagement

	Year 1		Year 2	
	Minimum–maximum (range)	Mean (SD)	Minimum–maximum (range)	Mean (SD)
Activity Settings				
Basics	.03–.36	.17(.08)	.00–.37	.16(.09)
Meals–Snacks	.00–.44	.15(.08)	.00–.32	.13(.08)
Whole Group Time	.00–.40	.12(.10)	.00–.65	.17(.14)
Free Choice/Center	.05–.81	.44(.17)	.00–.88	.40(.16)
Small Group Time	.00–.63	.09(.11)	.00–.52	.12(.11)
Individual Time	.00–.26	.01(.04)	.00–.27	.01(.03)
Outside Time	.00–.78	.26(.19)	.00–.80	.25(.14)
Child Engagement in Academic Activities				
Reads To	.00–.15	.03(.04)	.00–.22	.04(.06)
Pre-Read/Read	.00–.22	.03(.05)	.00–.15	.02(.03)
Letter/Sound Learning	.00–.14	.03(.04)	.00–.45	.03(.06)
Oral Language Development	.00–.38	.11(.10)	.00–.47	.10(.09)
Writing	.00–.09	.00(.01)	.00–.20	.03(.04)
Math	.00–.31	.07(.06)	.00–.47	.09(.09)
Science	.00–.40	.14(.09)	.00–.52	.15(.12)
Fantasy Play	.00–.51	.13(.10)	.00–.40	.11(.09)
Aesthetics	.00–.60	.16(.12)	.00–.57	.15(.12)
Gross Motor	.00–.36	.12(.09)	.00–.39	.12(.08)
Teacher Engagement				
Scaffolds	.00–.48	.14(.12)	.00–.52	.14(.11)
Didactic	.00–.65	.27(.17)	.00–.83	.33(.15)
Second Language	.00–.73	.10(.18)	.00–.67	.04(.10)
Facilitate Peer	.00–.09	.01(.02)	.00–.07	.00(.01)

Key: SD, standard deviation; Snapshot, Emerging Academics Snapshot (Ritchie, S., Howes, C.H., Kraft-Sayre, M., & Weiser, B. [2001].)

Table 1.8. Year 1 CLASS, AIS, and ECERS scores for all observed programs—range, mean, and standard deviation

	Year 1		Year 2	
	Minimum– maximum (range)	Mean (SD)	Minimum– maximum (range)	Mean (SD)
Positive Climate	4.13–6.86	5.75(0.59)	2.80–7.00	5.81(0.85)
Negative Climate	1.00–2.80	1.53(0.43)	1.00–3.56	1.22(0.51)
Teacher Sensitivity	2.00–6.60	5.16(0.79)	2.20–6.83	5.29(0.90)
Over-Control	1.00–3.50	1.44(0.45)	1.00–2.89	1.21(0.37)
Behavior Management	3.25–7.00	5.32(0.72)	2.10–7.00	5.49(1.03)
Productivity	2.00–6.13	4.27(0.89)	2.57–6.00	4.15(0.69)
Concept Development	1.00–3.38	1.84(0.49)	1.00–3.40	1.95(0.60)
Learning Formats	1.38–6.00	3.99(0.99)	1.00–5.20	3.46(0.95)
Quality of Feedback	1.00–4.75	2.18(0.92)	1.00–4.40	2.45(0.91)
Children's Engagement	3.88–7.00	5.83(0.62)	3.60–7.00	5.58(0.60)
CLASS Emotional Climate Composite	4.55–6.83	5.85(0.49)	3.76–6.97	6.05(0.60)
CLASS Instructional Climate Composite	2.70–5.38	3.62(0.51)	2.24–4.45	3.53(0.46)
AIS	3.75–6.14	5.17(0.43)	1.80–6.00	5.06(0.74)
ECERS Academic	1.91–5.09	3.41(0.72)	1.55–6.00	3.90(0.89)
ECERS Interaction	2.00–7.00	4.71(1.29)	1.33–7.00	5.41(1.53)

Key: SD, standard deviation. CLASS, Classroom Quality Observation System, 2001 version (La Paro, Pianta, Hamre, & Stuhlman, 2001); AIS, Adult Involvement Scale (Howes, & Stewart, 1987); ECERS, Early Childhood Environment Rating Scale–Revised (Harms, Clifford, & Cryer, 1998) and Early Childhood Environment Rating Scale–Extended (Silva, Siraj-Blatchford, & Taggart, 2003).

gross motor activities), and proportion of time observed in which children experienced interactions with their teachers that represented scaffolding, didactic instruction, facilitation of peer interactions, and communication in a language other than English. Table 1.8 includes all individual subscale scores for the CLASS, as well as two composite scores (Emotional Climate and Instructional Climate), and average scores for the Adult Involvement Scale and the two composite ECERS scales (ECERS Academic and ECERS Interactions). Data from these observational measures were used to answer each of the research questions that follow.

Question 1: What Are the Early Education Experiences of Children in Programs Serving Dual Language Learners?

The first question addressed in these analyses is concerned with describing the early education programs experienced by dual language learners.

First information is presented on program variation according to the proportion of "low English proficiency" (LEP) children in each classroom. LEP status is defined by the school district, and teachers are typically aware of the number of children with this classification in their classrooms. Then, similar descriptive data are presented with respect to the language diversity of classrooms.

Proportion of Low English Proficiency Children in Classroom

Teachers completed questionnaires each year describing, among other things, the demographic characteristics of their classrooms or programs. In Year 1, 44 teachers responded to the teacher questionnaire and reported the number of students in their classrooms who were designated as LEP. The number of LEP children in the Year 1 classrooms ranged from 0 to 27, with a mean of 4.6 and a wide variance ($SD = 6.4$). The proportion of LEP children as a function of the total classroom size was computed as the ratio of LEP to total children enrolled. Classrooms ranged from 0% to 100% LEP students, with a mean of 25% ($SD = 31\%$). The three program types varied significantly with respect to the proportion of LEP children enrolled ($F(2, 40) = 4.13, p < .05$). Public programs had the highest mean proportion of LEP students (43%) and were the only program type that had instances of 100% LEP. Private centers and family child care homes averaged 18% and 14% LEP, respectively.

Bivariate correlations between the proportion of LEP students and observed measures of classroom quality and children's experiences revealed very few significant associations. Out of 38 computed correlations, only 2 were statistically significant: A higher proportion of LEP students in the class was associated with more time being read to ($r = .33, p < .05$) and more time spent using computers ($r = .57; p < .001$).

A categorical variable was created from the Year 1 LEP proportion, indicating classrooms with no LEP students (38% of classrooms), less than 50% LEP (41% of classrooms), and more than 50% LEP (21% of classrooms). One-way ANOVAs compared the observed quality and experiences of children according to these three categories. None of these analyses revealed significant differences, with the exception of the use of computers, which was highest in classrooms with a majority of LEP students but still quite low overall (0.5% in no-LEP classes, 1% in low-LEP classes, and 6% of the time in majority-LEP classes was spent engaging with computers; $F[2, 40] = 10.4, p < .001$).

In the second year of the study, 66 teachers responded to the questionnaire items regarding the number of LEP students in their classes. They reported a range from 0 to 44 LEP students, with a mean of 5.2 ($SD = 8.7$). The proportion of LEP students in the classrooms serving the 4-year-old children ranged from 0% to 100% with a mean of 23% ($SD = 31\%$).

Again, public preschool programs had significantly higher proportions of LEP students (35%) than the private preschools or family child care programs (16% and 5%, respectively; $F[2, 59] = 4.14, p < .05$).

Bivariate correlations between the Year 2 LEP proportion and observed quality and child experiences showed more significant associations than in Year 1 (see Table 1.9). Higher proportions of LEP students were significantly associated with scores on the CLASS: better quality of feedback, less over-control, and higher scores on the instructional climate scale. LEP proportion was also associated with the amount of time classrooms spent in particular activity settings and academic activities. Classrooms with higher LEP proportion spent more time in whole-group activity settings and reading to children, engaged in oral language development and in aesthetics, but spent less time in social studies-related activities. In higher LEP classrooms, teachers engaged in more scaffolding as well as more didactic instruction, and the ECERS Academic Scale was higher.

Post hoc analysis explored whether these correlations were associated with the greater proportion of LEP students in public programs. Correlations run separately by program type illustrated that even within public programs, the proportion of LEP students was significantly correlated with several of these domains, supporting the previously described pattern (results not shown).

Classroom Language Diversity Children whose home language is not English may nonetheless not be identified by their teachers as LEP. Preschool-age children living in monolingual non-English or bilingual families may have made enough progress in their English language development not to qualify as LEP while still being considered ELL or DLL. Teachers provided information via questionnaire regarding the variety of languages spoken by children in their classrooms (although not the numbers of children speaking each language). Questions were worded to determine the presence or absence of each language (e.g., "Which languages are spoken by children in your classroom?"). Of the 46 classrooms with valid data for this question in Year 1, the vast majority indicated that their classroom had DLL students. Only 5 teachers indicated English as the only language spoken by students; 4 teachers indicated that Spanish was the only language spoken by students, and 37 indicated that English and at least one other language was spoken (21 English and Spanish; 2 English and another language; 14 English, Spanish, and another language). Non-Spanish foreign languages spoken by children in these classrooms included Arabic, Armenian, French, Swahili, Punjabi, Tagalog, Korean, and Chinese languages. From answers to these questions, we constructed variables describing each classroom as comprising no DLLs (English speakers

Table 1.9. Pearson correlations between Year 2 proportion of LEP children in classroom and observed features of the classroom (*n* = 50–62)

	r
CLASS	
Positive Climate	.27
Negative Climate	−.17
Teacher Sensitivity	.22
Over-Control	−.30[a]
Behavior Management	.23
Productivity	−.01
Concept Development	.27
Learning Formats	.19
Quality of Feedback	.43[b]
Children's Engagement	.08
Emotional Climate Composite	.24
Instructional Climate Composite	.30[b]
Adult Involvement Scale	.22
Snapshot Activity Settings	
Basics	−.02
Whole Group Time	.36[b]
Free Choice/Center	−.21
Small Group Time	.04
Outside Time	−.18
Snapshot Child Engagement	
Reads To	.29[a]
Preread/Read	.06
Letter/Sound Naming	.08
Oral Language Development	.28[a]
Writing	.21
Math	.24
Science	.20
Social Studies	−.26[a]
Aesthetics	.31[a]
Gross Motor	−.00
Snapshot Teacher Engagement	
Scaffolds	.43[b]
Didactic	.35[b]
Second Language	.07
Facilitate Peer	−.18
ECERS scales	
ECERS Interaction Scale	.28[a]
ECERS Academic Scale	.08

Key: n, number of classrooms; *r,* Pearson Product Moment Correlations; LEP, low English proficiency; CLASS, Classroom Assessment Scoring System (Pianta, La Paro, & Hamme, 2008); Adult Involvement Scale (Howes & Stewart, 1987); Snapshot, Emerging Academics Snapshot (Ritchie, Howes, Kraft-Sayre, & Weiser, 2001); ECERS, Early Childhood Environment Rating Scale–Revised (Harms, Clifford, & Cryer, 1998) and Early Childhood Environment Rating Scale–Extended (Silva, Siraj-Blatchford, & Taggart, 2003).

[a]$p < .05$; [b]$p < .01$

only; $N = 5$), DLL Spanish only (at least one Spanish-speaking child in the classroom and no other non-English languages spoken; $N = 25$), and DLL Other (at least one non-Spanish and non-English language spoken by students in the classroom; $N = 16$). Most of the DLL Other classrooms included Spanish-speaking children in addition to children speaking other non-English languages. The small number of no-DLL classrooms was unevenly distributed across program type, with the center-based programs particularly unlikely to have no DLL children (1 classroom each in the public and private center-based programs).

Among the Year 2 classrooms, 70 teacher responses were recoded into an analogous variable. Of these 70 classrooms, 10 contained no DLLs, 42 were DLL Spanish only, and 15 were classified as DLL Other. In these programs serving 4-year-olds, the no-DLL classrooms were more evenly distributed across program type, but public preschools had the highest proportion of classrooms with DLL children speaking languages other than Spanish. These data are presented in Table 1.10.

ANOVAs comparing mean scores on CLASS, Snapshot, AIS, and ECERS scores by classroom language diversity were conducted to determine whether there were average differences in classroom quality and children's experiences associated with the language diversity of their classrooms. In Year 1, there were no significant differences according to these categories (results not shown). In Year 2, there were a few significant associations. Two constructs from the CLASS showed significant variation according to these categories: Learning formats scores were significantly higher in classrooms with Spanish speakers in comparison to those with no DLLs or DLLs speaking other languages ($F[2, 52] = 3.55$, $p < .05$), and

Table 1.10.   Language diversity by program type

	Program type (n of classrooms)			
	Public	Private	Family child care	Total
Year 1 classroom language diversity				
No DLLs	1	1	3	5
DLL Spanish only	6	12	7	25
DLL Other	8	4	4	16
Total	15	17	14	46
Year 2 classroom language diversity				
No DLLs	4	4	2	10
DLL Spanish only	19	20	3	42
DLL Other	12	5	1	18
Total	35	29	6	70

Key: n, number of classrooms; DLL, dual language learner.
Note: Ns do not match total number of observed programs because language diversity information came from teacher questionnaires, with a lower response rate.

overcontrol scores were higher for classrooms with no DLLs than for Spanish-only DLL classrooms ($F(2, 52) = 4.90$, $p < .05$). DLL Other classrooms spent singnificanly less time in social studies activities (8%) than no-DLL and Spanish-only DLL classrooms (15% and 16%, respectively; $F[2, 63] = 3.31$, $p > .05$). Finally, ECERS Interaction scores were highest in classrooms that included Spanish-speaking DLLs but not other-language DLLs ($F[2, 54] = 3.16$, $p < .05$).

Classroom Experiences of Spanish-Speaking Dual Language Learning Children   The preceding analyses describe how classrooms varied according to their demographic makeup with respect to the number of DLL children in the classroom. This question was also examined from the individual-child perspective, comparing the experiences of the target children in our study who were Spanish-speaking DLLs and those who were from monolingual English-speaking families. When children were in their 3-year-old year of preschool, only a few differences in experiences were found between these two groups. Individual children's time-use data from the Snapshot measure showed that Spanish DLLs spent a higher proportion of their day outside than monolingual English-speaking children (28% of the day for Spanish DLLs and 22% for monolingual English [$F(1,118) = 4.04$, $p < .05$; 95% confidence intervals (CIs) 23%–33% and 17%–27%, respectively]). Although there was overall a very low proportion of time spent using computers, the Spanish DLLs spent more time using computers than monolingual English speakers (3% versus 1% [$F(1,118) = 4.48$, $p < .05$; 95% CIs 1%–5% and 0%–2%, respectively]). Finally, there was a marginally significant difference in the amount of non-English used by adult staff with the children depending on their language background. Interestingly, monolingual children did experience small amounts of non-English, but Spanish-speaking DLLs experienced somewhat more non-English (9% for Spanish DLLs versus 4% for monolingual English speakers [$F(1,118) = 3.77$, $p = .055$; 95% CIs 4%–13% and 2%–7%, respectively]).

In terms of observed classroom characteristics, there were no significant differences between the experiences of DLL and monolingual children in the complexity of adult interaction observed with the AIS and no differences on the two ECERS composites (Academic and Interactions). There were also no significant differences for these two groups in CLASS composite scores, but two individual CLASS scales did show differences: Overall, the DLL children experienced classrooms higher in both positive climate and children's engagement scores. For positive climate, the average for Spanish DLLs was 5.81 but 5.57 for monolingual children (F[1,118] = 4.44; $p < .05$; 95% CIs 5.56–5.96 versus 5.41–5.73). Note that these groups are both experiencing relatively high levels of positive climate. Classroom-level children's engagement scores were also high in both groups but higher in the classrooms experienced by Spanish DLL children (5.89) compared to monolingual children (5.58) ($F[1,118] = 7.48$; $p < .01$; CIs 5.73–6.04 and 5.41–5.74, respectively).

For the children attending preschool and family child care programs during their 4-year-old year, there were virtually no differences in the experiences of quality or the patterns of time use for Spanish DLLs and monolingual English-speaking children. There were no differences in Adult Involvement, CLASS scores, or ECERS scores. Time-use patterns measured with the Snapshot also showed no differences in experiences for DLL versus monolingual children, except in the area of non-English use by adult staff. DLL children experienced more instances of non-English use (5% versus 2% for monolingual children; $F[1,157] = 5.37$; $p < .05$; 95% CIs 3%–8% and 0%–3%, respectively).

Question 2: What Are the Patterns of School Readiness Skill Development for Dual Language Learning Children?

Our second research question focuses on the trajectories of school-readiness skill development for DLL preschool-age children. For these analyses (Fuligni, Howes, Lara-Cinisomo & Karoly, 2009, 2010), all children in our study were examined, including those who did not attend a licensed early learning program and those who only enrolled in a preschool program in the second year of the study. Children's language, literacy, and numeracy skills were measured three to four times (depending on the assessment) from the beginning of the study through the end of kindergarten. Individual children's trajectories in each area were modeled via MPlus Growth Modeling analysis using individually varying times of assessment as the time scores. This procedure treats individual times of measurement as a level of analysis nested within individual children, to estimate a latent variable accounting for patterns of change over time, or growth (Muthén & Muthén, 1998–2010). In addition, the ratio of children's family income to needs and maternal education (measured from parent interviews) were included in the modeling to control for socioeconomic differences between DLL and monolingual children.

Within this low-income sample of children, all were on average performing below national norms based on their standard scores on the language assessments and the Woodcock-Johnson Applied Problems test (administered in the child's best language). For instance, average English receptive vocabulary (PPVT-IIIA) standard scores at age 3 were below 80 (well over a full standard deviation below the norm), 80 at the end of preschool, and just over 90 by the end of kindergarten. Children's math reasoning (Applied Problems) standard scores were also just below 90 points at the end of the 3- and 4-year-old years and rose to be comparable with national norms (just above 100) by the end of kindergarten. Multiple-group growth-curve analyses allowed us to estimate these trajectories separately for the Spanish DLL and monolingual English-speaking children. Even after controlling for differences in socioeconomic factors, the Spanish DLL children appeared to have more delays in language and math skills than the monolingual English-speaking children.

Question 3: Do Early Education Experiences Support the School Readiness of Dual Language Learning Children?

Finally, in analyses reported elsewhere (Fuligni et al., 2009, 2010), the experiences of children in these diverse early learning settings were used to predict the growth factor (slope) in the school-readiness trajectories described previously. Four specific observed factors were selected for examination: whether or not the child attended an early learning program in Year 1 and/or Year 2, the Year 1 and Year 2 ECERS Interaction Scale scores, the Snapshot measurements in Year 1 and Year 2 of the proportion of time children experienced oral language development activities, and the Year 1 and Year 2 Snapshot measure of proportion of time children experienced letter/sound (phonics) activities.

Two-group growth-curve analyses were conducted using individually varying times of assessment and controlling for socioeconomic characteristics. In this type of analysis, the latent variable of growth over multiple observations of an individual child is estimated separately for specified groups—in this case, the monolingual versus the DLL children (Muthén & Muthén, 1998–2010). By assessing the effect of the observed predictors (e.g., whether the child was in a program in Year 1, time in oral language development) on the growth factor in each group, some differences in the effects of early learning programs on DLL and monolingual children were identified. The primary results of these analyses point to the importance of simply attending one of the observed programs rather than being in the comparison. Being in an early learning program during either the 3-year-old or 4-year-old year was associated with faster rates of development (regardless of starting status) in English receptive and expressive language scores and the Applied Problems score. Being in a program during the second year (age 4) was a predictor of growth rate in emergent literacy skills, but being in a program at age 3 was not. These effects of attending an early learning program during the 4-year-old year were particularly strong among the Spanish DLL children and nonsignificant when monolingual English speakers were examined separately.

Some observed characteristics of children's early learning experiences in these diverse settings were associated with children's growth trajectories. The amount of time spent in oral language development activities in Year 1 was strongly significantly associated with growth in English expressive vocabulary for the Spanish DLL children but not for the sample as a whole or the monolingual group separately. Growth in emergent literacy skills was significantly predicted by the amount of time in Year 2 spent in letter/sound activities for the monolingual English speakers but not for the DLL children. Finally, growth-curve analyses predicting the DLL children's development in Spanish receptive and expressive vocabulary skills did not show any effects of being in early learning settings nor of any of the specific observed features of children's experiences in these settings.

CONCLUSIONS

The analyses presented previously use data from a study of school-readiness experiences in a diverse sample of low-income children to explore issues related to DLLs in early education. Taken together, these results support a few tentative conclusions. First, these findings suggest very few differences in experiences in early learning programs for DLL and monolingual children. However, it must be noted that these analyses are influenced by the sampling design of the study. In the initial program sampling, children's language status was not a feature of the sampling method, and both DLL and monolingual children were likely to be selected from within the same classrooms or programs. Therefore great differences in the experiences of these two groups of children would not be expected. However, the second year of data provides an opportunity to see children's experiences in some programs other than those where they were originally sampled, because children were followed into any program they attended. Even fewer differences in DLL versus monolingual children's experiences in the second year were found. In both years, DLL children were observed in part- and full-day programs, in large and small classrooms, and in public, private, and home-based early learning settings. The early education experiences of monolingual and DLL children were compared in terms of the demographic makeup of their classrooms or programs and by exploring the experiences of individual children within their programs. Overall, the analyses suggest that most of the programs observed are serving a mix of DLL and monolingual children.

Together, these findings suggest no strong pattern of differences in children's experiences in early learning programs based on the language background of the children. In an urban setting serving a large population of DLLs and providing a great diversity in the types of early learning programs available, children are generally experiencing a similar mix of experiences and interactions, regardless of their language background. Public preschool programs tended to have the highest proportions of DLLs, and classrooms with more DLLs tended to spend more time in literacy and oral language activities.

A second major area of analysis addressed the development of school-readiness skills. Even among their peers in a variety of preschool programs serving low-income children, Spanish DLL children appear to have more delays in language development in both English and Spanish than monolingual children. This finding is not surprising, given the young age of these children who are still learning to master both their home language and that of the school culture. Discrepancies in school-readiness skills in the areas of math and literacy are also evident for DLL children (assessed in Spanish when applicable), but these are less striking, especially by the end of the kindergarten year. DLL children's Spanish-language skills did not show appreciable improvement during this time period, either. Early educators are correct to be particularly concerned about the language skills of DLL children as they enter kindergarten, as these skills are the foundation for the additional learning that needs to happen in elementary school. Without a rich vocabulary in any language, children are likely to be at a disadvantage for successful learning interactions with teachers and peers.

Results of ongoing analysis using observed features of early learning settings to help predict growth in school-readiness skills suggest that even within a very diverse sample of early learning programs with a wide range of quality and activities, Spanish DLLs who attend a program exhibit a particularly greater rate of development in comparison with Spanish DLLs who do not attend a prekindergarten program of some sort. The improvement in English-language, math, and emergent literacy skills attributable to early learning program attendance can help bring DLL children closer in achievement to their monolingual peers but typically only makes them comparable to monolingual children who did not attend preschool. Furthermore, the importance of oral language development activities to support the continued language development of DLLs in preschool is in contrast with the beneficial nature of phonics-type activities that support literacy development for monolingual but not DLL children. These findings suggest that early educators may need to differentiate activities more than they are currently doing to provide the most useful activities to promote school readiness for DLL children.

Finally, the lack of impact of program attendance and program quality on children's Spanish-language development should be addressed. The policy context in California emphasizes monolingual English education from kindergarten and considers English-language proficiency an important goal of prekindergarten early learning programs. However, more attention should be paid to the benefits of maintaining and supporting bilingual language development to promote cognitive flexibility, increased communication skills, and ongoing academic skill development while both English and Spanish (or other home languages) are still developing.

STUDY QUESTIONS

1. What are some of the multiple challenges that ELLs face when entering the formal education system?

2. Briefly describe the intent and methods of the LA ExCELS Study. What did it purport to examine?

3. What results did the LA ExCELS researchers obtain? Specifically, what did they discover with respect to the three questions enumerated at the beginning of the chapter?

REFERENCES

Droop, M., & Verhoeven, L. (2003). Language proficiency and reading ability in first- and second-language learners. *Reading Research Quarterly, 38,* 78–103.

Dunn, L.M., & Dunn, L.M. (1997). *Peabody Picture Vocabulary Test, IIIA.* Circle Pines, MN: AGS.

Dunn, L.M., Padilla, E.R., Lugo, D.E., & Dunn, L.M. (1986). *Test de Vocabulario en Imágenes Peabody (TVIP)* [Peabody Picture Vocabulary Test]. Circle Pines, MN: AGS.

Fuligni, A.S., Howes, C., Lara-Cinisomo, S., & Karoly, L. (2009, April). *Development of school readiness skills among at-risk English- and Spanish-speaking children with diverse preschool experiences.* Poster presented at the Biennial Meetings of the Society for Research in Child Development, Denver, CO.

Fuligni, A.S., Howes, C., Lara-Cinisomo, S., & Karoly, L. (2010). *Patterns of school readiness development among low-income monolingual and dual-language learners with diverse preschool experiences.* Manuscript in preparation.

Harms, T., Clifford, R.M., & Cryer, D. (1998). *Early Childhood Environment Rating Scale–Revised.* New York: Teachers College Press.

Howes, C., Burchinal, M., Pianta, R., Bryant, D., Early, D., Clifford, R., et al. (2008). Ready to learn? Children's pre-academic achievement in pre-kindergarten programs. *Early Childhood Research Quarterly, 23,* 27–50.

Howes, C., & Stewart, P. (1987). Child's play with adults, toys, and peers: An examination of family and child care influences. *Developmental Psychology, 23,* 423–430.

La Paro, K., Pianta, R.C., Hamre, B., & Stuhlman, M. (2001). *Early Elementary Classroom Quality Observation System.* Charlottesville: University of Virginia.

Loeb, S., Fuller, B., Kagan, S.L., & Carrol, B. (2004). Child care in poor communities: Early learning effects of type, quality, and stability. *Child Development, 75,* 47–65.

Los Angeles Unified School District. (2006). *R30 language census report for the district* (pp. 5–34). Retrieved March, 21, 2007, from http://search.lausd.k12.ca.us/cgi-bin/fccgi.exe?w3exec=r30s2.2007&which=ld.

Love, J., Kisker, E.E., Ross, C.M., Schochet, P.Z., Brooks-Gunn, J., Paulsell, D., et al. (2002). *Making a difference in the lives of infants and toddlers and their families: The impacts of Early Head Start, Vol. 1: Final technical report.* Princeton, NJ: Mathematica Policy Research.

Mason, J.M., & Stewart, J. (1989). *Story and print concepts: The CAP Early Childhood Diagnostic Instrument.* Iowa City, IA: American Testronics.

Muthén, L.K., & Muthén, B.O. (1998–2010). *Mplus user's guide* (6th ed.). Los Angeles: Author.

NICHD Early Child Care Research Network. (2000). The relation of child care to cognitive and language development. *Child Development, 71*, 960–980.

Perlman, M., Zellman, G., & Le, V. (2004). Examining the psychometric properties of the Early Childhood Environment Rating Scale–Revised (ECERS-R). *Early Childhood Research Quarterly, 19*(3), 398–412.

Reese, L., Garnier, H., Gallimore, H., Goldenberg, C. (2000). Longitudinal analysis of the antecedents of emergent Spanish literacy and middle-school English reading achievement of Spanish-speaking students. *American Educational Research Journal, 37*(3), 633–662.

Ritchie, S., Howes, C.H., Kraft-Sayre, M., & Weiser, B. (2001). *Emerging Academics Snapshot.* Unpublished measure, University of California, Los Angeles.

Schweinhart, L., Barnes, H., Weikart, D., Barnett, W.S., & Epstein, A. (1993). *The High/Scope Perry preschool study through age 27.* Ypsilanti, MI: High/Scope Press.

Silva, K., Siraj-Blatchford, I., & Taggart, B. (2003). *Assessing quality in the early years: Early Childhood Environment Rating Scale (ECERS-E).* Stoke-on-Trent, United Kingdom: Trentham Books.

Suarez-Orozco, C., & Suarez-Orozco, M. (2001). *Children of immigration.* Cambridge, MA: Harvard University Press.

Votruba-Drzal, E., Levine Coley, R., & Chase-Lansdale, P.L. (2004). Child care and low-income children's development: Direct and moderated effects. *Child Development, 75*, 296–312.

Woodcock, R.W., McGrew, K.S., & Mather, N. (2001). *Woodcock-Johnson Tests of Achievement.* Itasca, IL: Riverside.

Woodcock, R., & Muñoz-Sandoval, A.F. (1996). *Bateria Woodcock-Muñoz–Revisada* [Woodcock-Muñoz Battery–Revised]. Itasca, IL: Riverside.

2

The Importance of Sensitive Measurement Tools for Understanding What Instructional Practices Promote School Readiness for Dual Language Learners

Emily J. Solari, Susan H. Landry,
Tricia A. Zucker, and April D. Crawford

As the population of dual language learners (DLLs) grows nationwide, increasing attention has been drawn to the need to evaluate effective teaching practices and professional development models for this population of students. Nationwide statistics indicate that although 41% of teachers have taught DLLs, less than 13% have received any specialized training or professional development on how to effectively teach this population (National Center for Education Statistics, 2002). It is essential that early childhood teachers be well prepared for teaching DLLs because national statistics indicate that the population of DLLs is growing faster than the general population (Shore, 2001). Moreover, a growing body of research indicates that high-quality early childhood experiences improve child outcomes (Howes et al., 2008; LoCasale-Crouch et al., 2007; Mashburn et al., 2008; Peisner-Feinberg et al., 2001) and that the prekindergarten (pre-K) years represent a critical period of language development that forms the foundation for later language and literacy achievement (Leppänen, Niemi,

Aunola, & Nurmi, 2006; Snow, Tabors, Nicholson, & Kurland, 1995). This population of students remains understudied; therefore, little is known about what specific instructional methods or programs will best decrease the risk for failures in English and Spanish emergent literacy, language development, reading proficiency, and ongoing achievement in both language and literacy development (Greene, 1998; Slavin & Cheung, 2003).

To better understand the instructional methods that are effective with this population of young children, valid and reliable methods are needed for measuring what is happening in the classroom. Too often, researchers and practitioners simply use observation tools that were originally intended for use in monolingual classrooms to observe bilingual classrooms; however, these measures may not be sensitive to teacher practices that are effective for DLLs. Bilingual pre-K classrooms are inherently different than classrooms that are instructed in English only in their composition, population, instructional language, and overall academic goals; therefore, classroom observation systems that are sensitive to these differences are a necessity when conducting observations. One of the main differences between bilingual and monolingual classrooms is the language of instruction; *bilingual* inherently means that instruction is implemented in two languages, but how the two languages are used across the day varies greatly across pre-K classrooms both within schools and districts and across states. In addition to language of instruction, the makeup (e.g., ethnicity, socioeconomic status) of bilingual classrooms tends to be different from monolingual classrooms; therefore, it is important to measure and understand teaching behaviors that are sensitive to this population of students and that are shown to be effective in enhancing academic outcomes for these children.

Given the growing population of DLLs nationwide, it is crucial to invest resources to determine the most effect teaching practices to ensure school readiness for DLLs. Actual classroom instruction for DLLs varies greatly despite declared program philosophies and goals and with respect to differences in the specific curriculum implemented, instructional materials and aids (e.g., reading series adopted), fidelity of implementation of particular program principles and strategies, and overall quality of instruction offered by individual teachers (Padrón, 1994). Therefore, the development of effective classroom observation tools for bilingual classrooms is essential to further the field's knowledge of specific teaching practices that prepare DLL children for kindergarten entry.

One way to determine which instructional models and teacher behaviors are effective is through classroom observations that specifically target the quantity and quality of teacher behaviors that influence enhanced academic outcomes in bilingual pre-K classrooms. In research studies with DLL students, typically the implemented content or curriculum is described but not the explicit methods by which teachers, through their monitoring, their knowledge of student and domain, and their procedural effectiveness and efficiency, accommodate or fail to accommodate individual learners. Close observation of teaching practices that specifically targets intentional teachable moments between teachers and students is necessary to determine which teaching practices are effective for preparing DLL children for kindergarten.

Research on how to effectively teach DLLs has traditionally focused on the debate of which language should be used for instruction and program evaluations of policy initiatives rather than on understanding the role of instructional processes. This chapter instead emphasizes the quality of teacher–child interactions regardless of language of instruction, because these proximal processes provide the mechanism for influencing children's development (Bronfenbrenner & Morris, 2006) and school readiness. Specifically, the chapter concentrates on teaching practices and professional development for DLL teachers that have been shown to be essential for cognitive school readiness.

Bilingual classroom observation tools must be able to accomplish two important goals. First, the measure must be sensitive to teacher change across the school year that is a result of systematic professional development. Second, the measure must be linked to measurable school-readiness academic variables. Oftentimes, in professional development research, the link between classroom and teacher observation is missing, leaving researchers and practitioners wondering if teacher change and implementation of effective teaching practices are directly related to changes at the child level. Significant gains in child outcomes should be the ultimate goal of all professional development efforts, but many times these questions are not addressed in research or implementation of professional development programs.

In this chapter, the Bilingual Teacher Behavior Rating Scale (B-TBRS; Solari, Landry, Crawford, Gunnewig, & Swank, 2009) is described. This bilingual observation tool is a direct derivative of the Teacher Behavior Rating Scale (TBRS; Landry, Crawford, Gunnewig, & Swank, 2001). The theoretical framework for the B-TBRS and its psychometric properties are discussed. Finally, preliminary data that demonstrate the tool's sensitivity to teacher change over time and correlations with school-readiness skills in a population of DLL children are discussed.

THEORETICAL FRAMEWORK FOR THE BILINGUAL TEACHER BEHAVIOR RATING SCALE

The theoretical framework for the B-TBRS is derived from abundant empirical evidence regarding native English speakers' early language and literacy development as well as a growing body of evidence on the development of these skills in DLLs. Correlational and experimental research with both non-DLL and DLL populations indicates that skilled reading requires several critically important component skills—namely oral language (e.g., vocabulary, grammar), print knowledge, and phonological processing abilities. Children with more of these emergent literacy skills appear to profit more from reading instruction, learn to read sooner, and read better than do children with fewer of these skills (for reviews, see August & Shanahan, 2006; National Early Literacy Panel, 2008; Whitehurst & Lonigan, 1998, 2001).

When acquiring emergent literacy skills, DLLs bring an additional set of resources that are linked to their first language, including knowledge of a first language's morphology, phonological systems, semantics, and syntax. Along with these additional resources come challenges to literacy development in a second language, such as spelling pattern interference and limited vocabularies in the second language (Bialystok & Herman, 1999; Cobo-Lewis, Pearson, Eilers, & Umbel, 2002). Understanding the developmental pathways of cross-linguistic transfer between a child's first and second language can help inform instructional practice for DLL children and can identify factors that indicate risk status for young DLLs (e.g., Comeau, Cormier, Grandmaison, & Lacroix, 1999; Durgunoglu, 1998; Durgunoglu, Nagy, & Hancin-Bhatt, 1993; Geva & Siegel, 2000; Geva, Wade-Woolley, & Shany, 1997; Lindsey, Manis, & Bailey, 2003). These considerations were taken into account when designing the B-TBRS.

The B-TBRS includes nine subscales that measure instruction related to the following four broader domains: 1) classroom organization/management (e.g., classroom community, learning centers, lesson plans), 2) teacher sensitivity, 3) comprehension-related instruction (e.g., oral language, book reading), and 4) code-related instruction (e.g., phonological awareness, letter knowledge, writing). It is important that both code- and comprehension-related instruction are assessed because some evidence suggests that a simultaneous focus on comprehension-related skills along with code-related skills is a beneficial instructional format for DLLs (Solari & Gerber, 2008; Vaughn et al., 2006). Particular attention was given to the comprehension-related subscales of the B-TBRS because DLL children perform about one standard deviation below their monolingual peers on all aspects of vocabulary and reading comprehension (McLaughlin et al., 2000), and, although these students are learning vocabulary, their rate of acquisition is not fast enough to catch up with monolingual peers (August, Carlo, Dressler, & Snow, 2005; McLaughlin et al., 2000). Table 2.1 includes research evidence supporting the four domains measured with the B-TBRS, all of which are associated with children's outcomes.

Table 2.1. Research evidence for the theoretical framework of the Teacher Behavior Rating Scale (Landry, Crawford, Gunnewig, & Swank, 2001)

Domain	Research evidence
Classroom Organization and Management	Establishing classroom routines and organization in ways that value students and support literacy and language skills, such as using literacy-rich play centers (e.g., Christie & Enz, 1992; Morrow, 1991; Morrow & Rand, 1991) and providing access to books (DeTemple, 2001; Neuman, 1996; Whitehurst & Lonigan, 1998).
Teacher Sensitivity	Responding to children's behavioral and affective signals and providing children with guidance and feedback supports their behavioral and academic outcomes (Landry, Smith, Swank, & Guttentag, 2008; Taylor, Anthony, Aghara, Smith, & Landry, 2008).
Comprehension-Related Skills	Modeling language, asking questions, making comments, linking to previously learned words/concepts (Carlisle, Beeman, Davis, & Spharim, 1999; Dickinson & Tabors, 2001; Gelderen, 2004; McLaughlin et al., 2000), and sharing books (Mol, Bus, & de Jong, 2009; Senechal & Cornell, 1993; Silverman, 2007; Whitehurst, et al., 1988) all encourage children's language use and vocabulary development and may also be related to dual language learner decoding in the second language (Gottardo, 2002; Quiroga, Lemos-Britten, Mostafapour, Abbot, & Berninger, 2002).
Code-Related Skills	Engaging children in activities that promote print knowledge, (Bond & Dykstra, 1980; Mason, 1980; National Early Literacy Panel [NELP], 2008; Stevenson & Newman, 1998) phonological awareness (Anthony, Williams, McDonald, & Francis, 2007; Bradley & Bryant, 1985; Gerber et al., 2004; Leafstedt, Richards, & Gerber, 2004) and early writing (NELP, 2008; Matera & Gerber, 2008) supports children's later decoding skills.

DEVELOPMENT OF THE BILINGUAL TEACHER BEHAVIOR RATING SCALE

An emerging literature has provided the field with ideas about important classroom environment characteristics and teacher practices that seem to be important for both social and cognitive development and ultimately school readiness in young DLLs. Although this research has added much to the field, very little research has been conducted to directly assess the implementation of these factors in bilingual pre-K classrooms. Published teacher and classroom observation tools designed to specifically measure classroom and teacher characteristics in bilingual pre-K are not readily available and are therefore not widely used. Often observation tools designed for monolingual classrooms are used to observe bilingual classrooms. This practice does not capture language use in the classroom nor specific teaching practices that address the unique needs of DLLs.

In a recent pilot study, the B-TBRS was used to capture classroom environment characteristics and teacher practices that are directly related to student outcomes for DLLs. The B-TBRS was implemented in 24 bilingual classrooms in different communities in Texas in both the fall and spring of the 2009–2010 academic year. Teachers were involved in a comprehensive professional development program that directly taught teachers effective tools to work with young DLLs, provided ongoing in-class mentoring, and trained teachers to measure students' progress across the year using a progress-monitoring assessment available in both English and Spanish.

DESCRIPTION OF THE BILINGUAL TEACHER BEHAVIOR RATING SCALE

The B-TBRS is based on the TBRS (Landry et al., 2001), which was developed and validated for use in monolingual pre-K classrooms (Assel, Landry, & Swank, 2007). The TBRS and B-TBRS are unique because, unlike other teacher observation measures, they directly observe both classroom environment and specific teacher behaviors, what are often called teachable moments (i.e., interactions between teacher and student that explicitly teach one of the B-TBRS content areas). These teachable moments are measured in both quality and quantity across the four specific teaching domains described on page 49. The monolingual version of the TBRS has been shown to be sensitive to teacher change over time and to correlate with student academic outcomes (Assel et al., 2007).

The B-TBRS contains nine subscales and 72 items. The content areas include 1) Classroom Community, 2) Sensitivity, 3) Lesson Plans, 4) Learning Centers, 5) Book Reading, 6) Written Expression, 7) Oral Language, 8) Print and Letter Knowledge, and 9) Phonological Awareness (PA). Most items evaluate both quality and quantity of the observed behaviors. Quality is evaluated using a four-point rating scale (1 = *Low*, 2 = *Moderate Low*, 3 = *Moderate High*, 4 = *High*) for all subscales. Quantity of instructional opportunities is evaluated with a three-point rating scale (e.g., 1 = *Rarely*, 2 = *Sometimes*, 3 = *Often*), and frequency counts. See Table 2.2 for a detailed description of each content area.

Measuring both quality and quantity of teacher behaviors is an important element of the B-TBRS, as there may be discrepancies seen between the amount of time teachers engage in each activity and the quality of the instruction. In previous studies using the TBRS (Landry et al., 2001), the scores on quantity and quality for particular subscales have differed, although they usually show moderate to high correlations. If a teacher incorporates an instructional practice frequently across an observation but lacks attention to a full range of important instructional goals, the quantity

Table 2.2. Bilingual-Teacher Behavior Rating Scale (B-TBRS) subscales (Solari et al., 2009)

Subscale	Sample teaching behaviors rated	Quality maximum score	Quality maximum score[a]
1. Classroom Community	Establishes classroom routines, rules, and organization in ways that value students.	9[b]	20
2. Sensitivity	Uses responsive behaviors to children's behavioral and affective signals. Provides guidance and feedback.	36[b]	32
3. Lesson Plans	Evidence that learning objectives are linked to theme-related materials and activities. Teacher is observed implementing lesson plan activities.	9[b]	12
4. Learning Centers	Number of centers with clear boundaries that link to learning objectives and theme. Teacher explains center routines and how to use materials.	6[c]	28
5. Book Reading	Teacher discusses book features and vocabulary words. Encourages discussion about text. Reads with engaging voicing and appropriate pacing.	21[c]	28
6. Written Expression	Teacher models writing and provides a variety of opportunities to encourage early writing.	∞[d]	12
7. Oral Language	Encourages children's use of language by modeling language, asking questions, making comments, and linking to previously learned words/concepts. Engages children in multiple-turn conversations.	21[b]	28
8. Print and Letter Knowledge	Engages children in activities that promote print knowledge, including print concepts, letters, words, and letter-sound associations.	∞[d]	28
9. Phonological Awareness (PA)	Provides opportunities that follow the sequence of the PA developmental continuum (e.g., sentence segmenting, syllable blending and segmenting, phoneme blending, segmenting, manipulation), and activities are integrated into various learning situations.	∞[d]	28
Total Teaching Sum	Summary scores obtained by summing across subscale scores.	∞	216

[a]Based on 4-point rating scale on the quality of instructional practice: 1 = *Low*, 2 = *Moderate Low*, 3 = *Moderate High*, 4 = *High*.

[b]Based on 3-point quantity rating scale: 1 = *Rarely*, 2 = *Sometimes*, 3 = *Often*.

[c]Most items based on 3-point quantity rating scale, but some items based on 3-point rating of number of opportunities provided (e.g., 1 = *0 to 1 opportunities observed*, 2 = *2–3 opportunities observed*, 3 = *4+ opportunities observed*).

[d]Most items based on observed total frequency of instructional opportunities observed (range = 0 to ∞), but some items based on 3-point rating of number of opportunities provided.

score is higher than the quality score. In contrast, another teacher may be observed exposing children to a learning domain for only a brief period of time but carries out the activity in an effective manner. This would result in a low quantity score but a higher quality rating. When observing pre-K classrooms, it is important to measure both quality and quantity of instructional behaviors to obtain a comprehensive rating of the classroom and teachers.

The B-TBRS was designed to be conducted in a 2- to 2½-hour observation period. Observers are required to see at least one large-group and one small-group instructional period as well as transitions between activities. Observers are also required to examine teachers' weekly lesson plans and samples of student work.

One large difference between the TBRS and B-TBRS is that language of instruction is a coded variable on the B-TBRS. When observing each content area, the measure allows coders to provide a quality and quantity rating for each teachable moment in English, Spanish, and Dual. For example, if a teacher is instructing rhyming in English, the coder will code how many times this occurred and the quality of this instruction and vice versa for Spanish. Therefore, it is possible to code only one language under the rhyming section. However, if the teacher introduces the topic in the children's home language, and then allows the children to practice in both Spanish and English, this would be considered a Dual teaching moment. For example, the teacher begins a rhyming example in Spanish, and the students proceed to practice rhyming words in Spanish. The teacher then provides the students with examples in English and proceeds to have the children practice the skill in English. This would be coded as the same teachable moment because the same skill set is being instructed and the language of instruction would be Dual. Within the Dual code, coders provide both a quality and quantity for the instruction in both Spanish and English. Providing the option for Dual coding allows us to understand how often teachers are teaching the same skill in both languages. In addition, because we have a quality rating for both languages, we can determine if teaching performance is better in one language or equal across both languages.

There are several other noteworthy additions to the B-TBRS that make it different from the TBRS, given the unique instructional needs of DLLs. Specific topics have been added under the Oral Language section that directly relate to oral language support for DLL children. For example, coders are asked to observe if teachers help DLL children expand their oral responses and provide support for language development in their home language when a student does not understand in his or her second language. Items were also added to the Book Reading section to monitor teachers' comprehension questioning, as this promotes language use in the classroom. Also, the items are expanded in the General Teaching Behaviors subscale to address whether teachers are responsive to the needs of DLLs and allow appropriate accommodations for DLLs.

BILINGUAL TEACHER BEHAVIOR RATING SCALE TRAINING

Comprehensive, systematic training is required before observers are able to use the instrument reliably. There is a prescribed scope and sequence for training. First, trainees are presented with a didactic overview of the measure that includes introducing the purpose of the measure, procedures, and constructs that underlie the measure. Next, observers are taught about each subscale, and specific attention is paid to the scale used for each subscale and item.

After observers become familiar with the B-TBRS, they are asked to practice using the observation tool by watching videotaped classroom instruction. This part of the training is used for observers to practice coding particular subscales—for example, they watch a section of the teaching video in which the teacher is conducting a read-aloud and code that particular teaching sequence, or they spend time watching phonological awareness instruction. Practice is conducted by subscale so that trainees do not become overwhelmed with learning multiple scales at one time. During this time, extensive discussion occurs between an expert/master coder and trainees regarding the observed behaviors and appropriate codes.

When trainees have demonstrated their ability to reliably code videotaped teaching sessions, the next phase in training is live coding alongside a trained expert observer. This phase is required for the trainee to receive field certification on the observation tool. Following the live coding sessions, expert coders and trainees compare the coding of the trainee to the coding of the expert by calculating agreement for each subscale. Trainees are certified as reliable once they have achieved agreement within 1 point of an expert observer across a series of four classroom observations. Following the training period, 20% of the observations are double-coded to calculate inter-rater reliability, or agreement between coders. Inter-rater reliabilities across the subscales were high, ranging between .86 and .92; internal consistency, the correlation of items within the same subscale, was also high, at .89.

Professional Development Model Pilot Study

In 2002 a national evaluation of pre-K curricula (i.e., Preschool Curriculum Evaluation Research [PCER]) demonstrated that supplying teachers with professional development and a research-based curriculum does not guarantee that children will arrive at kindergarten with the skills necessary to succeed (PCER, 2008). Likewise, Hamre and colleagues (2010) indicated that providing teachers with sufficient materials and an evidenced-based curriculum is not enough to foster academic readiness skills of children in pre-K. Children have very different classroom experiences and academic outcomes even though classroom materials are the same. This calls for an increase in professional development for teachers, above and beyond the provision of a research-based curriculum.

The pilot study professional development for target teachers consisted of 1) comprehensive professional development (PD) classes, 2) ongoing in-class mentoring, and 3) the use of a technology-based progress-monitoring tool to assess children's growth over the school year. Comparison teachers only received the progress-monitoring technology. Mentors facilitated 14 PD classes (two 2-hour sessions devoted to each topic area) using a technology-enhanced PD course with small groups of teachers, because communities of teachers at the same grade level and using similar types of dual language instruction provided an ideal venue for teachers to exchange ideas and solve problems (Desimone, 1999; Vaughn & Coleman, 2004). Course content was available through an online source, which presented content areas provided in English and Spanish, model teaching video examples, and expert commentary responding to and further explaining the expert teaching examples. The courses in the study were similar to the online courses that proved to be effective in changing teaching behaviors in the study by Landry et al. (2009), but these courses featured multiple web-based video examples of both effective monolingual instruction and also bilingual instruction. Previous studies in various contexts showed that video exemplars help adults reflect on adult–child interactions (e.g., Blachowicz, Obrochta, & Fogelber, 2005; Hoffman, Roser, & Farest, 1988; Landry, Smith, Swank, & Guttentag, 2008; Pianta et al., 2008). In conjunction with the courses, teachers had access to online discussion forums linked to targeted instructional topics. Some evidence suggests that these forms of technology-enhanced discussion can support problem solving or debate of educational issues (see Gentry, Denton, & Kurz, 2008).

Teachers were randomly assigned to receive the aforementioned professional development and mentoring or continue their teaching practices in a comparison condition. As stated, teachers that were assigned to the target condition participated in ongoing professional development and received in-class mentoring, both with a focus on effective teaching practices for DLL children. All teachers, both target and control, were trained to use a digital progress-monitoring tool to monitor their students' progress across the year in the following constructs in both English and Spanish: phonological awareness, letter knowledge, and one-word picture vocabulary. The progress-monitoring tool used personal digital assistant (PDA) technology to allow teachers to sync their student scores with progress-monitoring software that instructs teachers on how to form ability-level grouping to better provide instruction for struggling learners.

The in-class mentoring component was designed to provide individualized support regarding implementation of a dual language early childhood curriculum and effective teaching practices. When mentors provide support that is embedded in the authentic context of the teacher's classroom, this type of practice-based learning is believed to support adult learning (Desimone, 2009; Neuman & Cunningham, 2009; Webster-Wright, 2009). The individualized feedback possible with mentoring appears to be critical aspect of improving teaching practices (Landry et al., 2006, 2009; Pianta et al., 2008; Wasik et al., 2006). In-class mentoring has been used in previous evaluations of professional development for DLL teachers because universally packaged professional development is often not feasible or relevant for these teachers (Calderón & Marsh, 1988).

Finally, mentors provided assistance in the use of a supplemental curriculum, associated materials, and a handheld PDA with software for conducting and analyzing progress-monitoring assessments. Mentoring is believed to provide a useful method for encouraging teachers to adopt new technologies, particularly if such practices are unfamiliar or likely to produce resistance (Onchwari & Keengwe, 2008), and use of a similar PDA tool in the Landry et al. (2009) study revealed that many pre-K teachers were unfamiliar with PDAs and computers. Comparison teachers only received the PDA tool and were provided with a brief initial training on how to use the tool and ongoing technical assistance throughout the year; however, they did not have access to a mentor who could support their interpretation and use of assessment data.

Specific Instructional Supports that Facilitate Cognitive Development for Dual Language Learners

The importance of a supportive classroom environment for appropriate cognitive development for school readiness has been a topic of early education researchers for many years. In the pilot study, several key elements of language and literacy development that are supported by empirical literature were implemented: 1) monitoring the progress of early literacy and language skills, 2) small-group ability-level grouping for instructional purpose with highly targeted instruction to promote literacy and language development, and 3) highly targeted instruction to promote literacy and language development.

Progress Monitoring for Early Literacy and Language Skills in English and Spanish   With states now focusing on scientifically based instruction and accountability in early education, the use of teacher-implemented short

assessments within the classroom have become more prevalent for informing more effective instruction (McConnell, 2000; Phaneuf & Silberglitt, 2003). Often referred to as progress-monitoring measures, the measures are usually very brief, often timed assessments with repeated administrations across the school year.

The use of progress-monitoring assessments is important mainly because teachers are able to make data-based decisions about instructional time. When teachers are able to track their students' progress across the school year, they can differentiate instruction and provide targeted instruction based on particular needs to individual students. Fortunately, research has identified the school-readiness domains that are critically important for academic success (e.g., oral language, letter knowledge, phonological awareness, and early mathematics). Children who master more of these rudimentary skills by kindergarten become better at literacy and mathematics than children who have not mastered them (Geary, 1994; National Early Literacy Panel, 2008; National Reading Panel, 2000; Whitehurst & Lonigan, 1998, 2001).

For DLL children, it is important to monitor development of these skills in both English and Spanish across the school year. When possible, there are several reasons why monitoring student progress in both the home language and school language(s) is important. First, students arrive at pre-K with a set of language and literacy skills that may not be apparent if they are only assessed in English. Depending on language of instruction of a classroom, it may be important to assess children in the their home language across the school year as well as English, or if students are in English immersion classrooms, it may be more appropriate to assess certain literacy skills in English—those that are directly taught, such as phonological awareness and letter knowledge—and assess oral language and vocabulary development in both their home language and English. Many times, decisions on language of assessment are made at the program level or school level, leaving wide variability in practice across the nation, but it is important to consider both programmatic goals and developmental appropriateness for individual students when deciding on language of assessment.

For example, if a DLL child is enrolled in an English immersion classroom, the programmatic goals are clear—students are immersed in English instruction from Day 1 with a goal of making the transition to English as soon as possible. However, knowledge of that student's ability levels at pre-K entry in his or her home language provides important instructional information for teachers. Extant research demonstrates that oral proficiency in a child's native language has been found to be predictive of later literacy outcomes, specifically phonological awareness (Durgunoglu, Nagy, & Hancin-Bhatt, 1993; Quiroga et al., 2002) and reading comprehension (Dufva & Voeten, 1999). Cross-linguistic correlations have been found between phonological awareness in a child's first and second language (Durgunoglu, 1998; Durgunoglu et al., 1993; Geva & Siegel, 2000; Geva, Wade-Woolley, & Shany, 1997; Lindsey, Manis, & Bailey, 2003; Oller & Eilers, 2002) and vocabulary levels (Carlisle et al., 1999; Ordonez, Carlo, Snow, & McLaughlin, 2002). Therefore, if it is possible to know a child's skill level in his or her home language, teachers can be provided with better data to plan instruction in both English and the home language, when possible and appropriate.

Small-Group Ability-Level Grouping   An additional benefit to monitoring progress across the school year is that it allows teachers to group students according to ability level for instructional purposes. This allows teachers to provide targeted instruction in particular academic skills for students who may be struggling. Highly targeted instruction in language and literacy should concentrate on areas of development that have been demonstrated to be predictive of later reading outcomes. Specifically, this includes oral language development including vocabulary, phonological awareness instruction, and alphabet knowledge. Children with more of these emergent literacy skills appear to profit more from reading instruction, learn to read sooner, and read better than do children with less of these skills. Small-group instruction has been demonstrated to be effective in promoting moderate to large gains in children's learning (Lonigan & Whitehurst, 1998; Starkey, Klein, & Wakeley, 2004). One important question examined in the meta-analysis that was the basis of the National Early Literacy Panel report (2008) was this: Which instructional practices were most likely to enhance early language and literacy skills? A major conclusion was that the interventions that produced large and positive effects on these skills were most often conducted as one-to-one or small-group activities. They tended to be directed by the teacher and engaged children in a targeted way in the use of particular skills. Other evidence for the importance of small-group approaches in pre-K comes from the PCER National Report, where it was reported that the most effective curriculum are those that emphasize the use of small-group instruction (PCER, 2008).

There is empirical support that describe how greater learning occurs by maximizing DLLs' engagement with small, homogenous instructional groups (Gersten & Geva, 2003). For DLL children, the benefit of ability-level grouping is multiplied, as children can be grouped based on ability level for a certain content area in addition to their language level. Researchers are now beginning to understand that for children to learn a second language and continue to advance in their first (home) language, specialized support from teachers is particularly important; an optimal approach is for this learning to occur in parallel to introducing and building the child's understanding and expressive skills in English.

Teacher Change over Time as Measured by the Bilingual Teacher Behavior Rating Scale

Comparisons between the target and comparison groups were conducted both pretest and posttest, which coincided with the beginning and end of the school year. A series of ANOVAs were conducted pretest to determine if there were significant pretest differences between the target and control groups. Pretest observations, utilizing the B-TBRS, indicated that there were no significant differences between the teachers assigned to the target condition and those assigned to the comparison condition at the start of the project. Posttest, a series of ANCOVA analyses were conducted to determine the effect of the intervention utilizing the pretest scores on the B-TBRS subscales. Posttest, significant differences were observed between the target and control teachers in the following domains: Overall Teacher Quality, $F(1, 20) = 4.62$, $p = .05$, $ES = .87$; Quality of Classroom Community, $F(1, 20) = 5.61$, $p = .03$, $ES = .92$; Oral Language Quality, $F(1, 20) = 4.32$, $p = .05$, $ES = 1.01$. Oral Language Quantity approached significance, $[F(1, 20) = 4.12$, $p = .058$, $ES = .92]$.

These results, although preliminarily, seem to indicate that teachers in the target condition performed better in the domains posttest when compared to the teachers in the comparison condition. These results are encouraging, as they indicate that the mentoring program, combined with professional development courses about early language and literacy instruction for DLLs, significantly increased competency in critical domains, such as quality of teachers' oral language instruction. The finding that teachers in the target group used higher quality oral language on the B-TBRS scale is of great practical importance, given how difficult it can be to teach teachers to model high-quality language and to elicit oral language from pre-K children in the classroom setting.

These results also indicated significant differences between the target and control groups in Quality of Classroom Community. This subscale of the B-TBRS measures common aspects of classroom community, such as how the classroom is set up, orienting children for expectations in the classroom, and the layout of the classroom. The significant increase in Quality of Classroom Community was perhaps a result of the professional development session on classroom management that explicitly addressed these topics. In addition, mentors were asked to help teachers arrange classrooms and organize supplemental materials in a manner that was conducive to children's learning and allowed children to engage in social and cognitive learning, which was likely to have influenced these findings.

Another encouraging finding was the significant difference between target and control teachers on overall teaching quality. This score is a total score of all the B-TBRS subscales. Improvement on this metric indicates that target teachers' classrooms showed greater improvement on the B-TBRS subscales at a greater rate than teachers in the control condition. It is likely that all aspects of the professional development model, from in-class mentoring to progress monitoring, influenced this score.

Relationship Between Bilingual Teacher Behavior Rating Scale and Student Data

In addition to examining teacher behavior changes across the school year, the study utilized the B-TBRS to investigate the relationship between the B-TBRS subscales and child outcomes. Specifically, simple Pearson correlations were examined between end-of-year child outcome data and the content areas observed by the B-TBRS. Table 2.3 includes only correlations between the B-TBRS content areas and child outcome data that were significant. Moderate significant correlations ($r = .41 - .69$) were found between many of the B-TBRS content areas and child outcomes in the same content areas. This first step in establishing the predictive validity of the B-TBRS is important, as it is essential that classroom observational tools are associated with child outcomes.

One interesting finding is the negative correlations between B-TBRS content areas in Spanish and child outcomes in English and vice versa. This suggests that in some content areas, when Spanish quality is better and quantity is higher, English child outcomes may suffer. The same is true when English quality is better and quantity is higher for Spanish outcomes. In one regard, this finding is not surprising, because teachers, similar to the children they instruct, typically have a dominant language. When this is the case, these teachers are more comfortable and better equipped to instruct in certain content areas in their dominant language and may have higher quality teachable moments in their dominant language. In addition, this finding suggests that despite program philosophies, actual implementation of bilingual instruction was not carefully balanced. It is important to note that if quality and quantity in both Spanish and English had not been separately measured, there would have been no evidence of this relationship between classroom instruction and student outcomes. More research is needed in the area, but this finding has potential to become an important mentoring tool to improve bilingual instruction in the future.

CONCLUSIONS

The B-TBRS was developed with two important goals in mind. The first is to be sensitive to teacher change over time. The pilot study data indicate that the measure could discriminate between teachers who received a comprehensive professional development program and those who did not in important content areas such as overall teaching quality and the quality

Table 2.3. Significant correlations between Bilingual-Teacher Behavior Rating Scale (B-TBRS) content areas and child outcomes (Solari et al., 2009)

	English BESA-M	Spanish BESA-M	English BESA-S	Spanish BESA-S	English EOWPVT	Spanish EOWPVT	English ROWPVT	Spanish ROWPVT	English PA	Spanish PA	English LK	Spanish LK
Classroom Community, Quality		.59[b]										.48[a]
Sensitivity, Quantity		.54[b]	.52[b]			.40[a]		.42[a]		.45[a]	.46[a]	
Sensitivity, Quality	.42[a]									.42[a]		.42[a]
English Book Reading, Quantity		−.40[a]										
English Book Reading, Quality		−.43[a]				−.48[a]		−.46[a]				
English Oral Language, Quantity		−.40[a]	.52[b]		.42[a]							
English Oral Language, Quality		−.40[a]	.53[b]			−.48[a]		−.47[a]				
English Print & Letter Knowledge, Quantity											.61[a]	−.66[a]
Spanish-Print and Letter Knowledge, Quantity											−.55[b]	.56[b]
English-Print and Letter Knowledge, Quality											.50[a]	−.51[a]

Spanish PA, Quantity				.43[a]		
English PA, Quantity			.45[a]			
Spanish PA, Quality				.48[a]		
English PA, Quality			.40[a]			
Total Teaching Sum, Quality	.61[b]	.42[a]			.43[a]	.42[a]	.41[a]
Total Teaching Sum, Quantity	.69[b]	.41[a]			.48[a]	.46[a]	.46[a]	.55[a]

Key: BESA-M, Bilingual English-Spanish Assessment–Morphosyntax and BESA-S, Bilingual English-Spanish Assessment–Semantics (Peña, Gutierrez-Clellen, Iglesias, Goldstein, & Bedore (n.d.); EOWPVT, Expressive One-Word Picture Vocabulary Test (Brownell, 2000a); ROWPVT, Receptive One-Word Picture Vocabulary Test (Brownell, 2000c); PA, phonological awareness; LK, letter knowledge.

[a]$p \leq .05$; [b]$p \leq .01$.

of overall language instruction. Although it is a bit discouraging that significant differences between target and control teachers across other content areas did not appear, because of the population of students in the study (DLLs), much of the professional development was concentrated on improving oral language instruction across all content area instruction.

The second goal of the B-TBRS is to capture critical teaching behaviors that have direct influence on student outcomes in bilingual pre-K settings. Of particular importance was to develop a measure that could be directly linked to student variables that are known to be important for cognitive development and school readiness in DLLs. The results indicate moderate correlations between subscales in the B-TBRS and language and literacy outcomes for DLLs.

The preliminary results with the B-TBRS are encouraging, but more research is needed with the tool to further examine its psychometric properties and usefulness in bilingual pre-K settings. Of particular importance will be to conduct analyses similar to those presented in this chapter with a larger sample of bilingual teachers and DLLs.

STUDY QUESTIONS

1. According to research with both DLL and non-DLL populations, what skills are crucial to reading proficiency? What advantages are enjoyed by children who have these skills?

2. What are the four broad domains that the B-TBRS measures?

3. Give several ways in which the B-TBRS differs from its predecessor, the TBRS.

4. Why is it important to monitor students' progress in both their home language and their school language(s)?

REFERENCES

Anthony, J.L., Williams, J., McDonald, R., & Francis, D.J. (2007). Phonological processing and emergent literacy in younger and older preschool children. *Annals of Dyslexia*, 57, 11–37.

Assel, M.A., Landry, S.H., & Swank, P.R. (2007). Are early childhood classrooms preparing children to be school ready? The CIRCLE Teacher Behavior Rating Scale. In L. Justice & C. Vukelich (Eds.), *Achieving excellence in preschool literacy instruction* (pp. 12–35). New York: The Guilford Press.

August, D., Carlo, M., Dressler, C., & Snow, C. (2005). The critical role of vocabulary development for English Learners. *Learning Disabilities Research & Practice*, 20(1), 50–57.

August, D. & Shanahan, T. (2006). *Developing literacy in second-language learners: Report of the National Literacy Panel on Language Minority Children and Youth.* Mahwah, NJ: Lawrence Erlbaum Associates.

Baumann, J.F., & Kameenui, E.J. (1991). Research on vocabulary instruction: Ode to Voltaire. In J. Flood, J.J.D. Lapp & J.R. Squire (Eds.), *Handbook of research on teaching the English language arts* (pp. 60–32). New York: MacMillan.

Bialystok, E., & Herman, J. (1999). Does bilingualism matter for early literacy? *Bilingualism: Language and Cognition, 2*(1), 35–44.

Blachowicz, C.L.Z., Obrochta, C., & Fogelberg, E. (2005). Literacy coaching for change. *Educational Leadership, 62,* 5–8.

Bond, G.L., & Dykstra, R. (1997). The cooperative research program in first-grade reading instruction. *Reading Research Quarterly, 32,* 34–27.

Bradley, L., & Bryant, P. (1985). Rhyme and reason in reading and spelling. In *International Academy for Research in Learning Disabilities monograph series, number 1.* Ann Arbor: University of Michigan Press.

Bronfenbrenner, U., & Morris, P. (2006). The bioecological mode of human development. In W. Damon & R.M. Lerner (Eds.), *Handbook of child psychology: Theoretical models of human development* (6th ed., pp. 79–28). Edison, NJ: Wiley.

Brownell, R. (2000a). *Expressive One-Word Picture Vocabulary Test (EOWPVT).* Novato, CA: Academic Therapy Publications.

Brownell, R. (2000b). *Expressive One-Word Picture Vocabulary Test: Spanish-Bilingual Edition (EOWPVT-SBE).* Novato, CA: Academic Therapy Publications.

Brownell, R. (2000c). *Receptive One-Word Picture Vocabulary Test (ROWPVT).* Novato, CA: Academic Therapy Publications.

Calderón, M., & Marsh, D. (1988, Winter). Applying research on effective bilingual instruction in a multi-district inservice teacher training program. *NABE Journal,* 13–52.

Carlisle J.F., Beeman, M.M, Davis, L.-H., & Spharim, G. (1999). Relationship of metalinguistic capabilities and reading achievement for children who are becoming bilingual. *Applied Psycholinguistics, 20,* 45–78.

Christie, J.F., & Enz, B. (1992). The effects of literacy play interventions on preschoolers' play patterns and literacy development. *Early Education and Development, 3*(3), 205–220.

Cobo-Lewis, A., Pearson, B.Z., Eilers, R.E., & Umbel, V.C. (2002). Effects of bilingualism and bilingual education on oral and written English skills: A multifactor study of standardized test outcomes. In D.K. Oller & R.E. Eilers (Eds.), *Language and literacy in bilingual children.* Clevedon, United Kingdom: Multilingual Matters.

Comeau, L., Cormier, P., Grandmaison, E., & Lacroix, D. (1999). A longitudinal study of phonological processing in children learning to read in a second language. *Journal of Educational Psychology, 91,* 29–43.

Desimone, L.M. (2009). Improving impact studies of teachers' professional development: Toward better conceptualizations and measures. *Educational Researcher, 38,* 18–99.

DeTemple, J.M. (2001). Parents and children reading books together. In D.K. Dickinson & P.O. Tabors (Eds.), *Beginning literacy with language: Young children learning at home and school* (pp. 31–51). Baltimore: Paul H. Brookes Publishing Co.

Dickinson, D.K., & Tabors, P.O. (2001). *Beginning literacy with language: Young children learning at home and school.* Baltimore: Paul H. Brookes Publishing Co.

Dufva, M., & Voeten, M.J.M. (1999). Native language literacy and phonological memory as prerequisites for learning English as a foreign language. *Applied Psycholinguistics, 20,* 329–348.

Durgunoglu, A.Y. (1998). Language and literacy development in Spanish and English, The U.S.A. context. In A.Y. Durgunoglu & L. Verhoeven (Eds). *Literacy development in a multilingual context: A cross-cultural perspective* (pp. 135–146). Mahwah, NJ: Lawrence Erlbaum Associates.

Durgunoglu, A.Y., Nagy, W.E., & Hancin-Bhatt, B.J. (1993). Cross-language transfer of phonological awareness. *Journal of Educational Psychology, 85*, 45–65.

Geary, D.C. (1994). *Children's mathematical development: Research and practical applications.* Washington, DC: American Psychological Association.

Gelderen, A. (2004). Linguistic knowledge, processing speed, and meta-cognitive knowledge in first- and second-language reading comprehension: A componential analysis. *Journal of Educational Psychology, 96*(1), 19–30.

Gentry, L.B., Denton, C.A., & Kurz, T. (2008). Technology-based mentoring provided to teachers: A synthesis of the literature. *Journal of Technology and Teacher Education, 16*(3), 339–373.

Gerber, M.M., Jimenez, T., Leafstedt, J., Villaruz, J., Richards, C.R., & English, J. (2004). English reading effects of small-group intervention in Spanish for K–1 English learners. *Learning Disabilities Research and Practice, 19*, 23–51.

Gersten, R., & Geva, E. (2003). Teaching reading to early language learners. *Educational* Leadership, *60*(7), 4–9.

Geva, E., & Siegel, L.S. (2000). Orthographic and cognitive factors in the concurrent development of basic reading skills in two languages. *Reading and Writing: An Interdisciplinary Journal, 12*, 1–30.

Geva, E., Wade-Woolley, L., & Shany, M. (1997). Development of reading efficiency in first and second language. *Scientific Studies of Reading, 1*(2), 119–144.

Gottardo, A. (2002). The relationship between language and reading skills in bilingual Spanish–English speakers. *Topics in Language Disorders, 22*, 46–70.

Greene, J.P. (1998). *A meta-analysis of the effectiveness of bilingual education.* Austin: University of Texas.

Hamre, B.K., Justice, L.M., Pianta, R.C., Kilday, C., Sweeney, B., Downer, J.T., et al. (2010). Implementation fidelity of MyTeachingPartner literacy and language activities: Association with preschoolers' language and literacy growth. *Early Childhood Research Quarterly, 25*(3), 329–347.

Hart, B., & Risley, T.R. (1995). *Meaningful differences in the everyday experience of young American children.* Baltimore: Paul H. Brookes Publishing Co.

Hoffman, J.V., Roser, N.L., & Farest, C. (1988). Literature-sharing strategies in classrooms serving students from economically disadvantaged and language different home environments. *Yearbook of the National Reading Conference, 37*, 33–37.

Howes, C., Burchinal, M., Pianta, R., Bryant, D., Early, D., Clifford, R. et al. (2008). Ready to learn? Children's pre-academic achievement in pre-kindergarten programs. *Early Childhood Research Quarterly, 23*, 27–50.

Landry, S.H., Anthony, J.L., Swank, P.R., & Montique-Bailey, P. (2009). Effectiveness of comprehensive professional development for teachers of at-risk preschoolers. *Journal of Educational Psychology, 101*, 44–65.

Landry, S.H., Crawford, A., Gunnewig, S., & Swank, P.R. (2001). *Teacher Behavior Rating Scale.* Unpublished research instrument, Center for Improving the Readiness of Children for Learning and Education, University of Texas Health Science Center at Houston.

Landry, S.H., Smith, K.E., Swank, P.R., & Guttentag, C. (2008). A responsive parenting intervention: The optimal timing across early childhood for impacting maternal behaviors and child outcomes. *Developmental Psychology, 44*(5), 133–353.

Landry, S.H., Swank, P.R, Smith, K.E., Assel, M.A., & Gunnewig, S.B. (2006). Enhancing early literacy skills for preschool children: Bringing a professional development model to scale. *Journal of Learning Disabilities, 39*, 30–24.

Leafstedt, J., Richards, C., & Gerber, M.M. (2004). Effectiveness of explicit phonological awareness instruction for at-risk English learners. *Learning Disabilities Research and Practice, 19*, 25–61.

Leppänen, U., Niemi, P., Aunola, K., & Nurmi, J. (2006). Development of reading and spelling Finnish from preschool to Grade 1 and Grade 2. *Scientific Studies of Reading, 10*(3), 3–30.

Lindsey, K.A., Manis, F.R., & Bailey, C.E. (2003). Prediction of first-grade reading in Spanish-speaking English-language learners. *Journal of Educational Psychology, 95*, 482–494.

LoCasle-Crouch, J., Konold, T., Pianta, R., Howes, C., Burchinal, M., Bryant, D., et al. (2007). Observed teaching quality profiles in state-funded pre-kindergarten programs and associations with teacher, program, and classroom characteristics. *Early Childhood Research Quarterly, 22*, 3–17.

Lonigan, C.J., Wagner, R.K., & Rashotte, C.A. (2002). *The Preschool Comprehensive Test of Phonological and Print Processing.* Tallahassee: Florida State University.

Lonigan, C.J., Wagner, R.K., Torgesen, J.K., & Rashotte, C.A. (2007). *Test of Preschool Early Literacy.* Austin, TX: PRO-ED.

Mashburn, A.J., Pianta, R.C., Hamre, B.K., Downer, J.T., Barbarin, O.A., Bryant, D., et al. (2008). Measures of teaching quality in prekindergarten and children's development of academic, language, and social skills. *Child Development, 79*, 732–749.

Mason, J.M. (1980). When children do begin to read: An exploration of four-year-old children's letter and word reading competencies. *Reading Research Quarterly, 15*, 20–27.

Matera, C., & Gerber, M.M. (2008). Effects of a literacy curriculum that supports writing development of Spanish-speaking English learners in Head Start. *NHSA Dialog, 11*, 25–43.

McConnell, S.R., McEvoy, M.A., & Priest, J.S. (2002). "Growing" measures for monitoring progress in early childhood education: A research and development process for individual growth and development indicators. *Assessment for Effective Intervention, 27*, 3–14.

McLaughlin, B., August, D., Snow, C., Carlo, M. Dressler, C., White, C., et al. (2000). Vocabulary improvement and reading in English language learners: An intervention study. *Proceedings of the Research Symposium on High Standards in Reading for Students from Diverse Language Groups: Research, Practice & Policy, USDOE/OBEMLA*, 12–43.

Mol, S.E., Bus, A.G., & de Jong, M.T. (2009). Interactive book reading in early education: A tool to stimulate print knowledge as well as oral language. *Review of Educational Research, 79*(2), 979–1007.

Morrow, L.M. (1991). *Literacy development in the early years.* Needham Heights, MA: Allyn & Bacon.

Morrow, L.M., & Rand, M. (1991). Promoting literacy during play by designing the early childhood classroom environment. *Reading Teacher, 44*, 396–402.

National Early Literacy Panel. (2008). *Report of the National Early Literacy Panel.* Washington, DC: National Institute for Literacy.

National Reading Panel. (2000). *Teaching children to read: An evidence-based assessment of the scientific research literature on reading and its implications for reading instruction.* Available at http://www.nichd.nih.gov/publications/nrp/report.cfm.

Neuman, S.B. (1996). Children engaging in storybook reading: The influence of access to print resources, opportunity, and parental interaction. *Early Childhood Research Quarterly, 11*(4), 495–513.

Neuman, S.B., & Cunninham, L. (2009). The impact of professional development and coaching on early language and literacy instructional practices. *American Educational Research Journal, 46,* 53–66.

Oller, D.K., & Eilers, R.E. (2002). *Language and literacy in bilingual children.* Clevedon, England: Multilingual Matters.

Onchwari, G., & Keengwe, J. (2008). The impact of a mentor-coaching model on teacher professional development. *Early Childhood Education Journal, 36,* 1–4.

Ordonez C.L., Carlo, M.S., Snow, C.E., & McLaughlin, B. (2002). Depth and breadth of vocabulary in two languages: Which vocabulary skills transfer. *Journal of Educational Psychology, 94,* 719–728.

Padrón, Y. (1994). Comparing reading instruction in Hispanic/limited English proficient schools and other inner-city schools. *Bilingual Research Journal, 18,* 4–6.

Peisner-Feinberg, E.S., Burchinal, M.R., Clifford, R.M., Culkin, M.L., Howes, C., Kagan, S.L., et al. (2001). The relation of preschool child-care quality to children's cognitive and social developmental trajectories through second grade. *Child Development, 72,* 153–553.

Peña, E.D., Gutierrez-Clellen, V., Iglesias, A., Goldstein, B., & Bedore, L.M. (n.d.). *Bilingual English-Spanish Assessment (BESA).* Unpublished test, University of Texas, Austin.

Phaneuf, R.L., & Silberglitt, B. (2003). Tracking preschoolers' language and pre-literacy development using a general outcome measurement system: One education district's experience. *Topics in Early Childhood Special Education, 23*(3), 114–123.

Pianta, R.C., Mashburn, A.J., Downer, J.T., Hamre, B. K., & Justice, L. (2008). Effects of Web-mediated professional development resources on teacher–child interactions in pre-kindergarten classrooms. *Early Childhood Research Quarterly, 23,* 43–51.

Preschool Curriculum Evaluation Research Consortium. (2008). *Effects of preschool curriculum programs on school readiness (NCER 2008–2009).* Washington, DC: U.S. Department of Education, National Center for Education Research.

Quiroga, T., Lemos-Britten, Z., Mostafapour, E., Abbott, & Berninger, V.W. (2002). *Relationships between first-language oral proficiency and word and pseudoword reading skills in English.* Mahwah, NJ: Report to the National Literacy Panel on Language-Minority Children and Youth. Document Number).

Senechal, M., & Cornell, E. (1993). Vocabulary acquisition through shared reading experiences. *Reading Research Quarterly, 28,* 36–60.

Shore, K. (2001, March). Success for ESL students. *Instructor, 110*(6), 30–33.

Silverman, R. (2007). Vocabulary development of English-language and English-only learners in kindergarten. *Elementary School Journal, 107*(4), 36–83.

Slavin, R.E., & Cheung, A. (2003). *Effective reading programs for English language learners: A best-evidence synthesis.* Baltimore, MD: Success for All Foundation. Document Number).

Snow, C.E., Tabors, P.O., Nicholson, P., & Kurland, B. (1995). SHELL: Oral language and early literacy skills in kindergarten and first-grade children. *Journal of Research in Childhood Education, 10,* 2–8.

Solari, E.J., & Gerber, M.M. (2008). Early comprehension instruction for Spanish-speaking English language learners: Teaching text level reading skills while maintaining effects on word level skills. *Learning Disabilities Research and Practice, 23,* 155–168.

Solari, E.J., Landry, S.H., Crawford, A., Gunnewig, S., & Swank, P.R. (2009). *Bilingual-Teacher Behavior Rating Scale.* Unpublished research instrument, Children's Learning Institute University of Texas Health Science Center at Houston.

Starkey, P., Klein, A., & Wakeley, A. (2004). Enhancing young children's mathematical knowledge through a pre-kindergarten mathematics intervention. *Early Childhood Research Quarterly, 19*, 9–20.

Stevenson, H.W., & Newman, R.S. (1986). Long-term prediction of achievement and attitudes in mathematics and reading. *Child Development, 57*, 646–659.

Taylor, H.B., Anthony, J.L., Aghara, R., Smith, K.E., & Landry, S.H. (2008). The interaction of early maternal responsiveness and children's cognitive abilities on later decoding and reading comprehension skills. *Early Education and Development, 19*(1), 188–207.

Vaughn, S., & Coleman, M. (2004). The role of mentoring in promoting use of research-based practices in reading. *Remedial and Special Education, 25*, 2–8.

Wasik, B.A., Bond, M.A., & Hindman, A. (2006). The effects of a language and literacy intervention on Head Start children and teachers. *Journal of Educational Psychology, 98*, 63–74.

Webster-Wright, A. (2009). Reframing professional development through understanding authentic professional learning. *Review of Educational Research, 79*, 702–739.

Whitehurst, G.J., Falco, F.L., Lonigan, C.J., Fischel, J.E., DeBaryshe, B.D., Valdez-Menchaca, M.C., et al. (1988). Accelerating language development through picture book reading. *Developmental Psychology, 24*(4), 55–59.

Whitehurst, G.J., & Lonigan, C.J. (1998). Child development and emergent literacy. *Child Development, 69*, 848–872.

Whitehurst, G.J., & Lonigan, C.J. (2001). Emergent literacy: Development from prereaders to readers. In S.B. Neuman & D.K. Dickinson (Eds.), *Handbook of early literacy research* (pp. 1–9). New York: The Guilford Press.

3

Preschool Classroom Experiences of Dual Language Learners

Summary of Findings from Publicly Funded Programs in 11 States

Virginia E. Vitiello,
Jason T. Downer, and Amanda P. Williford

Owing to shifting demographics in the United States, more and more American families are considered "language minority," indicating that for the members of these families, a language other than English is the primary language spoken at home. Nationwide, approximately 20% of children come from homes where a minority language is spoken, and about a quarter of children are not fully English proficient (National Center for Education Statistics [NCES], 2009). These children, commonly referred to as dual language learners (DLLs), face special challenges in school, as they must learn to be proficient in speaking, reading, and writing in English and

This chapter was supported in part by a grant awarded to Dr. Robert C. Pianta and colleagues by the Institute of Education Sciences, U.S. Department of Education (Grant R305A060021), as part of the National Center for Research on Early Childhood Education, and by the Institute of Education Sciences, U.S. Department of Education, through Grant R305B060009 to the University of Virginia. The opinions expressed are those of the authors and do not represent views of the U.S. Department of Education. We would like to acknowledge several colleagues who contributed to the work summarized in this chapter—Drs. Margaret Burchinal, Sam Field, Aki Hamagami, Michael L. Lopez, Robert Pianta, and Carollee Howes. In addition, portions of the data summarized in this chapter have been submitted for publication elsewhere: Burchinal, M., Field, S., López, M., Howes, C., & Pianta, R. (2011). Instruction in Spanish in pre-kindergarten and child outcomes for dual language learners. Manuscript submitted for publication (copy on file with author).

simultaneously learn the basic concepts appropriate for their grade level. An achievement gap between DLL students and native English speakers can be detected as early as preschool and persists through high school (Laosa & Ainsworth, 2007; U.S. Department of Education, 2008).

As the population of DLLs increases, there is a growing need for preschool programs to determine how best to support their development. Most DLLs are born in the United States to immigrant parents and start school in the American school system, so the majority of children who are DLLs are young in age—concentrated in the preschool and early elementary grades (Fortuny, Capps, Simms, & Chaudry, 2009; McBride, 2008). The expansion of publicly funded preschool has increased DLLs' access to affordable preschool programs (Laosa & Ainsworth, 2007), but simply providing access to preschool may not be enough to prepare these children for successful school entry and later school achievement. In this chapter, several special issues related to providing preschool education for DLLs are examined, including measuring program quality, identifying factors that contribute to the development of English language proficiency, and determining whether instruction in children's primary language is appropriate for preparing children for school. The analyses presented in this chapter focus on a subpopulation of DLLs: students who reside within families where the primary language spoken at home is likely to be Spanish. These analyses are based on data from two large-scale studies of public preschool programs: the National Center for Early Development and Learning's (NCEDL's) Multi-State Study of Pre-Kindergarten ("Multi-State Study") and the National Institute for Early Education Research (NCEDL–NIEER) State-Wide Early Education Programs Study ("SWEEP Study"). Combined, these studies include data from more than 700 public preschool classrooms and nearly 3,000 children. In the next three sections of this chapter, the importance of classroom quality, attaining English proficiency, and acquiring school-readiness skills for preschool DLLs is summarized.

CLASSROOM QUALITY

Teacher–child interactions have been repeatedly identified in the education and developmental literature as critical inputs into the learning process of young children (Brophy, 1986; Good, Wiley, & Florez, 2009; Hamre & Pianta, 2007; Howes & Ritchie, 2002). Children who attend preschool classrooms that provide cognitively stimulating, supportive, and language-rich interactions leave preschool with better academic and social school-readiness skills than children who attend lower quality classrooms (Howes et al., 2008; Mashburn et al., 2008). Though sometimes labeled differently across studies, these interactions have largely been conceptualized to fall into the three domains of emotional, organizational, and instructional supports, which have now been applied to a wide range of age groups using a variety of metrics (Brophy & Good, 1986; Pressley et al., 2003; Rimm-Kaufman, Curby, Grimm, Nathanson, & Brock, 2009; Soar & Soar, 1979). However, researchers, administrators, and policy makers have questioned whether this conceptualization of classroom quality holds across classrooms that are ethnically or linguistically diverse (Child Trends, 2009). This concern has become increasingly salient in recent years, as preschool programs have begun using measures of classroom quality for accountability purposes and to identify high- and low-quality programs (Howes et al., 2008).

If measures of classroom quality such as the Classroom Assessment Scoring System™ (CLASS™; Pianta, La Paro, & Hamre, 2008), a widely used measure of teacher–child interaction quality, are going to be used to determine classroom quality *across* ethnically and/or linguistically diverse classroom, it is important to validate that these measures are psychometrically consistent across classrooms. When a measure of classroom quality does assess a construct in similar ways across classrooms, policy makers and researchers can be more confident that this measure is valid for these diverse populations. Thus, the first study discussed in this chapter examined the validity of the CLASS (Pianta et al., 2008) across classrooms with different proportions of DLLs (Downer, López, Hamagami, Howes, & Pianta, 2009). The framework used to examine validity involved establishing that the measurement structure of the CLASS was invariant across linguistically diverse classrooms. Establishing measurement invariance, including identical structure and relations between indicators, provides initial evidence that an assessment taps into the same underlying construct across groups (see, e.g., Horn & McArdle, 1992). Later in the chapter, classroom quality and specific types of instruction within the classroom are examined in relation to English proficiency and acquisition of school-readiness skills, outcomes that are important for children to be successful as they enter into formal schooling.

ATTAINING ENGLISH PROFICIENCY

In addition to providing high-quality classroom experiences to preschoolers who are DLLs, English proficiency is yet another important factor affecting later academic outcomes. English proficiency is associated with better reading achievement in English, more complex use of academic English, and the ability to interact with peers in English (Genesee, Lindholm-Leary, Saunders, & Christian, 2005). Children from language-minority households who start kindergarten with full English proficiency make gains in reading that are similar to the gains made by children from English-only households, whereas non–English-proficient children lag

behind (Kieffer, 2008). Thus, one of the key areas of research for DLLs is determining factors that contribute to children becoming proficient in English.

Prior research has shown that several family factors, such as parent
English proficiency and parent involvement at school, contribute significantly to children's acquisition of English (Bleakley & Chin, 2008; Lahaie,
2008). From a policy perspective, however, it may be even more important
to consider policy-relevant aspects of the learning environment. In the
preschool context, the proportion of instruction provided in Spanish as
well as the quality of the classroom environment may be important contributors to children's English proficiency. The second study discussed
here using this dataset of state-funded preschool programs involved identifying whether and how these factors contributed to the likelihood of children attaining English proficiency by focusing on a subsample of children
who were not English proficient by the end of preschool (Burchinal, Field,
López, Howes, & Pianta, 2011).

DEVELOPING SCHOOL-READINESS
SKILLS IN ENGLISH AND SPANISH

Another important and related question is whether instruction in children's home language helps them develop school-readiness skills such as
preliteracy and math. Research has shown that some degree of Spanish instruction can be beneficial for young Spanish-speaking children. For example, prior analysis of the Multi-State/SWEEP data indicated that
Spanish-speaking children exposed to some Spanish instruction in preschool were rated by teachers as having better social skills and closer
teacher–child relationships than Spanish-speaking children exposed to little or no Spanish instruction, suggesting that using some Spanish may
have helped these children adjust to the social demands of the classroom
(Chang et al., 2007). Programs that intentionally combine instruction in
English and Spanish have been shown to lead to gains in language and literacy skills measured in English (e.g., Barnett, Yarosz, Thomas, Jung, &
Blanco, 2007). However, in existing public preschool programs, Spanish-
speaking children's exposure to instruction in Spanish is not tightly controlled across programs and depends on many factors (e.g., whether the
preschool teacher speaks the children's primary language, whether local
directive personnel promote the use of dual-language instruction), so it is
likely to vary significantly from classroom to classroom.

The third study discussed in this chapter, therefore, examined
whether the percentage of Spanish instruction, alone and in combination
with classroom quality, significantly predicted gains in math and preliteracy skills for Spanish-speaking children. A key factor is that children's
school readiness skills were assessed in Spanish or English, depending on

the child's level of English proficiency (Field & Burchinal, 2009). This enabled the study to examine school-readiness skills that children had acquired in Spanish that may, in theory, support later English-language skills (Cardenas-Hagan, Carlson, & Pollard-Durodola, 2007).

CONTENTS OF THIS CHAPTER

To summarize, this chapter discusses analyses that were conducted using data from two large-scale studies of public preschool programs in the United States and then presents a discussion of findings across the studies. The purpose of these analyses was to examine several issues that are particularly relevant to educating preschool DLLs, the majority of which, in the current study, were from Spanish-speaking families. Specific research questions addressed were the following:

1. Is the construct of teacher–child interaction quality, as measured by the CLASS (Pianta et al., 2008), equally valid across classrooms with different proportions of DLLs (Downer et al., 2009)?

2. Does the percentage of Spanish instruction and teacher–child interaction quality predict the likelihood of Spanish-speaking children becoming English proficient in preschool and kindergarten (Field & Burchinal, 2009)?

3. Does the percentage of Spanish instruction and teacher–child interaction quality predict math and preliteracy skills in Spanish-speaking preschool children (Burchinal et al., 2011)?

METHOD

Data for the analyses reported here came from two large-scale studies: the NCEDL's Multi-State Study and the NCEDL–NIEER SWEEP Study. These two studies had very similar research designs, and the samples were meant to be combined for data analysis so that results were representative of the country's well-established, state-funded preschool programs from the years 2001–2004.

Participants

The studies included a total of 2,983 children enrolled in 721 preschool classrooms in 11 states. At the time of data collection, the 11 states included in these studies served approximately 80% of children in the United States who were attending state pre-kindergarten (pre-K) programs.

The Multi-State Study involved a stratified sampling of 40 pre-K sites within six states during the 2001–2002 school year. The SWEEP Study involved a stratified random sample of 100 state-funded pre-K programs within five states during 2003–2004. In both studies, one classroom was randomly selected to participate within each preschool site.

Children eligible for participation were those who 1) had parental consent, 2) met the state's age criterion for kindergarten eligibility the following year, 3) did not have an individualized education program, and 4) spoke English or Spanish well enough to understand simple instructions. Four children were randomly selected to participate from each classroom, and whenever possible this included selection of two boys and two girls. Classes averaged 17.6 children (standard deviation [SD] = 4.5), so this sample represents approximately 22.8% of the population of children who attended each class. Table 3.1 presents descriptive characteristics of all participating children, teachers, and classrooms.

For the research questions described in this chapter, a point of interest is a subsample of children from this combined dataset—those children who were DLLs and spoke both Spanish and English. However, the specific sample characteristics and sizes for each set of analyses differed based on each of the research questions under consideration. Therefore, specific sample information is presented for each study when reporting the results.

Table 3.1. Descriptive statistics for the combined Multi-State/SWEEP data

Variable	n	%	M (SD)
Child and family characteristics			
Boy	1,459	49	
White	1,200	41	
Black/African American	533	18	
Hispanic/Latino	764	26	
Other race/ethnicity	401	14	
Maternal education (years)			12.65 (2.41)
Child from low-income family	1,605	58	
Spanish speaking	950	32	
Teacher and classroom characteristics			
Bachelor of arts degree or higher	496	69	
Average teacher–student ratio			8.65 (3.54)
Full day classroom	304	46	
Average % of children from low-income family			0.59 (.32)
Teacher speaks Spanish	950	37	

Key: n, number of children; %, percentage of the participants; M, mean; SD, standard deviation; SWEEP, State-Wide Early Education Programs Study.

Child and Family Demographics

Fifty-one percent of the children were girls. Children's ethnicities included Caucasian (40%), Hispanic/Latino (26%), African American (18%), and other race/ethnicity (16%). The average maternal education was 12.65 years, and 58% of families were at or below the federal poverty threshold.

Teacher and Classroom Characteristics

Teachers reported an average of about 13 years of experience teaching and 16 years of formal education. Most teachers were Caucasian (67%), with smaller percentages identified as African American (14%), Hispanic/Latino (11%), or other race/ethnicity (8%). Thirty-four percent of teachers either spoke Spanish or had a Spanish-speaking teaching assistant. A little more than half of the classrooms met for a half day (54%), 61% were located in a public school, and 16% received Head Start funding. There was an average of about nine children per adult in each classroom, and the classrooms largely served children from families with low socioeconomic status (59%).

Measures and Procedures

Data on children, families, teachers, and classrooms were collected through surveys, observations, and direct assessments. Information about these measures and how they were collected are organized by the following construct.

Child, Family, and Teacher Characteristics Demographic information about children, families, and teachers (e.g., sex, age, education, primary language) were collected through demographic questionnaires distributed at the start of the study. Teachers were also asked to report basic information about their classrooms (e.g., full or half day, percentage of DLLs).

Classroom Quality Classroom quality was assessed using two measures: the CLASS (Pianta et al., 2008) and the Emerging Academic Snapshot ("Snapshot"; Ritchie, Howes, Kraft-Sayre, & Weiser, 2001), both live-coded during classroom visits.

For the CLASS, trained observers rated classrooms and teachers on nine dimensions in 20-minute cycles during an observation day, with observations lasting from the time children arrived until they started nap (or left for the day in half-day programs). CLASS dimensions are rated on a 7-point scale, with higher scores indicating that the dimension is more characteristic of the classroom. The nine dimensions are Positive Climate (evidence of enthusiasm, enjoyment, and respect between teachers and children), Negative Climate (evidence of a negative emotional and social tone), Teacher Sensitivity (teachers provide comfort, reassurance, and encouragement to children), Overcontrol (classroom activities are highly structured or regimented), Behavior Management (teachers' use of preventive rather than reactive behavior-management strategies), Productivity (management of classroom time allows children to be consistently involved in varied learning activities), Instructional Learning Formats (teachers' use of strategies and materials to maintain children's attention, interest, and active engagement in classroom activities), Concept Development (teachers' use of instructional strategies that promote higher order thinking skills and creativity), and Quality of Feedback (teachers' use of verbal feedback about children's work, comments, and ideas).

Factor analyses of the CLASS have yielded three factors of teacher–child interaction quality (Hamre, Pianta, Mashburn, & Downer, 2007; Pakarinen et al., 2009). The first factor, Emotional Support, is the average of Positive Climate, Negative Climate (reversed), and Teacher Sensitivity. The second factor, Classroom Organization, is the average of Behavior Management, Productivity, and Instructional Learning Formats. The third and final factor, Instructional Support, is the average of Concept Development and Quality of Feedback. These scores were highly internally consistent in the Multi-State/SWEEP data (Cronbach's alpha coefficients were .89, .79, and .82, respectively). During training on the CLASS, data collectors watched and coded video segments that had been coded by CLASS experts and did live classroom observations with one of the measures' authors. During these sessions, data collectors averaged 86% agreement within one point of expert codes.

For the Snapshot, data collectors observed each participating child for 20 seconds and had 40 seconds to record the child's activity setting, engagement with activities, and adult–child interactions, before moving on to observe the next child (Ritchie at al., 2001). These 60-second cycles were conducted for a 20-minute block, and then observers had a 5-minute break before beginning another block. On average, children were observed and coded 46.7 times ($SD = 5$, range $= 20$–115).

The Snapshot consists of 28 binary items coded (as "present" or "absent") after each 20-second period. Observers also noted when interactions were conducted in a language other than English. The Snapshot scores of interest here included information about adult–child interactions that took place during instructional activity settings. In conjunction with codes representing the type of activity the child was engaged in, a Snapshot score was created to represent the percentage of non-English interactions children received during academic activities. Data collectors' average kappa with the expert coder was .77 ($SD = 0.17$) on the Second-Language code. Ratings were also created to represent the percentage of scaffolding interactions that children received, indicating that the teacher responded to the child by giving instructions or assistance or asking a question without elaboration (average kappa = .69, SD = 0.15). The ratings also indicated the percentage of elaborated instruction, coded when teachers engaged in conversation, demonstrated interest, or asked questions that allowed children to give more extensive responses (average kappa = .77, SD = 0.17).

Child Assessments   Direct assessments of each child's English proficiency, vocabulary, and math skills were collected during a 50-minute testing session in the fall and spring of preschool and again in the fall and spring of kindergarten. Assessments were conducted using English or Spanish versions of each measure, depending on children's English proficiency.

English Proficiency   The Preschool Language Assessment Scale (PreLAS) 2000 (Duncan & De Avila, 1998) was administered in English to determine whether children were proficient enough in English to be administered the English-language versions of the assessment battery. Three of the six subscales (Simon Says, Art Show, Human Body) of the PreLAS 2000 were administered and required children to respond to a set of instructions and verbally identify pictures. Children who scored at least 31 correct out of 40 received the assessments in English, whereas children who scored below 31 were given the assessments in Spanish. According to the authors of the PreLAS, the three subscales are internally consistent (Cronbach's alphas were .88 [Simon Says], .90 [Art Show], and .86 [Human Body]) and reliable (test–retest reliabilities were .89 [Simon Says], .94 [Art Show], and .91 [Human Body]). All children who spoke a language other than English at home were given the English PreLAS subscales as part of their assessment at the first wave of data collection (fall of preschool). When the children were tested again in the spring of preschool, fall of kindergarten, and spring of kindergarten, they were given the English PreLAS subscales again only if they had not passed the previous time.

Spanish Receptive Vocabulary   The Test de Vocabulario en Imágenes Peabody (TVIP; Dunn, Padilla, Lugo, & Dunn, 1986) was used to measure Spanish receptive vocabulary. In the TVIP, children are shown a set of four pictures and are asked to select the picture that best represents the meaning of a word spoken by the examiner. A standard score is computed for the scale, with a national mean of 100 and SD of 15. Cronbach's alphas on the fall and spring TVIP for the children in this study were 0.92 and 0.93, respectively.

English Receptive Vocabulary   The Peabody Picture Vocabulary Test–Third Edition (PPVT-III; Dunn & Dunn, 1997) was used to measure children's receptive vocabulary skills for those children tested in English. In this test, children are shown cards with four pictures. The examiner reads a word that corresponds to one of the pictures, and the child is asked to point to the picture that best represents the word. Raw scores were converted into standardized scores (mean [M] = 100, SD = 15) based on each child's chronological age. The PPVT-III demonstrates acceptable levels of test–retest reliability and split-half reliability and is strongly correlated with other measures of receptive language, achievement, and intelligence (Chow & McBride-Chang, 2003; Dunn & Dunn, 1997).

Spanish Math and Reading Skills   Two scales from the Bateria Woodcock-Muñoz: Pruebas de Aprovechamiento–Revisada (Woodcock & Muñoz-Sandoval, 1996) test were used to assess early math and reading skills for the Spanish-speaking children. The Problemas Aplicados scale examines the ability to analyze and solve math problems. Internal consistency reported by the measure's creators is .91 for 4-year-olds. The Indentificación de Letras y Palabras scale examines reading identification skills in identifying isolated letters and words that appear in large type. The child is not required to respond correctly with the meaning of any word. The measure's creators report internal consistency of .92 for 4-year-olds.

English Math and Reading Skills   Two subtests of the Woodcock-Johnson III: Tests of Achievement (Woodcock, McGrew, & Mather, 2001) were used to assess math and reading skills in the English-speaking children. Applied Problems (AP) was administered in both the Multi-State and SWEEP studies, and Letter–Word Identification (LW-ID) was administered in the SWEEP study only. The AP test measures early math reasoning and problem-solving abilities. It requires the child to analyze and solve math problems while performing relatively simple calculations. The LW-ID test measures prereading and reading skills. It requires children to identify letters and words appearing in large type. Both measures are widely used and have good psychometric properties.

RESULTS

Research Question 1: Is the Construct of Teacher–Child Interaction Quality Equivalent Across Linguistically Diverse Classrooms?

The first research question (Downer et al., 2009) examined whether the construct of classroom quality, measured using the CLASS, could be considered to measure equivalent constructs across classrooms that varied in linguistic composition. Analyses for this research question were based on the full, combined sample from the Multi-State and SWEEP studies. A broad set of criteria was used to identify Spanish-speaking DLLs: 1) parents reported that Spanish was spoken at home, 2) parents reported that Spanish was the child's first language, 3) the child had been administered the PreLAS language screener the fall of the study year, 4) the child's classroom consisted of 100% DLL children, and/or 5) the child was identified by his or her parents as Latino (Mexican, Puerto Rican, Cuban, or other Hispanic). Children were considered DLLs if they met one or more of these criteria. Thirty-two percent of the sample (n = 948 children) were identified as DLLs.

Using this information, classrooms were categorized into groups based on the proportion of DLLs within each classroom. The three resulting groups were 1) No DLL (no DLLs in a classroom), 2) Mid DLL (classrooms that had 1%–49% DLLs), and 3) Hi-DLL (classrooms that had 50% or more DLLs). The first group, No DLL, comprised 48.3% of the sample (348 classrooms); the second group, Mid DLL, comprised 35.5% of the sample (256 classrooms); the third group, Hi-DLL, comprised 14.2% of the sample (102 classrooms); and information on the percentage of dual language students was not available for 15 classrooms (2.0%).

Several multigroup confirmatory factor analyses were tested to determine whether the CLASS measured an equivalent construct of teacher–child interaction quality across groups. First, analyses were conducted to determine whether a one-, two-, or three-factor structure best fit the data. These initial models were constrained to be completely invariant, meaning that all parameters were set to be equal across groups. Based on commonly used fit indices, results indicated that the three-factor model provided the best fit, $\chi^2(93)$ = 200.0, Tucker-Lewis index (TLI) = .970, comparative fit index (CFI) = .967, root mean square error of approximation (RMSEA) = .071, standardized root mean square residual (SRMR) = .105, replicating findings from previous studies, which have shown that the CLASS dimensions capture the latent constructs of Emotional Support, Classroom Organization, and Instructional Support (Hamre et al., 2007). Figure 3.1 illustrates the single-group representation of this factor structure.

Next, different levels of invariance were tested to determine whether the constructs measured by the CLASS were fully equivalent across groups or only partially equivalent. All of the models fit the data reasonably well (e.g., all Tucker-Lewis indices were above .95, all RMSEAs were .08 or lower). The strict invariance model, which involved constraining factor loadings, intercepts, and error variances to be equal across groups, was selected as the best combination of fit and parsimony, $\chi^2(75)$ = 183.3, TLI = .963, CFI = .967, RMSEA = .080, SRMR = .082. The good fit of this model indicated that the CLASS observation had a similar measurement structure across groups of classrooms with different proportions of DLLs, providing evidence that it measured equivalent constructs across classrooms that were diverse in terms of linguistic composition. Thus, the

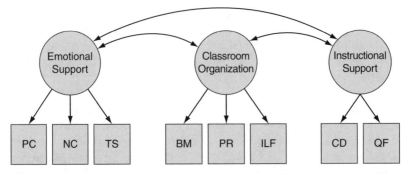

Figure 3.1. A path diagram for a confirmatory factor model for Classroom Assessment Scoring System (CLASS) domain variables. *Note:* This simplified path diagram shows only relations between dimensions and domains of the CLASS tool. Variances and error variances were tested but are not shown. (*Key:* PC = Positive Climate; NC = Negative Climate; TS = Teacher Sensitivity; BM = Behavior Management; PR = Productivity; ILF = Instructional Learning Formats; CD = Concept Development; QF = Quality of Feedback.) (From Downer, J., López, M., Hamagami A., Howes, C., & Pianta, R. [2009]. *The Classroom Assessment Scoring System in dual language learner classrooms: Factor structure and predictive validity.* Poster session presented at the 4th annual IES Research Conference, Washington, DC; adapted by permission.)

CLASS measured the key aspects of teacher–child interaction quality—emotional support, classroom organization, and instructional support—in the same way across these classrooms.

Research Question 2: What Factors Contribute to Attaining Proficiency in English?

To determine which factors predicted the attainment of English proficiency (Field & Burchinal, 2009), discrete time event history modeling (Allison, 1982) was conducted on data from the Multi-State Study only. Children were included in the analysis if they were administered the PreLAS English screener in the fall of preschool and did not demonstrate English proficiency at that time, resulting in a sample of 140 children (51% male). Data for these analyses included whether each child passed the PreLAS at each time point (spring of preschool, fall of kindergarten, spring of kindergarten), child sex, maternal education (years), baseline English proficiency in the fall of preschool, Snapshot scores (percentage of scaffolded instruction received by each child, percentage of elaborated instruction received by each child, and percentage of Spanish instruction received by each child), and CLASS scores of Emotional and Instructional Support. All continuous variables were centered at their means.

Logistic regression was used to determine whether these variables predicted the probability of a child attaining English proficiency at time t, conditional on the child not having attained proficiency at the prior time point. The model did not include an intercept but used dummy variables to represent the discrete time periods of risk, which allowed the hazard of passing the PreLAS to vary discretely over the time periods observed. Interaction effects were tested to determine whether the effects of Spanish instruction were moderated by the percentage of scaffolding, the percentage of elaborated instruction, or children's baseline English proficiency. Additional interactions tested whether the effects of classroom quality were moderated by children's baseline English proficiency and whether boys or girls were more likely to reach proficiency sooner.

Results of the logistic regression are presented in Table 3.2. Controlling for children's baseline English proficiency, the amount of Spanish instruction was significantly and negatively associated with the likelihood of attaining proficiency (-6.14, standard error $[SE] = 1.78$, $p < .001$). A significant interaction between baseline proficiency and Spanish instruction ($.43$, $SE = 0.19$, $p < .05$) indicated that the negative effect of Spanish instruction was more pronounced for children with lower baseline English. Although none of the other classroom variables were directly associated with increased likelihood of attaining proficiency, the percentage of elaborated interactions that children received had a marginally significant interaction with percentage of Spanish instruction (42.46, $SE = 22.00$, $p = .054$). This interaction effect indicated that higher levels of elaborated instruction mitigated the negative effect of Spanish instruction.

Research Question 3: What Factors Contribute to Academic School Readiness for Dual Language Learners?

The third research question (Burchinal et al., 2011) examined whether instruction in Spanish and classroom quality predicted DLLs' school-readiness outcomes at the end of preschool. The analyses examined a subsample of the combined Multi-State/SWEEP datasets, comprising Spanish-speaking children ($n = 357$, 53% male). These children included 273 children who did not demonstrate proficiency on the PreLAS English-language screener in the fall or spring of their prekindergarten year and 84 children who were not English proficient in the fall but were proficient in the spring. Data for these analyses included classroom Emotional and Instructional Support, whether any instruction was provided in Spanish, the percentage Spanish instruction, baseline English proficiency, and school-readiness assessments (receptive vocabulary, math, and reading), which were administered in English or Spanish, as appropriate.

Table 3.2. Logistic regression predicting the likelihood of children attaining English proficiency

Main effects	Estimate	SE	Wald 95% confidence limits		Chi-square	df
			Lower bound	Upper bound		
Time 1	−1.53	0.52	−2.56	−0.51	8.55**	1
Time 2	−0.34	0.57	−1.46	0.78	0.36	1
Time 3	0.95	0.66	−0.35	2.25	2.04	1
Mother's education	−0.13	0.11	−0.35	0.09	1.36	1
Baseline English proficiency	0.15	0.03	0.10	0.20	32.82***	1
% scaffolding interactions	7.27	5.28	−3.08	17.62	1.89	1
% elaborate interactions	3.23	4.53	−5.65	12.10	0.51	1
% Spanish instruction	−6.14	1.78	−9.63	−2.66	11.94***	1
Emotional support	−0.24	0.38	−0.98	0.50	0.39	1
Instructional support	−0.07	0.23	−0.52	0.38	0.09	1
Interactions						
% scaffolding × % Spanish	13.31	33.18	−51.72	78.34	0.16	1
% elaborate × % Spanish	42.46	22.00	−0.66	85.58	3.72†	1
Baseline English × % Spanish	0.43	0.19	0.05	0.81	4.89*	1
Baseline English × Emotional Support	−0.02	0.03	−0.08	0.05	0.32	1
Baseline English × Instructional Support	0.04	0.02	−0.00	0.08	3.13	1
Time 1 × boy	−0.68	0.58	−1.81	0.46	1.37	1
Time 2 × boy	−1.32	0.67	−2.63	−0.01	3.89*	1
Time 3 × boy	0.47	0.74	−0.98	1.91	0.40	1

From Field, S.H., & Burchinal, M. (2009). Developing school readiness in English and Spanish. Unpublished raw data; adapted by permission.

Key: *$p < .05$, **$p < .01$, ***$p < .001$, †$p = .054$. SE, standard error, df, degrees of freedom.

Note: Time 1 refers to the first assessment time point, Time 2 refers to the second assessment time point, and Time 3 refers to the third assessment time point.

Multilevel modeling was used to account for the nested structure of the data (children within classrooms). Two sets of models were run, the first examining outcomes for children who were tested both times in Spanish and the second to examine outcomes for children who were tested in Spanish in the fall and English in the spring. Both models controlled for child sex, baseline English proficiency, maternal education, and the child's fall score on the outcome measure. Interaction effects were tested to determine whether the effects of the presence and amount of Spanish instruction were moderated by classroom Emotional and Instructional Support.

For the children tested twice in Spanish, results suggested that there was a significant effect of percentage of Spanish instruction on children's reading scores (beta $[\beta]$ = 12.20, SE = 5.82, $p < .05$). Findings indicated that more Spanish instruction was associated with better reading readiness at the end of preschool for these children. There was also a significant interaction between the percentage of Spanish instruction and Emotional Support in predicting children's math scores (β = 22.40, SE = 8.50, $p < .01$). To interpret this, effect sizes were calculated for the percentage of Spanish instruction when Emotional Support was one SD above and below the mean. Results showed that Spanish instruction was negatively associated with math skills when Emotional Support was lower (effect size $[d]$ = .12) and positively associated with math skills when Emotional Support was higher (d = .18). Instructional Support did not significantly predict the outcomes alone or in combination and was therefore dropped from the models. None of the variables significantly predicted Spanish receptive vocabulary skills.

For the children tested in Spanish in the fall and English in the spring, the pattern of effects were different. The two Spanish-language variables—whether the child received Spanish instruction and the percentage of Spanish instruction—were significant, so percentage of Spanish instruction was dropped from the model to reduce potential collinearity. None of the interactions was significant, so these were also dropped. Results of the final model showed no effects of the classroom variables on children's school-readiness scores at the end of preschool.

DISCUSSION

Providing high-quality, appropriate preschool education to DLLs will become increasingly important as the population of DLLs in the United States increases. In accordance, the studies discussed in this chapter presented analyses that examined some of the key areas of concern for preschool children: assessing quality in diverse classrooms, identifying factors that predict English proficiency, and testing the effects of classroom variables on children's school-readiness outcomes.

Assessing Quality Across Diverse Classrooms

The first issue addressed in this chapter was whether estimates of classroom quality using the CLASS (Pianta et al., 2008) tap into equivalent constructs across linguistically diverse classrooms (Downer et al., 2009). Classroom quality is important for children from all ethnic backgrounds (Burchinal & Cryer, 2003), but high-quality programs are not equally available to all children—Hispanic children are less likely to be enrolled in center-based preschool, and the programs they do access tend to be of lower quality (Burchinal & Cryer, 2003; Laosa & Ainsworth, 2007; Magnuson & Waldfogel, 2005). One of the first steps in improving classroom quality is determining which programs provide children with high- and low-quality experiences. To do this effectively, assessments must be valid for diverse populations. Here, structural equation modeling confirmed that the factor structure of the CLASS was broadly equivalent across the three groups of classrooms, indicating that the CLASS observation measured qualitatively equivalent constructs across linguistically diverse classrooms.

Although these findings are limited to a single measure of classroom quality, they indicate that it is possible to validly assess at least some aspects of quality, in this case teacher–child interactions, across diverse classrooms (Downer et al., 2009). This adds to prior research that showed that other common measures of classroom quality were valid across Caucasian, African American, and English-speaking Hispanic populations of preschoolers (Hamre et al., 2007). An important contribution of this finding to existing knowledge is that the classroom-quality construct, which focused specifically on teacher–child interactions, was valid for classrooms with different proportions of DLLs. This information can ultimately be of use to the people involved in ensuring program quality; it suggests, for this measure, that high-quality interactions between children and teachers are structured similarly across classrooms with different linguistic compositions.

Classroom Factors that Support English Proficiency

Factors that contribute to English proficiency in preschool and kindergarten Spanish speakers were another issue addressed here. Results indicated that the most important predictor of reaching English proficiency was the percentage of teacher instruction that was provided in Spanish (Fields & Burchinal, 2009). The effect was negative, meaning that more instruction in Spanish was associated with a lower likelihood of attaining English proficiency. In addition, interaction effects suggested that as the amount of rich, elaborated instruction increased, the negative effect of Spanish instruction on English proficiency decreased and that the negative effect of Spanish instruction was stronger for children who had lower initial English scores.

These findings suggest that if the goal of a preschool program is to increase children's English language proficiency, less instruction provided in Spanish may be better for children's ability to attain proficiency in English. This effect was especially pronounced for children who began preschool with very low English proficiency; these children had the lowest likelihood of becoming English proficient. These findings must be considered within the context of a larger debate in education research about how best to support second-language proficiency in DLLs. U.S. schools have clearly rejected the idea that children with poor English-language skills can be educated entirely in English (McAndrew, 2009). In fact, in programs that have a DLL population that is predominantly from one language background, some instruction in children's primary language combined with English as a second language (ESL) instruction has proven effective (National Council of la Raza [NCLR], 2005). To best improve children's English proficiency, researchers suggest that educators consider children's current English level and other academic needs (NCLR, 2005). The findings presented here support that practice for preschool education, as well.

SPANISH INSTRUCTION FOR SPANISH-SPEAKING PRESCHOOLERS

The third research question addressed whether Spanish instruction contributed to better school-readiness outcomes among Spanish-speaking preschool children (Burchinal et al., 2011). For the group of children tested in Spanish in the spring, children made greater gains in reading when more of their instruction was in Spanish. For math, an interaction between Spanish-language instruction and emotional support in the classroom indicated that in less emotionally supportive classrooms, more Spanish instruction was associated with smaller math gains, whereas for more emotionally supportive classrooms, more Spanish instruction was associated with larger gains.

This set of analyses further emphasized the importance of providing some instruction in Spanish for children who have limited English proficiency. It also draws attention to the notion that for DLLs, it is important to consider achievement outcomes in the child's first language rather than focusing solely on English outcomes. Research on cross-linguistic transfer has suggested that increasing children's skills in their first language can lead to gains in English skills, as well (Cardenas-Hagan et al., 2007). School-readiness skills that children acquire in Spanish may support the acquisition of English school-readiness skills and later achievement, making it important to consider gains in skills measured in Spanish.

An additional contribution to existing knowledge was the examination of the role of classroom quality in preparing dual language preschoolers for school. Results suggested that quality is an important moderator of the effect of Spanish-language instruction on children's outcomes. This highlights the importance of using children's primary language to improve children's knowledge while they are becoming English proficient but further suggests that teachers' use of supportive and enriching interactions with children are important contributors to the effect of primary-language use on outcomes. Teacher–child interaction quality continues to emerge as an important element of the preschool experience, both for native English speakers and DLLs.

Limitations

The research discussed here makes substantial contributions to our understanding of DLL preschool education. Limitations to this work are important to note, though. First, because this research focused nearly exclusively on Spanish-speaking DLLs, the findings may not be generalizable to other populations. In particular, communities that have mixed dual-language populations rather than a homogenous population may face special challenges to the provision of high-quality, appropriate preschool education, especially because many programs attempt to incorporate a degree of home language instruction. Another limitation is that the data focuses on short-term school-readiness outcomes. Further studies that followed children from preschool into later grades provided additional insight into the effects that preschool experiences have on education outcomes.

In addition, the approach to measuring school readiness in the current studies did not fully address the dual development of skills in both English and Spanish for DLLs. Once screened for English proficiency, children were either given English or Spanish versions of school-readiness measures, never both. This greatly limits the capacity of these data to answer questions about how classroom context may differentially contribute to the development of skills in both languages simultaneously. For example, English proficiency levels in the Fall are known for Spanish-speaking DLLs, but Spanish language proficiency is only known for those children with lower English skills. This prompts the question, among others, about what types of classroom experiences best support young DLLs' development when they enter school with solid English and Spanish language skills.

Another shortcoming of the current work is the lack of depth of understanding of these young children's home environments. The NCEDL studies were focused on understanding the early classroom experiences of young, at-risk children and requested very little information from parents. Therefore, beyond simple information about what languages were spoken at home, nothing is known about the level of English and Spanish proficiency of adults in the home; whether parents were first-, second-, or third-generation immigrants; or parental attitudes toward dual (or single) language use in the household. These are all key factors in understanding what DLL children are bringing with them into their first classrooms that may interact with the experiences they have in preschool. Finally, the classroom observational data reported in this chapter largely address global elements of classroom quality rather than any DLL-specific instructional practices. Even the Snapshot's attempt to capture the amount of instruction provided in Spanish is a relatively coarse measure, underscoring the need for more rigorous attention to identifying and measuring early childhood teaching practices that are particularly relevant to DLL children or a subset of DLLs such as those with low incoming English proficiency.

Implications

Despite these limitations, several implications can be drawn from this work. Taken together, these results highlight the importance of primary-language use and classroom quality in educating young DLLs. The implications for policy and practice are nuanced, however.

First, it appears that common conceptualizations of quality that underscore the importance of interactions and enriching experiences in preschool are structured similarly across classrooms with high and low proportions of DLLs. Although the findings are limited to a single measure of classroom quality, the results suggest that it is possible to compare classroom quality using a common definition of the term that applies across diverse classrooms. One direction for future research will be to focus observations of quality specifically on the factors that make classrooms appropriate for DLLs. As more is learned about the factors that contribute to the development of language proficiency and other school-readiness skills, observations that address these factors will be increasingly important to ensuring quality in linguistically diverse settings.

Second, these results suggest that the use of children's primary language can have both positive and negative effects. On one hand, too much exposure to the primary language (in these analyses, Spanish) can slow children's acquisition of English. On the other hand, to effectively teach school-readiness skills like math and reading to DLLs, some instruction in their primary language appears desirable. Policy makers, program administrators, and teachers will need to carefully balance these competing needs when structuring language use and instruction in preschool classrooms. Children's initial English proficiency should play an important role in decision making, as children with low English proficiency at the beginning of preschool could benefit most from mixed exposure to English and non-English instruction.

Third, these results underscore the importance of high-quality interactions within the classroom. In particular, teachers' creation of warm, supportive relationships and sensitivity to individual children's academic and emotional needs are particularly important for learning math when combined with appropriate use of children's primary language. Educating teachers about providing high-quality interactions to DLLs will be an important aspect of improving preschool experiences for these children and can draw from recent work in the field that suggests that these types of interactions are amenable to intensive professional development opportunities (Pianta, Mashburn, Downer, Hamre, & Justice, 2008; Raver et al., 2008). Future studies in this area should continue to examine the interaction between quality and primary language instruction and move toward building a set of principles in this area that can guide preschool practice.

CONCLUSION

With the expected growth in the population of DLLs in the United States, providing effective preschool experiences for these children will become increasingly important. The research presented here provides some guidance in this area and suggests areas for further work in both public policy and research. By adding to our understanding of how best to educate preschool DLLs, we will be better able to structure preschool experiences to meet their needs.

STUDY QUESTIONS

1. The chapter presents data from three analyses of public preschool programs. What issues did these analyses examine?

2. What results did the researchers obtain? Specifically, what did they discover with regard to teacher–child interaction quality, Spanish instruction, and English proficiency in DLLs?

REFERENCES

Allison, P.D. (1982). Discrete-time methods for the analysis of event histories. *Sociological Methodology, 13*, 61–98.

Barnett, W.S., Yarosz, D.J., Thomas, J., Jung, K., & Blanco, D. (2007). Two-way and monolingual English immersion in preschool education: An experimental comparison. *Early Childhood Research Quarterly, 22*, 277–293.

Bleakley, H., & Chin, A. (2007). What holds back the second generation: The intergenerational transmission of language human capital among immigrants. *Journal of Human Resources, 43*, 267–298.

Brophy, J. (1986). Teacher influences on student achievement. *American Psychologist, 41*, 1069–1077.

Brophy, J., & Good, T.L. (1986). Teacher behavior and student achievement. In M.C. Wittrock (Ed.), *Handbook of research on teaching* (3rd ed., pp. 398–375). New York: Macmillan.

Burchinal, M.R., & Cryer, D. (2003). Diversity, child care quality, and developmental outcomes. *Early Childhood Research Quarterly, 18*, 401–426.

Burchinal, M., Field, S., López, M., Howes, C., & Pianta, R. (2011). Instruction in Spanish in pre-kindergarten and child outcomes for dual language learners. Manuscript submitted for publication (copy on file with author).

Cardenas-Hagan, E., Carlson, C.D., & Pollard-Durodola, S.D. (2007). The cross-linguistic transfer of early literacy skills: The role of initial L1 and L2 skills and language of instruction. *Language, Speech, and Hearing Services in Schools, 38*, 249–259.

Chang, F., Crawford, G., Early, D., Bryant, D., Howes, C., Burchinal, M., et al. (2007). Spanish-speaking children's social and language development in pre-kindergarten classrooms. *Early Education and Development, 18*, 243–269.

Child Trends. (2009). *What we know and don't know about measuring quality in early childhood and school-age care and education settings* (Publication #2009-12). Washington, DC: Office of Planning, Research, and Evaluation.

Chow, B.W.-Y., & McBride-Chang, C. (2003). Promoting language and literacy development through parent–child reading in Hong Kong preschoolers. *Early Education and Development, 14*, 233–248.

Downer, J., López, M., Hamagami, A., Howes, C., & Pianta, R. (2009). *The Classroom Assessment Scoring System in dual language learner classrooms: Factor structure and predictive validity.* Poster session presented at the 4th Annual IES Research Conference, Washington, DC.

Duncan, S., & De Avila, E. (1998). *PreLAS 2000 technical report.* Monterey, CA: CTB/McGraw Hill.

Dunn, L.M., & Dunn, L.M. (1997). *Examiner's manual for the Peabody Picture Vocabulary Test, Third Edition.* Circle Pines, MN: American Guidance Service.

Dunn, L., Padilla, E., Lugo, D., & Dunn, L. (1986). *TVIP—Test Vocabolario en Imagenes Peabody.* Circle Pines, MN: American Guidance Service.

Field, S.H., & Burchinal, M. (2009). [Developing school readiness in English and Spanish]. Unpublished raw data.

Fortuny, K., Capps, R., Simms, M., & Chaudry, A. (2009). *Children of immigrants: National and state characteristics.* Washington, DC: The Urban Institute.

Genesee, F., Lindholm-Leary, K., Saunders, W., & Christian, D. (2005). English language learners in U.S. schools: An overview of research findings. *Journal of Education for Students Placed at Risk, 10*, 363–385.

Good, T.L., Wiley, C.R.H., & Florez, I.R. (2009). Effective teaching: An emerging synthesis. *International Handbook of Research on Teachers and Teaching, 21*, 803–816.

Hamre, B.K., & Pianta, R.C. (2007). Learning opportunities in preschool and early elementary classrooms. In R. Pianta, M. Cox, & K. Snow (Eds.), *School readiness and the transition to kindergarten in the era of accountability* (pp. 49–84). Baltimore: Paul H. Brookes Publishing Co.

Hamre, B.K., Pianta, R.C., Mashburn, A.J., & Downer, J.T. (2007). *Building and validating a theoretical model of classroom effects in over 4000 early childhood and elementary classrooms.* Manuscript submitted for publication.

Horn, J.L., & McArdle, J.J. (1992). A practical and theoretical guide to measurement invariance in aging research. *Experimental Aging Research, 18*, 1096–4657.

Howes, C., Burchinal, M., Pianta, R., Bryant, D., Early, D., Clifford, R., et al. (2008). Ready to learn? Children's pre-academic achievement in pre-kindergarten programs. *Early Childhood Research Quarterly*, *23*, 27–50.

Howes, C., & Ritchie, S. (2002) *A matter of trust: Connecting teachers and learners in the early childhood classrooms.* New York: Teachers College Press.

Kieffer, M.J. (2008). Catching up or falling behind? Initial English proficiency, concentrated poverty, and the reading growth of language minority learners in the United States. *Journal of Educational Psychology*, *100*, 851–868.

Lahaie, C. (2008). School readiness of children of immigrants: Does parental involvement play a role? *Social Science Quarterly*, *89*, 684–705.

Laosa, L.M. & Ainsworth, P. (2007). Is public pre-K preparing Hispanic children to succeed in school? *Preschool Policy Brief, 13.* New Brunswick, NJ: National Institute for Early Education Research.

Magnuson, K.A. & Waldfogel, J. (2005). Early childhood care and education: Effects on ethnic and racial gaps in school readiness. *Future of Children*, *15*, 169–196.

Mashburn, A.J., Pianta, R.C., Hamre, B.K., Downer, J.T., Barbarin, O., Bryant, D., et al. (2008). Measures of classroom quality in prekindergarten and children's development of academic, language, and social skills. *Child Development*, *79*, 732–749.

McAndrew, M. (2009). Ensuring proper competency in the host language: Contrasting formula and the place of heritage languages. *Teachers College Record*, *111*, 1528–1554.

McBride, A. (2007). Addressing achievement gaps: The language acquisition and educational achievement of English-language learners. *Policy Notes: News from the ETS Policy Information Center*, *16*(2).

National Center for Education Statistics. (2009). *The condition of education 2009.* Washington, DC: U.S. Department of Education. Retrieved January 7, 2010, from http://nces.ed.gov/pubsearch/pubsinfo.asp?pubid=2009081.

National Council of la Raza. (2005). *Education English language learners: Implementing instructional practices.* Providence, RI: Education Alliance at Brown University.

Pakarinen, E., Lerkkanen, M-K., Poikkeus, A-M., Kiuru, N., Siekkinen, M., Rasku-Puttonen, H., et al. (2009). *A validation of the Classroom Assessment Scoring System in Finnish kindergartens.* Manuscript submitted for publication.

Pianta, R., Mashburn, A., Downer, J., Hamre, B., & Justice, L. (2008). Effects of Web-mediated professional development resources on teacher–child interactions in pre-kindergarten classrooms. *Early Childhood Research Quarterly*, *23*, 431–451.

Pianta, R.C., La Paro, K.M., & Hamre, B.K. (2008). *Classroom Assessment Scoring System™ (CLASS)™: Pre-K.* Baltimore: Paul H. Brookes Publishing Co.

Pressley, M., Roehrig, A., Raphael, L., Dolezal, S., Bohn, C., Mohan, L., et al. (2003). Teaching processes in elementary and secondary education. In W. Reynolds & G. Miller (Eds.), *Handbook of psychology: Vol. 7, Educational psychology* (pp. 153–176). Hoboken, NJ: John Wiley & Sons.

Raver, C.C., Jones, A.S., Li-Grining, C.P., Metzger, M., Smallwood, K., & Sardin, L. (2008). Improving preschool classroom processes: Preliminary findings from a randomized trial implemented in Head Start settings. *Early Childhood Research Quarterly*, *23*, 10–26.

Rimm-Kaufman, S.E., Curby, T.W., Grimm, K., Nathanson, L., & Brock, L.L. (2009). The contribution of children's self-regulation and classroom quality to children's adaptive behaviors in the kindergarten classroom. *Developmental Psychology*, *45*, 958–972.

Ritchie, S., Howes, C., Kraft-Sayre, M., & Weiser, B. (2001). *Emerging Academics Snapshot.* Los Angeles: University of California at Los Angeles.

Soar, R., & Soar, R. (1979). Emotional climate and management. In P. Peterson & H. Walberg (Eds.), *Research on teaching: Concepts, findings, and implications* (pp. 97–119). Berkeley, CA: McCutchan.

U.S. Department of Education. (2008). *National assessment of educational progress in reading and mathematics, 2007.* Washington, DC: Author.

Woodcock, R.W., McGrew, K.S., & Mather, N. (2001). *Woodcock-Johnson III: Tests of Achievement.* Itasca, IL: Riverside.

Woodcock, R.W., & Muñoz-Sandoval, A.F. (1996). *Bateria Woodcock-Muñoz: Pruebas de Aprovechamiento–Revisada.* Itasca, IL: Riverside.

4

The Role of Teacher–Child Relationships in Spanish-Speaking Dual Language Learners' Language and Literacy Development in the Early Years

Youngok Jung, Carollee Howes, Deborah Parrish, Heather Quick, Karen Manship, and Alison Hauser

This chapter examines the role of teacher–child relationships in Spanish-speaking dual language learners' (DLLs') early language and literacy development. In particular, it examines whether teacher–child relationships moderate the associations between children's literacy engagement in classrooms and their language and literacy outcomes. A total of 90 Spanish-speaking DLLs (4–5 years old) and their mothers who were enrolled in family literacy programs participated. Children were observed in their classrooms for their engagement with literacy activities and assessed in the fall and spring of the preschool year for their language and literacy skills. Teachers rated their relationships with individual children on closeness and conflict. Descriptive findings revealed that Spanish-speaking DLLs

This chapter was prepared with partial support from the National Center for Research on Early Childhood Education (NCRECE). It was supported by Grant R305A060R21, administered by the Institute of Education Sciences, U.S. Department of Education. However, the contents do not necessarily represent the positions or policies of the U.S. Department of Education or NCRECE, and endorsement by the federal government or NCRECE should not be assumed. The research reported herein was supported by First 5 LA.

are more likely to develop conflicted relationships with their teachers when there is an ethnicity/language match between teachers and children. Multilevel regression analyses revealed that children's literacy engagement was positively related to their story and print knowledge. In addition, the examination of interaction between literacy engagement and teacher–child relationships found that conflicted relationships with teachers may forfeit benefits of literacy instructions provided in school.

How do teacher–child relationships affect children's development of early language and literacy skills? Children who have conflicted relationships with their teachers are a concern to parents and teachers alike. Decades of research in brain development and developmental psychology demonstrate the predictability of teacher–child relationships for children's school adjustment and academic success (e.g., Mashburn & Pianta, 2006; Meisels, 1999). In addition, the National Association for the Education of Young Children (NAEYC; 1996)—the nation's leading organization of early childhood education—clearly indicated that social relationships with adults influence children's language and cognitive development and calls for teachers to establish positive, personal relationships with children to foster their development. Yet, the formation of close relationships with teachers has been challenged by federal and state school accountability initiatives, which lead schools and teachers to focus on the curriculum that is tested at the expense of other curriculum, including relationship building with teachers. More than three quarters of young children attend child care programs for some portion of the day (Barnett & Yarosz, 2004) and the number increases every year. Moreover, earlier teacher–child relationships formed in preschool are more closely related to children's language and social development than later ones formed in elementary school (Burchinal et al., 2002). This chapter extends the correlational findings of current literature on the role of teacher–child relationships in children's development by examining pathways of which teacher–child relationships influence children's language and literacy development. This chapter especially focuses on immigrant low-income Spanish-speaking DLLs enrolled in family literacy programs.

THEORETICAL AND CULTURAL BACKGROUND

Drawing on the continuity in the quality of parent–child and teacher–child relationships, teacher–child relationships can be viewed in the context of attachment theory (Howes & Hamilton, 1992, 1993; Lynch & Cicchetti, 1992). According to Bowlby (1969), secure attachment with mothers provides children with protection, security, and trust, which facilitate their exploration of new environments and management of stressful events. Teacher–child relationships, although differing in some ways (e.g., affection, duration), provide parallel assistances to children's social and academic functioning in school. Close, low-conflict relationships with teachers help children adjust to the social demands in the classroom and provide stability and organization to the learning process, which facilitate children's attainment of social and academic skills required in school (Bowlby, 1982; Bretherton, 1990; Main, Kaplan, & Cassidy, 1985).

In Latino culture, having good relationships is as important as learning academic skills. *Educación*—the Spanish word for *education*—includes learning in school as well as raising well-behaving individuals, putting equal emphasis on academic training, relationship building, and moral development (Valenzuela, 1999). Thus, well-educated children are not only expected to display proficiency in the academics but also act accordingly in school, respecting others and social expectations. Moreover, Latino parents believe that children with good morality do well in school. That is, a child who knows how to respect and treat others is more likely to learn easily (Reese, Balzano, Gallimore, & Goldenberg, 1995). Taken together, teacher–child relationships are expected to make a change in the effectiveness of classroom instructions and the efficacy of children's learning in classrooms. Particularly in Latino culture, where having a good relationship is as important as attaining academic skills, teacher–child relationships are expected to exert even greater influence on the relation between classroom instruction and child outcomes.

ROLE OF TEACHER–CHILD RELATIONSHIPS IN CHILDREN'S LANGUAGE AND LITERACY DEVELOPMENT

In research, the teacher–child relationship is often defined as a multidimensional construct that is characterized by the degree of closeness and conflict within the interpersonal interactions between teachers and children (Birch & Ladd, 1997; Pianta, 1994; Pianta, Steinberg, & Rollins, 1995). *Closeness* refers to the degree of warmth, open communication, and positive interactions between the teacher and child, and *conflict* refers to the level of negativity within teacher–child interactions (Birch & Ladd, 1997; Mashburn & Pianta, 2006).

Strong positive relationships with teachers characterized by closeness are positively related to children's short- and long-term academic competencies, including their language and literacy (Birch & Ladd, 1997; Brophy-Herb, Lee, Nievar, & Stollak, 2007; Hamre & Pianta, 2001; Howes et al., 2008; Pianta & Stuhlman, 2004). For instance, Burchinal and colleagues (2002) found that teacher-reported closeness with students was positively related to growth in children's receptive vocabulary and reading abilities from preschool to second grade, specifically for African American children and children whose parents reported more authoritarian attitudes. Howes et al. (2008) studied teacher–child relationships of children ($N = 2,800$) enrolled in prekindergarten (pre-K) programs in 11 states and found that after controlling for child/family characteristics (e.g., age, sex, income) children who had close relationships with teachers tended to have better alphabet knowledge, higher reading skills, and more advanced language and literacy skills than those who had conflicted relationships with teachers.

Problematic relationships with teachers, characterized by high levels of conflict, are related to children's academic and social difficulties and, ultimately, greater problems with school adjustment (Baker, 2006; Justice, Cottone, Mashburn, & Rimm-Kaufman, 2008; Ladd & Burgess, 2001). Ladd and Burgess (2001) examined environmental factors that influenced school adjustment of kindergarten children ($N = 200$) and identified that children who had more conflicts in relationships with their teachers were also less engaged in the classroom and at increased risk for poor academic achievement. Baker (2006) examined the relationship between teacher–child relationships and school adjustment for elementary-age children ($N = 1,310$) and found that higher levels of conflict in teacher–child relationships were negatively and robustly associated with children's language and reading skills, prosocial competence, and classroom adjustment.

These results show links between different qualities of teacher–child relationships and children's development, including their language and literacy development. Although informative, these findings are restricted due to the correlational nature of the investigations. In this study, the teacher–child relationship was viewed in the context of teacher–child interactions around literacy engagement and considered as a moderating factor between classroom instructions and child outcomes.

CLASSROOM QUALITY, LITERACY ENGAGEMENT, RELATIONAL FUNCTIONING, AND EARLY LANGUAGE AND LITERACY DEVELOPMENT

Recent research has explored classroom environments that are directly linked to children's academic achievement, including language and literacy skills. Thus far, classroom quality and literacy engagement have gained empirical supports. Classroom quality defined as children's direct experiences in classrooms has been found to be associated with children's development (Mashburn, 2008; Mashburn et al., 2008). For instance, Mashburn et al. (2008) examined 2,439 children in 671 pre-K classrooms in 11 states and found that children who attended pre-K classrooms with higher quality showed faster rates of development in academics and social competence. Specifically, the quality of instructional climate was positively associated with children's proficiency in receptive language, expressive language, rhyming, and letter naming. Furthermore, classroom quality is linked to teacher–child relationships, with significant associations between emotional support and positive teacher–child relationships (Hamre & Pianta, 2005).

Literacy engagement, a systematic instruction embedded in daily routines in a form of classroom activities, has been identified as an effective teaching strategy that can increase children's core literacy knowledge and skills (National Reading Panel, 2000; Snow et al., 1998). Notwithstanding the variability in the definition of literacy engagement, two studies (Hughes & Kwok, 2007; Ponitz, Rimm-Kaufman, Grimm, & Curby, 2009) examined children's classroom engagement and found that literacy engagement was significantly associated with children's reading skills. Furthermore, they identified that classroom engagement mediated the relation between teacher–child relationships and children's reading skills. Wingfield et al. (2008) also found significant associations between reading engagement and reading outcomes among fourth graders.

In the current study, children's classroom engagement was observed, especially in language and literacy activities, and examined how the extent of child's literacy engagement was related to their early language and literacy skills after taking into account classroom quality. By controlling classroom quality, an attempt was made to identify the ways in which individual classroom experiences influence children's early language and literacy development. The hypothesis formulated was that the effectiveness of literacy engagement was mediated through the quality of teacher–child relationships and tested such meditational relations.

EXAMINATION OF THIS STUDY

Couched in the attachment theory (Bowlby, 1969), Pianta (2004, 2006) argues that teacher–child relationships support children's language and literacy development in two ways. First, they support the development of basic learning processes such as focusing attention on learning, communicating effectively, maintaining interest in learning, and engaging in critical reasoning, largely through oral language and nonverbal interactions. Children who have positive relationships with their teachers not only enjoy attending to their teachers and engaging in extended communications and interactions with them, but they also regard teachers as transmitters of meaningful information. Second, teacher–child relationships influence the intentionality of language and literacy instruction. In teacher–child interactions serving this function, the teacher provides explicit instruction in language and literacy skills (e.g., rhyme, vocabulary).

This study examined the extent to which teacher–child relationships contributed to the language and literacy skills of Spanish-speaking DLLs in early education programs as well as the extent to which the quality of teacher–child relationships, which is defined as teachers' perceptions of their relationships with a child on conflict and closeness, moderated the associations between the intensity of children's engagement with language and literacy activities and their language and literacy development. Specifically, based on Pianta's framework (2004), it was hypothesized that 1) teacher–child relationships were associated with children's language and literacy skills as well as the intensity of their engagement with language and literacy activities in classrooms, and 2) the associations between the intensity of children's engagement with language and literacy activities and their language and literacy skills would be moderated by teacher–child relationships. That is, there would be varying associations between the intensity of children's engagement with language and literacy activities and children's language and literacy outcomes when the quality of teacher–child relationship is considered. Thus, the contribution of classroom language and literacy instruction to children's language and literacy skills was expected to be more positive and stronger when children form close relationships with their teachers than when conflicted relationships are formed.

Participants

Ninety 4- and 5-year-old children (41 females; $M = 4.52$ years) in 23 family literacy programs participated in this study. Programs were recipients of local family literacy program expansion and enhancement grants in the greater Los Angeles area heavily populated by immigrant Latino families. The programs were selected based on the severity of enrolled families' needs in income, literacy, employment, housing, and English proficiency and were provided with financial and technical support. All of the programs provided families with comprehensive family literacy services at no cost with goals of promoting children's school readiness, particularly English language and literacy skills, as well as parental support for children's learning and development. Participating children were drawn from a larger program evaluation study ($N = 319$) that examined school readiness of DLLs enrolled in family literacy programs in the greater Los Angeles area. This analysis included only 90 children who were rated on the Student–Teacher Relationship Rating Scale (STRS; Pianta, 2001), participated in the classroom observation, and assessed in the fall and spring for language and literacy skills. According to parent interviews, all of the children spoke Spanish as a primary home language, and the majority of them (98%) were introduced to English in the early education portion of family literacy programs. About 70% of the children came from households that had lived in the United States for 1–5 years (69%), had household income less than $20,000 (75%), and had maternal education of high school or less (69%). Table 4.1 shows descriptive information of participating children and their families.

Table 4.1. Descriptive statistics for participants' demographics

	N	Frequency	Proportion
Age			
Child's sex	88		
Girl		41	47%
Boy		47	53%
Immigration history (years living in the United States)			
Less than 1 year	74	2	3%
1–2 years		27	37%
3–5 years		24	32%
6–10 years		12	16%
More than 10 years		6	8%
Entire life		3	4%
Income	67		
$10,000 or less		10	15%
$10,001–$20,000		40	60%
$20,001–$40,000		15	22%
$40,001 or more		2	3%
Maternal education	67		
Less than 6th grade		6	9%
6th–12th grade (no diploma)		14	21%
High school/general equivalency diploma		26	39%
Some college (no degree)		11	16%
Associate/bachelor's degree		4	6%
Graduate/professional degree		6	9%
English spoken at home	90		
Yes		2	2%
No		88	98%

Note: $N = 90$.

n, the number of participants who responded to related parent interview questions.

Procedures and Measures

Data collection for this study took place during the 2003–2004 school year. In Fall 2003 and Spring 2004, direct assessments were conducted of the children's language and literacy skills for pretest and posttest child outcomes. Extensive classroom observations (via the Classroom Assessment Scoring System [CLASS] [La Paro & Pianta, 2000] and Emerging Academic Snapshot ["Snapshot"] [Ritchie, Howes, Kraft-Sayre, & Weiser, 2001]) were made in the early spring of 2004 after the programs were offered for at least 2 months. The observation of the children in their early childhood classrooms took place during a single day, starting from the time the children arrived in school until they went to nap. Throughout the observation day, observers rated the teacher, child, teacher–child interactions, and classroom activities on the dimensions included in the CLASS and Snapshot in repeated cycles. The mean length of observation was 3.6 hours (standard deviation [*SD*] = 1.1) with a range of 2.5 hours and 5.4 hours. Parent interviews and teacher reports on teacher–child relationships, ethnicity, and language also took place in Spring 2004.

Parent Interview   Parent interviews were conducted and information was obtained regarding families' sociodemographic characteristics and migration history—income, home language, parent education, and the number of years that the family had lived in the United States.

Teacher–Child Relationships   In the spring, teachers rated the quality of their relationships with children, using the short version of Student–Teacher Relationship Scale (STRS; Pianta, 2001). The STRS measures teachers' perceptions of their relationships with students in the area of closeness and conflict on a five-point Likert scale (1 = *definitely does not apply;* 2 = *not really;* 3 = *neutral, not sure;* 4 = *applies somewhat;* and 5 = *definitely applies*). The closeness subscale indicates the extent of warmth, positive emotions, trust, and open communications in the teacher–child relationships (e.g., "I share an affectionate, warm relationship with this child"; Cronbach's alpha = .91). The conflict subscale indicates the extent of negativity and disharmony in teacher–child relationships (e.g., "This child and I always seem to be struggling with each other"; Cronbach's alpha = .94). The STRS has shown associations with children's academic and social functioning in pre-K through elementary grades (Hamre & Pianta, 2001; Pianta, La Paro, Payne, Cox, & Bradley, 2002).

Quality of Classroom Environment   The CLASS (La Paro & Pianta, 2000)[1] is an observational measure that examines the quality of teacher–child interactions in two domains: Emotional Climate and Instructional Climate. A trained observer rated early education classrooms of family literacy programs on the five scales of Emotional Climate and four scales of Instructional Climate every 20 minutes followed by 10 minutes of scoring time throughout the observation period. Each scale was rated on a 1 to 7 low-to-high scale, with 1 or 2 indicating low ranges, 3–5 indicating medium ranges, and 6 or 7 indicating high ranges. Classroom scores for the two domains were computed as average ratings across the subscales and observations. An average of seven CLASS observations (*SD* = 2.53) were made, with a range between 4 and 17 observations.

---

[1]The data were collected prior to the publication of the revised CLASS (Pianta, La Paro, & Hamre, 2004).

Emotional Climate assesses the quality of teachers' support for children's social and emotional functioning. It is a composite mean score of the following five scales: Positive Climate, Negative Climate (reversed), Teacher Sensitivity, Overcontrol, and Behavior Management. Data were combined at the classroom level. The internal consistency reliability in this sample for the socioemotional climate scales was .95.

Instructional Climate assesses the quality of instructional support provided in early childhood education classrooms based on how teachers scaffold children's cognitive and language development. It is a composite mean score of the following four scales: Productivity, Concept Development, Instructional Learning Format, and Quality of Feedback. The internal consistency reliability in this sample for the instructional climate scales was .92.

Literacy Engagement   Snapshot (Ritchie, Howes, Kraft-Sayre, & Weiser, 2001) was used to assess the extent of child's engagement with a teacher in the following literacy and language activities: read to, preread/read, letters and sound, and oral language development. The Snapshot is a time-sampling measure that captures children's moment-to-moment experiences within their early education classrooms. When the observation began, the data collector observed a child for 20 seconds and coded for 40 seconds whether the child had been engaged with a teacher in any of the literacy activities (0 = *not observed*, 1 = *observed*). The data collector then observed each of the other study children in the classroom before coming back to the first child. This process was repeated throughout the observation period. Later, the proportion of a day that a child was engaged with a teacher in literacy activities was computed by dividing the frequency of observed literacy activities by the total number of times the child was observed. An average of 32 Snapshot (SD = 12.43) observations was made on each of the 90 study children with a range between 12 and 81 observations.

Child Assessments   Children's language and literacy skills were assessed in the fall and spring, using a combination of standardized and unstandardized instruments used widely in the field (Howes et al., 2008). The child assessment included assessments of each child's English proficiency, Spanish receptive language, and story and print concept and comprehension. The assessment was conducted by a trained data collector and took 30–45 minutes to complete.

The PreLAS 2000 Duncan & DeAvilla, 1998) examine young children's oral language proficiency in English. In this study, children were tested in two subscales measuring receptive oral language skills (Simon Says and the

Human Body), and one subscale measuring expressive oral language skills (Art Show). Children were tested individually and asked to respond to the examiner's verbal requests. The highest possible score was 40, and reliability coefficients for this sample were in the .80s and .90s.

The Test de Vocabulario en Imagenes Peabody (TVIP; Dunn et al., 1986) is a short, general Spanish verbal ability test that measures children's listening comprehension skills of spoken words. The word knowledge assessed by the TVIP is called "receptive vocabulary" to differentiate it from the more active vocabulary skills required to formally define a word or use it appropriately in a sentence. The TVIP assesses children's knowledge of the meaning of words by asking them to say, or indicate by pointing, which of four pictures best shows the meaning of a word that is said aloud by the examiner. A series of words is presented, ranging from easy to difficult for children of a given age, each accompanied by a plate consisting of four line drawings. As a majority of the children remained Spanish speakers over the course of family literacy programs, their receptive language skills were assessed in TVIP instead of Peabody Picture Vocabulary Test–Third Edition (Dunn & Dunn, 1997). Reliability coefficient for this sample was .89.

The story and print knowledge assesses children's book knowledge (e.g., where the front of a book is), print knowledge (e.g., directionality of reading), and reading comprehension skills. It is adapted from earlier pre-reading assessment procedures developed by Teale (1988) and Mason and Stewart (1989). The child was handed a children's storybook upside down and backward. For story and print concept, the assessor noted whether the child turned the book around to put it upright with the front cover on top. Then the child was asked to identify where the name of the book was written, where the material to be read began, and in what direction the reading proceeded. For story and print comprehension skills, the assessor read the story to the child and asked basic questions about the content of the story and the mechanics of reading. Children who experience frequent story reading by their parents or teachers are more likely to be able to answer such questions (e.g., Bus, van IJzendoorn, & Pellegrini, 1995). The highest possible score was 11 for story and print concept and 4 for story and print comprehension. Reliability coefficients in this sample for the subtests and for the whole were in the .60s.

Teacher Ethnicity and Language   Information was obtained regarding teachers' ethnicity and capability of speaking English or Spanish. A calculation was made to determine whether the teachers' ethnicity and language were matched to those of the child ($n = 73$) or not matched ($n = 13$).

Data Collector Training and Interrater Reliability   In the summer before the study began, data collectors who were bilingual in Spanish and

English and had at least bachelor of arts degrees were hired and received training on the measures for 2 months. They were trained to use the observational measures and conduct the child assessments and parent interviews in Spanish and English. Training was given by researchers who had extensive knowledge and experiences with the child assessment measures and parent interviews and had been certified to train others to use the CLASS and Snapshot by the measure developers. For the CLASS and Snapshot, data collectors' weighted kappas with a trainer were between .65 and .81. For the child assessment and parent interview, data collectors demonstrated competency and 100% accuracy in the administration and scoring.

RESULTS

Descriptives

Teachers rated the level of closeness that they perceived in their relationships with children high ($M = 3.91$, $SD = 0.82$), with a range between 1 and 5. Teachers' ratings on conflict were low ($M = 2.00$, $SD = 0.70$), with a range between 1.5 and 4. Refer to Table 4.2 for teachers' ratings on their relationships with children in closeness and conflict.

The quality of early education programs assessed using the CLASS was in the mid- to high range. The programs were rated in the upper midrange ($M = 5.36$, $SD = 0.78$) on the domain of Emotional Climate and in the lower midrange on the domain of Instructional Climate ($M = 3.54$, $SD = 0.79$). In terms of literacy engagement, children spent about 30% ($SD = 30\%$) of a day engaged in literacy and language activities. See Table 4.3

Table 4.2.   Descriptive statistics for teacher–child relationships on closeness and conflict

	N	M	SD	Minimum	Maximum
Closeness	90	3.91	.82	1.00	5.00
Conflict	90	2.00	.70	1.50	4.00

Key: SD, standard deviation; *N*, number of individual children rated on Student–Teacher relationship scale; *M*, mean.

Table 4.3.   Descriptive statistics for the quality of classroom environment and literacy engagement

	N	M	SD	Minimum	Maximum
Emotional Climate	23	5.36	.78	3.92	6.44
Instructional Climate	23	3.54	.79	1.50	5.16
Literacy engagement[a]	90	.30	.30	0.00	1.00

[a]Indicates the proportion of a day children were engaged in literacy and language activities.

Key: SD, standard deviation; *N* (= 23) indicates the number of programs observed using Classroom Assessment Scoring System; *N* (= 90) indicates the number of children who were observed using Snapshot; *M*, mean.

for mean scores of the quality of early education programs and the proportion of a day children engaged in literacy activities.

t-tests were conducted to examine how the language/ethnicity match between teachers and children were associated with the quality of teacher–child relationships and child outcomes. First, the ethnicity and primary language of teachers and children were reviewed, and the results indicated that 86% of the teacher–child dyad (*n* = 77) had a match in their language/ethnicity, and 14% (*n* = 13) did not have a match. Independent sample *t*-tests were then conducted to compare the mean scores of closeness and conflict and child outcomes of the ethnicity/language matching group with those of the nonmatching group. The results (Table 4.4) showed that the conflict scores were different, $t(84) = 3.35, p < .01$, indicating that the teachers perceived to have more conflicted relationships with children who were from same ethnic/language background. No differences were observed in child outcomes by the language/ethnicity match between teachers and children.

Second, a family index variable was created based on the parent's income, education, and immigration history. Higher scores on the index indicated longer immigration history than the median number of years living in the United States (3–5 years), lower annual household income than the median reported income ($10,000–$20,000), and lower levels of education than the median parent education (high school/general equivalency diploma). Scores ranged from 0 to 3 ($M = .69; SD = 0.76$). Correlational analyses found significant associations between the index and story and print scores ($r = .28, p < .01$). No relations were observed between the index and the quality of teacher–child relationships.

Correlational analyses (Table 4.5) were conducted between teachers' perceptions of their relationships with children on closeness and conflict and child outcomes. Significant correlations were observed between closeness and children's Spanish receptive language ($r = .38, p < .01$) and conflict and children's English proficiency ($r = -.22, p < .05$). Children with whom teachers perceived to have closer relationships scored higher on Spanish

Table 4.4.   Closeness and conflict by ethnicity/language match between teachers and children

	Ethnicity/ language match		Nonethnicity/ language match		Independent samples *t*-test	
	M	*SD*	*M*	*SD*	*df*	*t*
Closeness	3.84	.83	4.02	.63	84	−.76
Conflict	2.15	.66	1.49	.61	84	3.35*

*p < .01.
Key: *SD*, standard deviation; *df*, degrees of freedom; *t*, *t* statistic; *M*, mean.

Table 4.5.   Correlations between teacher–child relationships and child outcomes

	1	2	3	4	5
1. Closeness	—	−.18	.05	.38**	.11
2. Conflict		—	−.22*	−.07	−.13
3. English proficiency			—	.03	.47**
4. Spanish receptive language				—	.32*
5. Story and print knowledge					—

*$p < .05$, **$p < .01$.

receptive language assessment. Children with whom teachers perceived to have more conflicted relationships showed lower proficiency in English oral language.

Finally, an examination was conducted to determine whether the quality of teacher–child relationships moderated the relations between literacy instructions and child outcomes and accounted for any child outcomes. Family index, pretest outcomes, the intensity of literacy instructions, the quality of teacher–child relationships on closeness and conflict, interaction terms between literacy instruction and teacher child relationships, and the quality of classroom Emotional and Instructional climate were entered into a multilevel regression model. Accounting for the nesting of children in the same classroom, multilevel modeling in Mplus (Muthén & Muthén, 2008) analyses was used with the quality of classroom climate variables as the classroom-level covariates. A random intercept was estimated for each classroom, resulting in the estimation of separate variance terms at the classroom and child level and of the intraclass correlation. All variables were centered at the group mean so the main effects for a predictor were evaluated at the mean of the other variables included in interactions with that predictor. Centering makes coefficients meaningful and reduces multicollinearity problems in the data (Aiken & West, 1991; Neter, Wasserman, & Kutner, 1989). All two-way interactions between literacy instruction, closeness, and conflict were tested, and only the interaction between conflict and literacy instruction was found to be significant. Among all interaction terms, only this interaction was included in the final model. Examination of coefficient scores indicated that the quality of teacher–child relationship on conflict had a moderate effect for the relation between literacy instructions and children's story and print knowledge. Children who had less conflicted relationships with teachers and more literacy instructions had greater gains in story and print knowledge. However, the quality of teacher–child relationship did not have significant moderator effects for other child outcomes. Table 4.6 shows the results of the multilevel modeling, listing the coefficients, standard errors, and the variance components.

Table 4.6.   Results from multilevel regression models predicting spring child outcome scores

		English proficiency	Spanish receptive language	Story and print knowledge
Intercept	B	50.66**	88.96**	11.64**
	(SE)	(19.27)	(11.49)	(2.16)
Fall test score	B	1.22**	.83**	.35**
	(SE)	(.22)	(.07)	(.10)
Index	B	.39	−.66	−1.15*
	(SE)	(1.28)	(1.92)	(.61)
Literacy engagement	B	5.68	−6.70	10.28*
	(SE)	(5.75)	(4.88)	(4.66)
Closeness	B	.97	4.40*	4.89
	(SE)	(5.54)	(1.95)	(1.63)
Conflict	B	−.91	−.48	−1.34*
	(SE)	(2.69)	(1.80)	(.58)
Literacy* conflict	B	5.71	5.71	−3.06*
Center for Learning and Autism Support Services (CLASS) Emotional Support	(SE)	−6.16	16.16	−1.49
	B	3.16	6.04	.86
Center for Learning and Autism Support Services (CLASS) Instructional Support	(SE)	(5.59)	(4.64)	(.66)
	B	2.34	9.07	−.52
Standardized root mean residual (SRMR)	(SE)	(4.36)	(5.01)	(.55)
Between class variance		.10	.26	.28
Between student variance		.01	.27	.26
Intraclass correlation		.08	.06	.36
N		90	90	90

*$p < .05$, **$p < .01$.

Key: B, coefficient; SE, standard error; N, number of individual children included in the analysis.

DISCUSSION

The current study provided partial evidence to confirm the interconnections across teacher–child relationships, literacy instruction, and children's language and literacy development among Spanish-speaking DLLs. Descriptive findings revealed that Spanish-speaking DLLs are at higher risk of developing low-quality relationships with their teachers when there is an ethnic/linguistic teacher–child match. In addition, they spent about 30% of their day in early education classrooms engaged in literacy and language learning activities. Multilevel regression analyses, which took into account children's nesting in classrooms, revealed that literacy engagement was positively related to children's story and print knowledge. However, the examination of interaction between literacy engagement and teacher–child relationships suggested that conflicted teacher–child relationships might compromise benefits of literacy instructions provided in school for DLLs' language and literacy development.

Descriptive statistics showed that the relationships between teachers and Spanish-speaking DLLs enrolled in family literacy programs are generally close ($M = 3.91$, $SD = 0.82$), with low levels of conflict ($M = 2.00$, $SD = 0.70$). Nonetheless, the teacher–child relationship scores are noteworthy when compared to those of at-risk preschool-age children. Justice et al. (2008) examined the teacher–child relationships of mostly English-speaking at-risk children and concluded that the relationships were also close ($M = 4.40$, $SD = 0.50$) and free of conflict ($M = 1.70$, $SD = 0.88$). The comparison of the two scores shows that those Spanish-speaking children in family literacy programs are experiencing relatively lower quality relationships with their teachers than other at-risk children. The children in the current study are also considered as at-risk populations based on their ethnicity, home language, and household income. Considering the predictability of teacher–child relationships for at-risk children's developmental outcomes (e.g., Cicchetti & Lynch, 1993; Burchinal et al., 2002), the current finding suggests that teachers working with Spanish-speaking DLLs may benefit from participating in professional development in relationship-building skills.

Correlational results identified two interesting associations between teacher–child relationships and child outcomes, although the directions were not identified. First, closeness was positively correlated with children's Spanish receptive language skills but not with other language and literacy outcomes. This finding is similar to that of Burchinal et al. (2002) and Justice et al. (2008), which found significant correlations between closeness and receptive language skills. In particular, Burchinal and colleagues found that the associations between closeness and receptive language skills were especially stronger for children of color than Caucasian children. The positive associations between closeness and receptive language skills are important because receptive language skill is one of the best indicators of children's overall language competence as well as one of the best predictors of later academic competence (Bee et al., 1982; National Research Council, 2000).

Second, conflict was negatively correlated with children's English oral language competency. Previous research suggests that children's language competence contributes to the formation of teacher–child relationships (see Justice et al., 2008). Language serves as a medium through which relationships are formed between individuals; thus, children with low language competence tend to develop more conflicted relationships with teachers (Justice et al., 2008; Pence & Justice, 2007). This study indicated that incongruence between children's primary language and classroom language might have teachers perceive children's language competence lower than their actual competence. Together, these findings suggest that the quality of relationships that children develop with their teachers have implications for children's language development.

Teacher–child language/ethnicity match was associated with higher teacher ratings on conflict. This is contradictory to the findings of Zimmerman, Khoury, Vega, Gill, and Warheit (1995) and Saft and Pianta (2001), which suggest that ethnic match between teachers and children are negatively associated with teacher ratings on conflict. This contradiction might be due to the difference in the composition of study participants. Teachers participated in the current study were mostly Latino, whereas those in Zimmerman et al. and Saft and Pianta were mostly Caucasian. Thus, it is likely that teachers of different ethnicities might have interpreted children's behavior differently (Saft & Pianta, 2001). In Latino culture, children are expected to respect others and engage in proper behaviors, if not, they are assumed to lack values that support success in school (Valenzuela, 1999). In Latino culture, children are expected to show respect for others and social expectations in school (Valenzuela, 1999). Latino teachers' cultural knowledge of children's expected behaviors in school might make teachers more sensitive to children's inappropriate behaviors and take children's appropriate behaviors for granted.

Classroom language might have influenced teachers' higher ratings on their relationships with children in conflict. Examining Spanish-speaking prekindergartners from the National Center for Early Development and Learning's Multi-State Pre-Kindergarten Study and the Study of State-Wide Early Education Programs (Early et al., 2005), Chang et al. (2007) noted that that Latino children tend to be rated higher on problem behaviors and conflicted relationships with teachers when their teachers speak more English in classrooms. Furthermore they were reported to have more positive and close relationships with their teachers and peers when their teachers speak more Spanish in classrooms. As the participating programs were designed to enhance Spanish-speaking DLL's English language and literacy proficiency, English was spoken as a primary language of classrooms; thus, children's interactions in classrooms in Spanish must have been limited. Chang et al. (2007) reported that Spanish-speaking DLLs generally experienced less than 20% of their interactions in classrooms in Spanish, with about a quarter of them (23%) experiencing interactions in English only. Given that Latino children who experienced interactions in more Spanish than English tended to have more positive experiences in classrooms and favorable social and academic outcomes in schools, this finding adds to concerns of researchers who demands further investigations of the impact of classroom language and teacher–child ethnicity match on child development.

Teacher–child relationships on conflict moderated the effects of literacy engagement on children's story and print knowledge. That is, literacy engagement had a less positive impact on children when the quality of teacher–child relationships was more conflicted. This finding is in line with previous research that claims that teacher–child relationships contributed to children's academic competence through children's classroom engagement (Hughes & Kwok, 2007; Ponitz et al., 2009). For instance, Hughes and Kwok found that teacher–child relationships contributed to children's reading gains through positive associations with their classroom engagement. This finding provides additional evidence that the development of high-quality teacher–child relationships is important in the classroom. Nonetheless, it should be noted that no other moderating effects of teacher–child relationships on other language and literacy outcomes were found.

A few limitations of the current study need to be noted. First, despite the wide range of immigration history, income, and parental education included, the participants were fairly homogeneous in terms of their primary language, enrollment in family literacy programs, and residential environments. Thus, one should take caution in interpreting the current findings and applying them to other DLLs. Second, teacher–child relationships were measured using a teacher rating measure, without an observation of actual teacher–child interactions. Nonetheless, a few studies have found consistency between teacher ratings and their behaviors (Howes, Phillipsen, & Peisner-Feiberg, 2000; Pianta et al., 1995). Third, children were observed on only one day during the school year. This short length of observation has a potential to weaken the predictability of these measures for child outcomes (Ponitz et al., 2009). Finally, proportions of teacher–children interactions in classrooms in Spanish and English and their relations to teachers' perceptions of their relationships with children and child outcomes were not examined. Among Spanish-speaking DLLs, higher proportions of teacher–child interactions in Spanish showed higher positive associations with teachers' ratings on their relationships with children and children's social and behavioral competence. Future studies need to further examine whether teacher–child ethnicity/language match and teachers' language use are differently associated with children's social interactions as well as their development.

STUDY QUESTIONS

1. Describe some ways in which good teacher–child relationships are related to students' academic success. Describe some ways in which teacher–child relationships are related to students' academic difficulties.

2. Which aspects of classroom environments have been empirically shown to be associated with children's positive development and increases in their literacy knowledge and skills? Why?

3. Briefly summarize the constructs examined in this study. What was the researchers' reasoning to link them to DLL children's language and literacy development?

4. Briefly describe the results the researchers obtained. What conclusions did they reach about teacher–child relationships and children's language and literacy development in DLL populations?

REFERENCES

Aiken, L.S., & West, S.G. (1991). *Multiple regression: Testing and interpretations.* Newbury Park, CA: Sage.

Baker, J.A. (2006). Contributions of teacher–child relationships to positive school adjustment during elementary school. *Journal of School Psychology, 44,* 211–229.

Barnett, W.S., & Yarosz, D.J. (2004). *Who goes to preschool and why does it matter?* New Brunswick, NJ: National Institute for Early Education Research.

Bee, H.L., Barnard, K.E., Eyres, S.J., Gray, C.A., Hammond, M.A., Spietz, A.L., et al. (1982). Prediction of IQ and language skill from perinatal status, child performance, family characteristics, and mother–child interaction. *Child Development, 53,* 1134–1156.

Birch, S.H., & Ladd, G.W. (1997). The teacher–child relationship and children's early school adjustment. *Journal of School Psychology, 35,* 61–79.

Bowlby, J. (1969). *Attachment and loss: Vol. 1. Attachment.* New York: Basic Books.

Bowlby, J. (1982). *Attachment and loss: Vol 1. Attachment* (Rev. ed.). New York: Basic Books.

Bretherton, I. (1990). Open communication and internal working models: Their role in the development of attachment relationships. In R.A. Thompson (Ed.), *Socioemotional development: Nebraska Symposium on Motivation: (Vol. 36,* pp. 57–113). Lincoln: University of Nebraska Press.

Brophy-Herb, H., Lee, R.E., Nievar, M.A., Stollak, G. (2007). Preschoolers' social competence: Relations to family characteristics, teacher behaviors and classroom climate. *Journal of Applied Developmental Psychology, 28,* 134–148.

Burchinal, M.R., Peisner-Feinberg, E., Pianta, R., & Howes, C. (2002). Development of academic skills from preschool through second grade: Family and classroom predictors of developmental trajectories. *Journal of School Psychology, 40,* 415–436.

Bus, A.G., Van IJzendoorn, M.H., & Pellegrini, A.D. (1995). Storybook reading makes for success in learning to read. A meta-analysis on intergenerational transmission of literacy. *Review of Educational Research, 65,* 1–21.

Chang, F., Crawford, G., Early, D., Bryant, D., Howes, C., Burchinal, M., et al. (2007). Spanish speaking children's social and language development in prekindergarten classrooms. *Journal of Early Education and Development, 18*(2), 243–269.

Cicchetti, D., & Lynch, M. (1993). Toward an ecological/transactional model of community violence and child maltreatment: Consequences for children's development. *Psychiatry, 53,* 96–118.

Duncan, S., & DeAvilla, E. (1998). *PreLAS 2000.* Montgomery, CA: McGraw-Hill.

Dunn, L.W., & Dunn, L. M. (1997). *Peabody Picture Vocabulary Test–III.* Circle Pines, MN: American Guidance Service.

Dunn, L.M., Padilla, E.R., Lugo, D.E., & Dunn, L.M. (1986). *Test de Vocabulario en Imágenes Peabody: Adaptación Hispanoamericana.* Circle Pines, MN: American Guidance Service.

Early, D., Barbarin, O., Bryant, B., Burchinal, M., Chang, F., Clifford, R., et al. (2005). Pre-kindergarten in eleven states: NCEDL's Multi-State Study of Pre-kindergarten and State-Wide Early Education Program (SWEEP) Study. Retrieved December 1, 2008, from http://www.fpg.unc.edu/ncedl/pdfs/ SWEEP MSsummary final.pdf.

Hamre, B.K., & Pianta, R.C. (2001). Early teacher–child relationships and the trajectory of children's school outcomes through eighth grade. *Child Development, 72,* 625–638.

Hamre, B.K., & Pianta, R.C. (2005). Can instructional and emotional support in the first-grade classroom make a difference for children at risk of school failure? *Child Development, 76,* 949–967.

Howes, C., Burchinal, M., Pianta, R.C., Bryant, D., Early, D., Clifford, R., et al. (2008). Ready to learn? Children's pre-academic achievement in pre-kindergarten programs. *Early Childhood Research Quarterly, 23,* 27–50.

Howes, C., & Hamilton, C.E. (1992). Children's relationships with caregivers: Mothers and child care teachers. *Child Development, 63,* 859–866.

Howes, C., & Hamilton, C.E. (1993). The changing experience of child care: Changes in teachers and in teacher–child relationships and children's social competence with peers. *Early Childhood Research Quarterly, 8,* 15–32.

Howes, C., Phillipsen, L., & Peisner-Feinberg, E. (2000). The consistency and predictability of teacher–child relationships during the transition to kindergarten. *Journal of School Psychology, 38,* 113–132.

Huges, J., & Kwok, O. (2007). Influence of student–teacher and parent–teacher relationships on lower achieving readers' engagement and achievement in the primary grades. *Journal of Educational Psychology, 99,* 39–51.

Justice, L.M., Cottone, E.A., Mashburn, A., & Rimm-Kaufman, S.E. (2008). Relationship between teachers and preschoolers who are at risk: Contribution of children's language skills, temperamentally based attributes, and gender. *Early Education and Development, 19,* 600–621.

Ladd, G.W., & Burgess, K.B. (2001). Do relational risks and protective factors moderate the linkages between childhood aggression and early psychological and school adjustment? *Child Development, 72,* 1579–1601.

La Paro, K.M., & Pianta, R.C. (2000). *Classroom Assessment Scoring System.* Charlottesville: University of Virginia.

Lynch, M., & Cicchetti, D. (1992). Maltreated children's reports of relatedness to their teachers. In R.C. Pianta (Ed.), *Beyond the parent: The role of other adults in children's lives* (pp. 81–107). San Francisco: Jossey-Bass.

Main, M., Kaplan, N., & Cassidy, J. (1985). Security in infancy, childhood, and adulthood: A move to the level of representation. In I. Bretherton & E. Waters (Eds.), Growing points of attachment theory and research. *Monographs of the Society for Research in Child Development, 50*(1–2, Serial No. 209), 66–104.

Mashburn, A.J. (2008). Quality of social and physical environments in preschool and children's development of academic, language, and literacy skills. *Applied Developmental Science, 12,* 113–127.

Mashburn, A.J., & Pianta, R.C. (2006). Social relationships and school readiness. *Early Education and Development, 17,* 151–176.

Mashburn, A.J., Pianta, R., Hamre, B.K., Downer, J.T., Barbarin, O., Bryant, D., et al. (2008). Measures of classroom quality in pre-kindergarten and children's development of academic, language and social skills. *Child Development, 79,* 732–749.

Mason, J.M., & Stewart, J. (1989). *The CAP Early Childhood Diagnostic Instrument* (Prepublication ed.). Chicago: American Testronics.

Meisels, S.J. (1999). Assessing readiness. In R.C. Pianta & M.J. Cox (Eds.), *The transition to kindergarten* (pp. 39–66). Baltimore: Paul H. Brookes Publishing Co.

Muthén, B.O., & Muthén, L.K. (2004). Mplus (Version 3.11) [Computer software]. Los Angeles: Author.

National Association for the Education of Young Children. (1996). *Developmentally appropriate practice in early childhood programs serving children from birth through age 8.* Washington, DC: Author.

National Reading Panel. (2000). *Teaching children to read: An evidence-based assessment of the scientific research literature on reading and its implications for reading instruction.* Retrieved August 18, 2009, from http://www.nichd.nih.gov/publications/nrp/report.cfm.

National Research Council. (2000). *Eager to learn: Educating our preschoolers.* Washington, DC: National Academy Press.

Neter, J., Wasserman,W., & Kutner, M.H. (1989). *Applied linear regression models.* Homewood, IL: Richard D. Irwin.

Pence, K.L., & Justice, L.M. (2007). *Language development from theory to practice.* Upper Saddle River, NJ: Merrill-Prentice Hall.

Pianta, R.C. (1994). Patterns of relationships between children and kindergarten teachers. *Journal of School Psychology, 32,* 15–32.

Pianta, R.C. (2001). *The Student–Teacher Relationship Scale.* Lutz, FL: Psychological Assessment Resources.

Pianta, R. (2004). Relationships among children and adults and family literacy. In B. Wasik (Ed.), *Handbook on family literacy programs* (pp. 175–192). Mahwah, NJ: Lawrence Erlbaum Associates.

Pianta, R.C. (2006). Teacher–child relationships and early literacy. In S. Neuman & D. Dickinson (Eds.), *Handbook of early literacy research* (Vol. 2, pp. 149–162). New York: Guilford.

Pianta, R.C., La Paro, K.M., & Hamre, B.K. (2008). *Classroom Assessment Scoring System™ (CLASS)™:* Baltimore: Paul H. Brookes Publishing Co.

Pianta, R.C., La Paro, K.M., Payne, C., Cox, M.J., & Bradley, R. (2002). The relation of kindergarten classroom environment to teacher, family, and school characteristics and child outcomes. *The Elementary School Journal, 102,* 225–238.

Pianta, R.C., Steinberg, M., & Rollins, K. (1995). The first two years of school: Teacher–child relationships and deflections in children's classroom adjustment. *Development and Psychopathology, 7,* 295–312.

Pianta, R.C., & Stuhlman, M. (2004). Teacher–child relationships and children's success in the first years of school. *School Psychology Review, 33,* 444–458.

Ponitz, C.C., Rimm-Kaufman, S.E., Grimm, K.J., & Curby, T.W. (2009). Kindergarten classroom quality, behavioral engagement, and reading achievement. *School Psychology Review, 38,* 102–120.

Reese, L., Balzano, S., Gallimore, R., & Goldenberg, C. (1995). The concept of *educación*: Latino family values and American schooling. *International Journal of Educational Research, 23,* 57–81.

Ritchie, S., Howes, C., Kraft-Sayre, M., & Weiser, B. (2001). *Teacher Involvement Scale–Pre Academic Scale.* Unpublished manuscript.

Saft, E.W., & Pianta, R.C. (2001). Teachers' perception of their relationships with students: Effects of child age, gender, and ethnicity of teachers and children. *School Psychology Quarterly, 16,* 125–141.

Snow, C.E., Burns, M.S., & Griffin, P. (1998). *Preventing reading difficulties in young children.* Washington, DC: National Academy Press.

Teale, W.H. (1988). Developmentally appropriate assessment of reading and writing in the early childhood classroom. *Elementary School Journal, 89,* 173–183.

Valenzuela, A. (1999). *Subtractive schooling: U.S. Mexican youth and the politics of caring.* Ithaca: State University of New York Press.

Wingfield, A., Guthrie, J.T., Perencevich, K.C., Taboada, A., Klauda, S.L., McRae, A., et al. (2008). Role of reading engagement in mediating effects of reading comprehension instruction on reading outcomes. *Psychology in the Schools, 45,* 432–445.

Zimmerman, R.S., Khoury, E.L., Vega, W.A., Gill, A.G., & Warheit, G.J. (1995). Teacher and parent perceptions of behavior problems among a sample of African American, Hispanic, and non-Hispanic students. *American Journal of Community Psychology, 23,* 181–197.

II

Describing the Language and Literacy Practices in Classrooms with Dual Language Learners

5

The Language Interaction Snapshot (LISn)

A New Observational Measure for Assessing Language Interactions in Linguistically Diverse Early Childhood Programs

Sally Atkins-Burnett, Susan Sprachman,
Michael López, Margaret Caspe, and Katie Fallin

The focus of this chapter is the development of the Language Interaction Snapshot (LISn), a new measure of the quality of the language environment in classrooms serving dual language learners (DLLs) developed by staff from Mathematica Policy Research for the Universal Preschool Child Outcomes Study (UPCOS). (The LISn [Atkins-Burnett, Sprachman, & Caspe, 2010] is an adaptation of the Child–Caregiver Observation System [Boller,

The research reported herein was supported by First 5 LA. We thank First 5 LA for their contribution to advancing knowledge in this critical area. We thank the Los Angeles Universal Preschool programs, families, and children for their participation in this study. Additional information about the LISn can be found on the First 5 LA Web site in the UPCOS reports: http://www.first5la.org/research/UPCOS.

This chapter was prepared with partial support from Mathematica Policy Research and from the National Center for Research on Early Childhood Education (NCRECE). It was supported by Grant R305A060021, administered by the Institute of Education Sciences, U.S. Department of Education. However, the contents do not necessarily represent the positions or policies of the U.S. Department of Education or NCRECE, and endorsement by the federal government or NCRECE should not be assumed.

Sprachman, & the Early Head Start Research Consortium, 1998]). (See Figure 5.1; this copy of the LISn is provided for reference within chapter context only and may not be reproduced or used for clinical or educational purposes.)

The LISn is designed to examine the child-specific language interactions within the classroom. This allows examination of how the language environment differs for children, particularly in classrooms that include DLLs. The LISn focuses on individual child-level interactions and the language provided to specific children by the lead teacher and other adults in the classroom, as well as the language or languages used by the child. Because most early childhood classrooms spend a limited amount of time in large group activities, the majority of the interactions are not shared by all the children in the class. In many linguistically diverse classrooms, there may be considerable variability in the match between the children's home language and the teacher's or other adult's own linguistic proficiency, thereby influencing the way in which language interactions may occur. Thus, the LISn allows examination of the variability of language interactions experienced by different children within the same classroom. These data can then be aggregated to the group or classroom level to describe the average language experiences of the children in a classroom and to look at variation in the experiences across classrooms.

As part of UPCOS, Mathematica field staff conducted classroom observations in the spring of 2007 in 97 preschool classrooms. The UPCOS is a descriptive study of the Los Angeles Universal Preschool (LAUP) network. LAUP includes preschools serving culturally and linguistically diverse families in public and private schools, community-based programs, and Head Start centers. All LAUP programs must meet requirements regarding teacher credentials, class size, child–adult ratios, and adequate ratings of the early childhood environment. One of the goals of the study was to describe the classroom quality and instructional environments in LAUP.

A subsample of 18 programs was selected for a pilot of the LISn in the spring of 2007. The classrooms were selected to include a mix of children in three groups: 1) primarily English speakers, 2) primarily Spanish speakers, and 3) monolingual Spanish speakers. Concurrently, American Institutes for Research (AIR) staff conducted a pilot of the LISn in 26 classrooms that were part of their Preschool for All study for First 5 San Francisco. Based on the findings from the Spring 2007 pilot, the LISn was revised, and a second pilot was conducted in the fall of 2009. In the winter of 2010, observers began collecting additional LISn data in 40 center-based classrooms and 20 family child care programs in LAUP. In this chapter, findings from the first pilot (Spring 2007) and preliminary findings from the most recent pilot (Fall 2009) with the revised measure are reported. This chapter begins with the rationale for focusing on the language environment in the classroom

LANGUAGE INTERACTION SNAPSHOT (LISn) I

CHILD ID: |_|_|_|_|_|_|_|_|_| CODING PERIOD: START: |_|_| : |_|_| AM/PM
ENTER THE SNAPSHOT NUMBER FOR THIS CHILD: |_|_| END: |_|_| : |_|_| AM/PM

CODE E = English; O = Other language; M = Multiple languages in one utterance	I			2			3			4			5		
A. FOCUS CHILD TALKS TO															
a. To Lead Teacher	E	O	M	E	O	M	E	O	M	E	O	M	E	O	M
b. To Other Adult	E	O	M	E	O	M	E	O	M	E	O	M	E	O	M
c. Other Children/Group	E	O	M	E	O	M	E	O	M	E	O	M	E	O	M
B. LEAD TEACHER VERBAL COMMUNICATION DIRECTED TO FC/FC WITH GROUP															
a. Repeats or confirms	E	O	M	E	O	M	E	O	M	E	O	M	E	O	M
b. Elaborates or builds (also code one of four below)	E	O	M	E	O	M	E	O	M	E	O	M	E	O	M
c. Gives directions	E	O	M	E	O	M	E	O	M	E	O	M	E	O	M
d. Requests language (contextualized)	E	O	M	E	O	M	E	O	M	E	O	M	E	O	M
e. Provides information, names, labels (contextualized)	E	O	M	E	O	M	E	O	M	E	O	M	E	O	M
f. Provides/elicits information (decontextualized)	E	O	M	E	O	M	E	O	M	E	O	M	E	O	M
g. Reads	E	O	M	E	O	M	E	O	M	E	O	M	E	O	M
h. Sings	E	O	M	E	O	M	E	O	M	E	O	M	E	O	M
i. Other Talk	E	O	M	E	O	M	E	O	M	E	O	M	E	O	M
C. OTHER ADULT VERBAL COMMUNICATION DIRECED TO FC/FC GROUP															
a. Repeats or confirms	E	O	M	E	O	M	E	O	M	E	O	M	E	O	M
b. Elaborates or builds (also code one of four below)	E	O	M	E	O	M	E	O	M	E	O	M	E	O	M
c. Gives directions	E	O	M	E	O	M	E	O	M	E	O	M	E	O	M
d. Requests language (contextualized)	E	O	M	E	O	M	E	O	M	E	O	M	E	O	M
e. Provides information, names, labels (contextualized)	E	O	M	E	O	M	E	O	M	E	O	M	E	O	M
f. Provides/elicits information (decontextualized)	E	O	M	E	O	M	E	O	M	E	O	M	E	O	M
g. Reads	E	O	M	E	O	M	E	O	M	E	O	M	E	O	M
h. Sings	E	O	M	E	O	M	E	O	M	E	O	M	E	O	M
i. Other Talk	E	O	M	E	O	M	E	O	M	E	O	M	E	O	M
(FOR OFFICIAL USE ONLY) TOTAL TALK	E	O	M	E	O	M	E	O	M	E	O	M	E	O	M
NOTES:															

Figure 5.1. Language Interaction Snapshot (LISn). (From *Language Interaction Snapshot + End of Visit Ratings (LISn + EVR)*, by S. Atkins-Burnett, S. Sprachman, and M. Caspe, 2010, Princeton NJ: Mathematica Policy Research; used by permission. © Developed by Mathematica Policy Research under contract with First 5 LA. May be used by license only. The LISn measure used by and/or referenced herein was developed by Mathematica Policy Research, Inc. and funded by First 5 LA. Neither Mathematica Policy Research, Inc. nor First 5 LA endorse the content herein. Any potential users must sign a sublicense agreement with Mathematica Policy Research, Inc. and have at least one member of their team become certified in the measure and pay the costs of that training. The Sublicense agreement is granted royalty-free. Any research product(s), data, knowledge, or other intellectual property resulting from the use of the LISn must include the legend: *The LISn measure used by and/or referenced herein was developed by Mathematica Policy Research, Inc. and funded by First 5 LA. Neither Mathematica Policy Research, Inc. nor First 5 LA endorse the content herein.*)

(continued)

Figure 5.1. *(continued)*

LANGUAGE INTERACTION SNAPSHOT (LISn) I

CODE E = English; O = Other language; M = Multiple languages in one utterance	6	7	8	9	10	Totals OFFICE ONLY
A. FOCUS CHILD TALKS TO						E O M
a. To Lead Teacher	E O M	E O M	E O M	E O M	E O M	
b. To Other Adult	E O M	E O M	E O M	E O M	E O M	
c. Other Children/Group	E O M	E O M	E O M	E O M	E O M	
B. LEAD TEACHER VERBAL COMMUNICATION DIRECTED TO FC/FC WITH GROUP						E O M
a. Repeats or confirms	E O M	E O M	E O M	E O M	E O M	
b. Elaborates or builds (also code one of four below)	E O M	E O M	E O M	E O M	E O M	
c. Gives directions	E O M	E O M	E O M	E O M	E O M	
d. Requests language (contextualized)	E O M	E O M	E O M	E O M	E O M	
e. Provides information, names, labels (contextualized)	E O M	E O M	E O M	E O M	E O M	
f. Provides/elicits information (decontextualized)	E O M	E O M	E O M	E O M	E O M	
g. Reads	E O M	E O M	E O M	E O M	E O M	
h. Sings	E O M	E O M	E O M	E O M	E O M	
i. Other Talk	E O M	E O M	E O M	E O M	E O M	
C. OTHER ADULT VERBAL COMMUNICATION DIRECED TO FC/FC GROUP						E O M
a. Repeats or confirms	E O M	E O M	E O M	E O M	E O M	
b. Elaborates or builds (also code one of four below)	E O M	E O M	E O M	E O M	E O M	
c. Gives directions	E O M	E O M	E O M	E O M	E O M	
d. Requests language (contextualized)	E O M	E O M	E O M	E O M	E O M	
e. Provides information, names, labels (contextualized)	E O M	E O M	E O M	E O M	E O M	
f. Provides/elicits information (decontextualized)	E O M	E O M	E O M	E O M	E O M	
g. Reads	E O M	E O M	E O M	E O M	E O M	
h. Sings	E O M	E O M	E O M	E O M	E O M	
i. Other Talk	E O M	E O M	E O M	E O M	E O M	
(FOR OFFICIAL USE ONLY) TOTAL TALK	E O M	E O M	E O M	E O M	E O M	E O M
NOTES:						

SNAPSHOT CONTEXT – CODE FOR THE 5 MINUTE OBSERVATION

A. CLASSROOM CONTENT
(CODE ALL ACTIVITIES IN WHICH FOCUS CHILD WAS INVOLVED)

ACTIVITY ONE	
1. ☐ Writing/copying	6. ☐ Singing
2. ☐ Sounds	7. ☐ Aesthetics
3. ☐ Non Print (oral language/vocabulary)	8. ☐ Science/Nature
4. ☐ Print Related	9. ☐ Social Studies
5. ☐ Math, Colors	10. ☐ Fine Motor
Numbers	11. ☐ Gross Motor
	12. ☐ Other *(Specify)* _____

ACTIVITY TWO	
1. ☐ Writing/copying	6. ☐ Singing
2. ☐ Sounds	7. ☐ Aesthetics
3. ☐ Non Print (oral language/vocabulary)	8. ☐ Science/Nature
4. ☐ Print Related	9. ☐ Social Studies
5. ☐ Math, Colors	10. ☐ Fine Motor
Numbers	11. ☐ Gross Motor
	12. ☐ Other *(Specify)* _____

B. CLASSROOM ACTIVITY STRUCTURE
(CODE ALL TYPES OF GROUPINGS AND TYPES OF ACTIVITIES IN WHICH FOCUS CHILD WAS INVOLVED)

1. ☐ Whole Group Activity	4. ☐ Free Choice/Centers
2. ☐ Small Group Activity	5. ☐ Routine
3. ☐ Individual Time	6. ☐ Meals/Snacks
	7. ☐ Recess/Outside

C. FOCUS CHILD ENGAGEMENT
How much of the 5 minutes . . .

	None of the Time	Some of the Time	Half of the Time	Most of the Time	All of the Time
C1. Was focus child engaged with materials and activities?	1 ☐	2 ☐	3 ☐	4 ☐	5 ☐
C2. Was the teacher's attention directed specifically to the focus child?	1 ☐	2 ☐	3 ☐	4 ☐	5 ☐
C3. Was focus child in a group with English speakers?	1 ☐	2 ☐	3 ☐	4 ☐	5 ☐

D. SUSTAINED CONVERSATIONS
How many times did the focus child participate in sustained conversations . . .

	None	Once	More than Once
D1. With lead teacher?	1 ☐	2 ☐	3 ☐
D2. With other adult?	1 ☐	2 ☐	3 ☐
D3. With other children?	1 ☐	2 ☐	3 ☐

and then provides an overview of the LISn, including the justification for selecting the coding categories. Next, the evolution of the LISn is described—what was learned in the initial piloting of the LISn and how the measure and procedures have been revised. Finally, the lessons learned and what additional work awaits are discussed.

THE CRITICAL ROLE OF LANGUAGE ENVIRONMENT FOR DEVELOPMENT

An ever-increasing percentage of children in the United States are DLLs. Children of immigrants comprise more than 20% of the children in the United States (Federal Interagency Forum on Child and Family Statistics, 2007), and many of these children are DLLs. Many DLLs live in families with fewer socioeconomic advantages, and they often enter school with fewer academic skills than English-speaking children (Cosentino de Cohen & Clewell, 2007; Lee & Burkham, 2002). Fortunately, preschool can make a difference in the skills that these children bring to kindergarten (Gormley & Gayer, 2005; Gormley, Gayer, Phillips, & Dawson, 2005; Loeb, Fuller, Kagan, & Carrol, 2004). Given the large number of DLLs and their greater need for educational support, it is particularly important to understand what constitutes a high-quality early childhood program for these children.

Almost all learning in school is dependent on language. Teachers and children use language to encode ideas and concepts and to communicate them to one another. As children progress through school, oral language is increasingly supplemented by written language or text. In the preschool years, most language development occurs through oral language and text that is read aloud. Children are exposed to a variety of ideas and concepts through descriptions and discussions of their daily experiences as well as through the use of literacy materials that are read aloud and discussed with them. Basic concepts such as size, shape, color, spatial relations, and categories of objects are easily embedded within the context of daily routines. Adults use a variety of types of discourse in talking with children and responding to children's communication. Adults also provide activities and experiences that expand the child's world beyond everyday experiences. Language is used to represent these experiences, allowing them to be discussed in other contexts and drawn upon in the future.

The link between language and later academic success is evident in the breadth of children's vocabulary and language proficiency. Children's vocabulary in preschool predicts their later ability to comprehend texts in elementary and middle school (Chall, Jacobs, & Baldwin, 1990; Dickinson, McCabe, Anastasopoulos, Peisner-Geinber, & Poe, 2003). Vocabulary knowledge represents the extensiveness of background knowledge and concept development that children acquire. This background is needed to attach meaning to text and to provide a basis for learning in the content areas. It is likely that the specific language in which this information is first learned may not matter nearly as much as whether children are provided with a rich array of language and literacy experiences, even if initially provided only in their home language. In a large-scale study of second-generation immigrants, Portes and Rumbaut (2001) concluded that maintaining home culture and language was related to higher academic achievement.

Unfortunately, preschool teachers often receive little guidance in how to support the development of children's vocabulary. In a review of 10 curriculum programs that were used in the Early Reading First program, Neuman and Dwyer (2009) found that only two curricula systematically addressed instruction in vocabulary in an average week of lessons, and only one program used what were considered developmentally appropriate activities (using visual and concrete aids) to support understanding of the meaning of words.

Little is known about the typical language environments of classrooms that include DLLs. Most of the literature examining instruction for DLLs involves studies of different types of interventions in classrooms at a macro level, such as monolingual versus bilingual environments (Slavin & Cheung, 2005), and most research on quality in classrooms focuses on the interactions with the primary teacher. There is anecdotal information that in many classrooms it may be more likely that the assistant teacher may be the more fluent speaker of the child's non-English language. With a national shortage of bilingual teachers, programs hire a teacher who may only speak English and then hire someone to assist in the classroom who knows the language the children speak. It is not clear whether the majority of the language interaction for DLLs occurs with the lead teacher, with the assistant teacher, or with peers. Similarly, it is not known what language(s) are used for those interactions with different conversational partners or for interactions within different contexts (e.g., academic or instructional activities versus more casual conversations around daily routines and transitions).

The language environment of DLLs is influenced by many factors, such as the match between child language and teacher language, adult fluency in the child's language, policy decisions about the use of a home language versus use of English, and family preferences. Some families want their children to acculturate quickly to the mainstream culture and view English as an important part of ensuring success in the United States. In some areas of the country, there are clear policy mandates for providing instruction in elementary schools primarily or only in English and so preschools are focused on helping children to acquire English before going to kindergarten. It is not clear whether this is at the expense of developing more sophisticated vocabulary and background knowledge in their home language as a way of supporting the longer term academic achievement and acquisition of English. Preschool teachers need to re-spond to competing philosophies and beliefs about how best to support the development of young DLL children. In addition, in many areas, there is a shortage of bilingual early childhood teachers, making it difficult to implement instruction in the home languages of children.

THE IMPORTANCE OF CAPTURING LANGUAGE USE IN A STUDY OF PROGRAMS THAT SERVE A HIGHLY DIVERSE POPULATION

The design of UPCOS included examining the quality of the preschool ex-periences. (In addition to classroom observations, UPCOS included parent and teacher interviews, child assessments, and teacher ratings of socioemo-tional development. See Love et al. [2009] for a full description of the study.) After a review of classroom observation tools, the Classroom Assessment Scoring System™ (CLASS™; Pianta, LaParo, & Hamre, 2008) was selected as the measure of overall quality, but there was interest in examining whether there were differences in what individual children or subgroups of children experienced within classrooms. A large part of the quality of the environment rests on the interactions between the adults and the children, including inter-actions taking place in multiple languages. When the children speak a lan-guage or languages that are different from the language used by the adults in the classroom, the quality of their experiences might differ—for example, in the level of cognitive demand and instructional support or in the emotional support for learning received by the children. Similarly, when there are dis-tinct linguistic subgroups of children within any given classroom, the type and quality of interactions and experiences also might vary accordingly.

Studies of early childhood settings often collect information about the number of adults and the number of children in each classroom. The as-sumption is that a better adult-to-child ratio (with more adults available for fewer children) leads to more interactions between adults and children and more positive outcomes for children. This is not necessarily the case for all children, particularly when one or more of the adults do not speak the same language as the child. With limited availability of bilingual teachers, the teachers in the classroom may not speak the child's primary language, or the adult who is fluent in the language other than English may be the adult with the more limited background in child development and education.

Capturing the diverse use of languages within classrooms was crit-ical for UPCOS, because LAUP serves a highly diverse population and individual preschools and family child care providers employ varied ap-proaches and curricula to meet the needs of the children. The sample of children in UPCOS in 2007 included 1,657 children, with only 41% using English only. Among the lead teachers in UPCOS, 45% spoke only English at home, 41% spoke Spanish and English at home, and 2% spoke

Spanish at home. This presented a unique opportunity to examine the use of two languages within a classroom, particularly how teachers use different languages when the classroom includes children who are DLLs.

For our 2007 pilot, classrooms were selected in which English-primarily, Spanish-primarily, and Spanish-only children (the determination of language group was based on a series of questions asked of parents on the permission slips) could be purposely sampled. The children in the subsample were primarily Latino (84%), with more than half speaking either Spanish only (22%) or primarily Spanish (32%) at the beginning of the school year. Spanish was reported as the first language for 56% of the sample. Approximately half the sample was male. More than half of the sample came from homes in which the mother's education was a high school diploma or less (59%).

On average, the teachers were experienced and educated. More than half of the teachers involved in the pilot study subsample worked in preschool for more than 9 years (range 2–22 years). More than 40% had a bachelor's degree or greater, another 32% reported an associate's degree, and 17% reported some college (without degree completion). More than half of the teachers reported reading to children and making instructional presentations in both English and Spanish (57%).

OVERVIEW OF THE LANGUAGE INTERACTION SNAPSHOT

The LISn captures the different types of naturally occurring talk between a particular focus child and others (lead teacher, other adults, or peers), as well as the different languages used in these interactions. The measure can be conducted with repeated observations throughout the observation period with one focus child or with alternating observations of a number of children. Each 5-minute coding snapshot is conducted with one child as the focus, and the researcher can combine multiple snapshots to obtain a picture of the use of the range of languages used within the classroom.

The LISn uses a time sampling method. Observers code all the categories of talk by language and conversational participant in a 30-second observation cycle. This is repeated 10 times for a child within a 5-minute period that is referred to as a snapshot. In the Spring 2007 pilot, in each 30-second cycle observers observed for 20 seconds and then recorded for 10 seconds. In the fall of 2009, continuous recording in each 30-second cycle was utilized in some of the classrooms. The observers reported that it was easier to code continuously because it was difficult to stop and start coding, even with the audio cues that were provided (observers found it troubling to ignore interactions during the record phase).

Within each 30-second observation cycle, the LISn observers code the language used by each adult and the target child (English, other language, mixed utterances), as well as the types of language each adult uses with the child. The LISn is not designed to count the specific number of interactions of each type of talk during the observation period but to provide a snapshot of the periodicity of types of interactions in each language, across the different observation cycles. Because of this, during each 30-second observation cycle, each type of talk in a particular language is only coded once. For example, a teacher might sing a song in English and the assistant teacher might lead the song in Spanish within the same coding segment. As long as the child is included in the group in which this is occurring, both of these would be coded on the snapshot by adult and language—in this case, the observer would code "Singing Spanish" for the assistant teacher and "Singing English" for the lead teacher. The child talk is coded in relation to the conversational partner(s)—that is, teacher, other adult, or peer—and the language used. If a child speaks to the teacher in English and to one peer in Spanish and one peer in English, then all three of these would be coded for that 30-second time period. However, if the child spoke three times to the teacher in English in one 30-second cycle, this is coded only one time for that observation cycle.

For each 5-minute snapshot, the observer notes the nature of all the language interactions in 30-second observation cycles. For each 30-second observation cycle, the observer codes whether the teacher or another adult repeats or confirms child language, elaborates or builds on child language, asks questions or otherwise requests language, gives directions, provides contextualized information, provides decontextualized information, or reads to or sings with the children, indicating the language(s) in which the interaction occurred.

At the end of the 5-minute time period, observers also indicate the context for the interaction (e.g., fine motor activity, routines, large-group time), indicate whether sustained interactions took place (sustained interactions are interactions with more than two complete conversational turns about a topic), and complete ratings of the frequency with which the child was in a group that included children who were English speakers, was engaged with the activities, and had the teacher's attention directed specifically toward the target child during the observation period.

After the two pilots, the End of Visit Ratings (EVR; Atkins-Burnett et al., 2010) were added to capture additional information about the instructional interactions associated with supporting DLLs in the classroom and about the social and emotional classroom climate. More explanation of this section is provided later in the chapter in the section on the evolution of the LISn.

The current definitions of the categories of teacher and other adult language coded during each snapshot are provided in Table 5.1. Appendix 5A contains definitions of these codes used in the initial pilot in 2007. It is important to note that the majority of the findings presented in this chapter are based on the 2007 definitions.

Table 5.1. Language Interaction Snapshot codes for teacher or other adult verbal communication, 2009

Code	Definition
Response to child language	
Repeats or confirms	This code is used to represent occasions in which the teacher repeats or confirms the focus child's utterance (e.g., when the child says, "milk" and the teacher says, "Yes, it's milk.").
Elaborates or builds	This code is used when the teacher responds to what the focus child says by building on the child's comment (e.g., if the child says, "milk" and the teacher says, "You opened the carton of milk yourself."). *Note: This code must be used with one of the four codes below to indicate how the teacher elaborates.*
Types of teacher language	
Requests language	This code is used to capture a teacher's eliciting a response from a child, usually in the form of a question (e.g., "What is this called?").
Gives directions (contextualized)	This code is used when the teacher requests information of the child that is connected to a physical cue in the environment, a facial expression or physical movement. This type of talk can be coded either as part of an elaboration, or as initiated spontaneously by the teacher. The question being asked must be contextualized in order for you to use this code (e.g., while looking at a red block, the teacher asks, "What color is this?").
Provides information, names, labels (contextualized)	This code is used when the teacher provides information to the child that is connected to a physical cue in the environment, a facial expression or physical movement. In other words, the teacher is providing information about things that are present at that time and giving the child contextual cues about what it is she is talking about. Often this code is used when teacher talk is in the form of instructing or guiding (e.g., "The lowercase *b* looks like a line with a ball. Watch how I make it.").
Provides/elicits information (decontextualized)	This code is used when the teacher provides or elicits information and the meaning of the information is conveyed solely by language. For this code, the child needs to carry the picture in his or her head. In terms of the hierarchy of our codes, this is considered a more cognitively advanced utterance. This code is most clearly recognized in the form of telling a story, recounting past events. The information might also be about a feeling or preference about something when the object is not present.

(continued)

Table 5.1. (continued)

Other classroom talk	
Reading	This code is used when the teacher is reading a book with the focus child either individually or in a group (including whole group).
Singing	This code is used when the teacher sings with the focus child either individually or in a group.
Other	This code is used to capture any type of language the teacher might use that falls outside one of the codes already discussed (e.g., "please," "thank you," or "wow").

From *Language Interaction Snapshot (LISn) Field Procedures and Coding Guide*, by S. Sprachman, M. Caspe, and S. Atkins-Burnett, 2009, Princeton NJ: Mathematica Policy Research; reprinted by permission. © Developed by Mathematica Policy Research under contract with First 5 LA.

RATIONALE FOR THE LANGUAGE INTERACTION SNAPSHOT CATEGORIES

In selecting categories of language for measurement, we wanted to maintain the ability to look at both the responsivity of the language in the classroom (i.e., how the adults respond to children's talk) as well as examine some of the complexity of the language, in particular, whether the language made connections to prior or future experiences or only referred to vocabulary and concepts that were present at the time of the discussion. The use of decontextualized language, talking about things not present at the time, teaches children to use language to represent ideas and events across time and space. Research found a relationship between decontextualized language use in the preschool years and reading comprehension in Grade 4 (Dickinson & Sprague, 2001; Snow, Dickinson, & Tabors, n.d.). Understanding decontextualized language is the essence of school literacy, because academic text often communicates about things not actually present.

When learning a new language, the context is important for understanding the communication. It was anticipated that the group conversations in the classroom in English would include mainly contextualized information to support the acquisition of English by the DLLs. For individual interactions with children, it was anticipated that decontextualized talk would occur in the primary language of the child. The LISn was designed to capture the prevalence of both contextualized and decontextualized talk as well as the language in which each type of talk occurred.

The design of the time-sampled codes on the LISn did not allow examination of the extent to which conversations with children were extended or sustained—did teachers ask and respond to questions and comments about a single topic for more than two complete conversational turns? Because a sustained conversation might cross the cycles of observation, information was collected about the frequency of sustained conversations at the end of each 5-minute snapshot.

Although there was interest in collecting information about additional categories of language, such as the novelty of the vocabulary used, the burden on assessors to code the language, the type of interaction, the conversational participant, and whether the conversation was sustained was already sufficiently cognitively demanding and reliability might suffer with the addition of more categories. In fact, the initial pretesting included additional categories, but some of them needed to be collapsed to gain rater reliability during live coding—for example, whether the teacher read informational text or narrative text was collapsed into "reading." To ensure high reliability in coding, the number of coding categories was limited. As noted previously, the results of the 2007 pilot led to further refinements of the categories and the definitions of the categories to ensure that important differences were captured.

DEVELOPMENT OF THE MEASURE— EVOLUTION FROM THE FIRST PILOT

In the Spring 2007 pilot of the LISn, three snapshots were collected for each of three children in 18 preschool classrooms with high proportions of DLLs. The sample of 54 children was purposive—one child was primarily an English speaker, one child was primarily a Spanish speaker, and one child was a Spanish-only speaker at the beginning of the year. CLASS observations and LISn observations were alternated. Observers completed a minimum of three CLASS observations per classroom and three LISn observations for each focus child.

Observer Training

To allow the observer to code not only what language is used but how that language is used, a high degree of fluency in the languages of the classroom is required. For the UPCOS pilot, observers were fluent in English and Spanish. Results indicated that although high fluency supports reliable coding of the categories, it can also make it more challenging for some extremely fluent observers to note which language they are hearing. One of our trainees, who was bilingual from birth, found it difficult to code when children and adults were speaking Spanish versus English (although she was reliable on coding the categories of talk). She did not easily categorize words as one language or the other. Because she might miss potentially important differences in how different languages were used in the classroom, she could not be certified on the LISn.

Observers in the 2007 pilot conducted both the CLASS and the LISn and needed to be reliable on both measures. Separate certifications were conducted for each measure, with high reliability on the CLASS a prerequisite for consideration as a LISn observer. The training for both measures is intensive. The training for the CLASS lasted 3.5 days, with 2 days of classroom training, 1 day of field practice, and a half day of field reliability.

Four of the most reliable CLASS observers were then selected for LISn training. This group of four met for three half-day sessions. In addition, observers worked independently at home coding transcripts and video-tapes on two evenings for additional practice. On the final morning of training, the team met in groups of two at an LAUP center in downtown Los Angeles to establish field reliability with the lead trainer (this is commonly referred to as establishing reliability with the gold standard).

LISn observer inter-rater reliability was established by using both videotape and field methods and calculated the percentage agreement between each observer and the gold standard observer separately for the child and teacher components and the English, Spanish, and mixed-language verbal interactions. The interrater agreement was high for the overall coding (96%). Due to concern that the low incidence of other language or mixed-language utterances inflated the rates of agreement, the agreement for the incidences of English and Spanish, and by category, was computed separately. No matter how the agreement was computed, the average agreement was greater than 85% with only two categories of talk in English with less than 80% agreement.

Revisions to Protocols and Second Pilot   Thus, the first pilot provided information about what was feasible to code reliably and what items needed to be revised as well as what additional information were to be obtained. For example, the 2007 pilot indicated a very low frequency of elaboration of child language, so the observer training about when to code "elaboration" was strengthened to ensure that the low incidence was not a function of poor observer training. Initially, we asked only about the number of sustained conversations, not whether these occurred with the lead teacher, assistant teacher, or a peer (we defined *sustained conversations* as more than two conversational turns on the same topic). This was revised to include information about the conversational partner as well as ensure that observers recognized when a sustained conversation occurred. Other revisions and additions were made to the definitions and exercises in training materials.

Our analysis of the 2007 pilot study and observation of video data indicated a need to make revisions to the definitions for codes related to giving directions, contextualized and decontextualized language. The codes for giving directions and providing contextualized information had the lowest interrater agreement (77% and 78%, respectively). In talking with observers, it became clear that they needed a clearer distinction between routine directions and instructional directions that provide information. Training was strengthened to improve reliability. On the training videotapes, much of the decontextualized language that was used in the classroom occurred as requests for language (e.g., "What did you eat for breakfast?" or "What did you see at the beach?"). Based on this, request for language was revised to include only requests that were contextualized. Any request for language that was decontextualized was then coded with decontextualized language. Requests for language and giving information are used now to designate contextualized interactions, and the code for decontextualized language includes both questions and providing information.

For the Fall 2009 pilot, four observers were trained to conduct the LISn with the revised coding scheme and additional training materials. (Additional observers were trained for the winter 2010 study, and observers were trained for other studies as well.) The revised training materials included additional exercises, particularly around coding elaboration and decontextualized versus contextualized language, and video of additional bilingual preschool classrooms with exemplars of decontextualized talk and elaboration. Field reliability at the end of training in both English and Spanish was more than 95% exact agreement between the observers and the gold standard. When calculating agreement based only on the cycles in which a specific category was observed, inter-rater agreement ranged from 84% to 92% with the gold standard. All individual codes had greater than 85% agreement except the two codes that were noted only one time (total across six observations) by the gold standard observer: decontextualized language and elaborates. Although these remain difficult for observers to identify, they were also very-low-frequency occurrences in the classrooms used for establishing field reliability. Particular attention is paid to this when monitoring quality in the ongoing data collection.

The most recent change for the Winter 2010 observations was to include EVR (see Appendix 5B) to provide information about the specific instructional practices used by the teacher to support language development, many that are particularly relevant for DLLs, as well as information about social and emotional climate and use of time. The first section of the EVR asks about practices such as effectively using pictures, objects, gestures, and vocal emphasis to support meaning, providing clear instructions, engaging in meaningful conversations, intentionally teaching both basic concepts and more sophisticated words, using routines to support children, and encouraging peer interactions that support language development. The second section of the EVR asks about areas such as classroom behavior and management, adult–child relationship, peer interaction, child engagement, and use of learning time. Each statement about the adult instructional practices or the social emotional climate is rated by how characteristic the descriptors are of the classroom that was observed, with ratings from 1 (*not at all*) to 4 (*extremely characteristic*). Each point along the scale is described in the coding guide—that is, an anchor is provided for each point on the rating scale. Observers used the EVR during LISn observations for the first time in winter 2010. With the strong focus of the LISn on the adult–child interactions, observers reported that it was relatively easy to code.

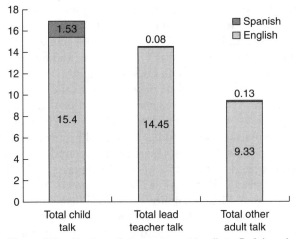

Figure 5.2. Number of time points with talk in English and Spanish by Speaker (Spring 2007 data).

Information Provided by the Language Interaction Snapshot

The LISn provides a variety of information, including language used, categories of talk used in each language, and differences in talk by context. It allows researchers to look at the proportion of observed talk in each language by the child with different conversational partners (peer, teacher, or other adult) and by the adult conversational partner—that is, the lead teacher or the other adult who talks with the child (see Figure 5.2 for an example from the 2007 pilot).

One can look at the patterns of use of English and Spanish at different times in the day—that is, within different activity settings. At the end of each 5-minute period, information was collected about the context for the communication. Keeping in mind that some 5-minute periods had more than one activity and which talk occurred during which activity could not be separated, estimates were observed of the mean amount of talk in each language when children had at least one observation in an activity setting.

For example, there was more teacher talk when the child's observations included individual time or large-group times. Child talk in both languages was observed more frequently when the observation included outside time, and teacher talk in English was observed more frequently when the child's observation included a large group or routine, whereas more teacher talk in Spanish was observed when a small group time was included.

Beyond the amount of language, the LISn collects data on what types of information are being communicated in each language by the teacher and the other adults. In the pilot sample, more than half of the lead teacher

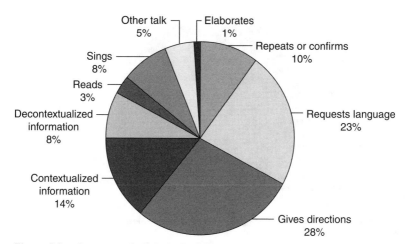

Figure 5.3. Categories of talk by lead teacher in English.

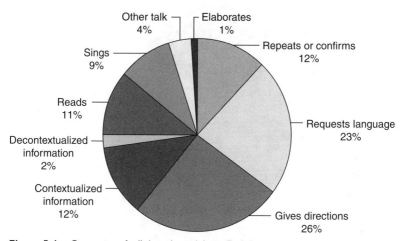

Figure 5.4. Categories of talk by other adults in English.

communication in English was giving directions and requesting language (usually asking questions), whereas decontextualized language represented less than 10% of the talk in either language. In the spring of 2007, approximately 14% of the lead teacher communication was giving information in context, and 3% of the communication was reading. The communication from the other adults had a similar level of diversity in the type of talk occurring in English (see Figures 5.3 and 5.4), suggesting that the assistant teachers' communications in English follow a pattern similar to those of the lead teachers' communication.

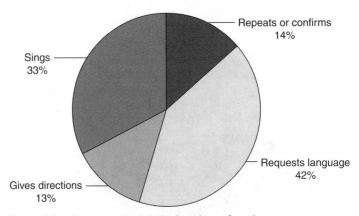

Figure 5.5.   Categories of talk by lead teacher in Spanish.

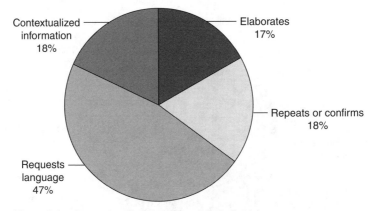

Figure 5.6.   Categories of talk by other adults in Spanish.

When the talk in Spanish was examined in the spring pilot, much lower rates of use of Spanish and less diversity in the types of communication in Spanish when compared to English were observed, and differences were found in how teachers and other adults in the classroom used Spanish (see Figures 5.5 and 5.6). The majority of the Spanish communication by the lead teacher was singing and requests for language, with 9% repeating child language and 9% giving directions. For the other adult, more than half of the Spanish was also requesting language from the child, but greater percentages of the more responsive types of talk were also observed in Spanish used by the other adult—repeating or confirming and elaborating on child language. Spanish was also used to give information in context (18% of the Spanish by the other adult).

With differences in the amount of talk in different contexts as well as differences noted in who talked more in the varied contexts, the research team wondered whether some of the results were attributable to the limited number of snapshots per child and the differences in the context of the observations. In the Fall 2009 pilot, LISn observations were collected continuously so that each child was observed every 15–20 minutes, and the observations were increased to five to six snapshots per child by the end of the morning. Thus, the language interactions in all of the activities in each classroom were captured. Observers reported that, in most cases, each child was observed in each type of activity structure.

The preliminary analysis of pilot data in the fall of 2009 suggests that any study of teacher talk in bilingual classrooms should take into account that there may be differences in the distribution of talk in fall and spring. The data indicated differences in the distribution of use of both English and Spanish with the teachers who were sampled in the fall using Spanish more frequently than those sampled in the spring. However, in English, most of the differences between our spring pilot in 2007 and the fall of 2009 pilot were noted in the categories of talk that were refined before the fall pilot (see Figure 5.7). For example, the amount of talk coded as elaboration increased from 1% to 6% of the talk, whereas repeats or confirms decreased from 10% to 5% of the talk.

Not all the differences can be attributed clearly to the types of changes that were made to the coding categories. Based on the changes made to the

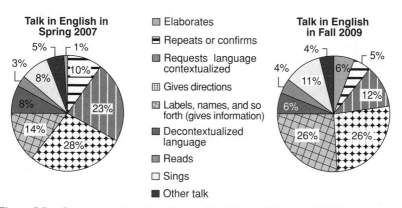

Figure 5.7. Comparison of teacher talk in English in Spring 2007 and Fall 2009.

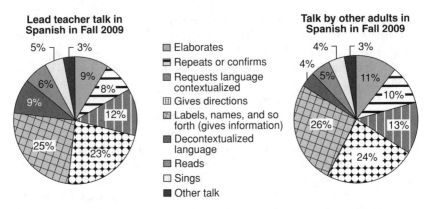

Figure 5.8. Comparison of talk by lead teacher and other adults in Spanish in Fall 2009.

definitions, it was hypothesized that the percentage of decontextualized language would increase and the percentage of requests for language would decrease. Although the percentage of talk in English devoted to requesting language from children (now limited to contextualized language) decreased from 23% to 12% of the talk, the percentage of talk in English devoted to providing decontextualized information decreased a little (8% in Spring 2007 and 6% in Fall 2009), and the amount of contextualized talk increased from 14% to 26%. In this case, it is difficult to disentangle the influence of changes in the category definitions and the sampling of teachers from potential differences in the teacher talk in fall and spring, but it is suggestive of greater use of labeling and contextualized language in the fall by teachers.

The Fall 2009 pilot indicated more frequent use of Spanish by teachers and more diversity in what is said in Spanish by both lead teachers and other adults (see Figure 5.8). In addition, this pilot indicated a pattern in the data that the research team had anticipated seeing in the earlier pilot— the percentage of decontextualized language used by the lead teacher was greater in Spanish (9%) than in English (6%). Both the lead teacher and the other adults used more decontextualized talk in Spanish than in English in the Fall 2009 pilot.

By increasing the number of snapshots collected in the Fall 2009 pilot, more talk overall was captured for each child. Children were observed in a variety of settings, with each child observed every 20 minutes. Thus, the activity setting was much less likely to influence comparisons across children in the type and amount of talk that was observed. This may also have influenced the changes in the distribution of talk from the Spring 2007 to Fall 2009 pilot.

RELATIONSHIP OF THE LANGUAGE INTERACTION SNAPSHOT AND THE CLASSROOM ASSESSMENT SCORING SYSTEM

Initial evidence of the validity of the LISn was obtained in the UPCOS 2007 pilot by examining relationships of the LISn variables with the CLASS scores obtained during the same observation period. The different categories of talk on the LISn as well as a measure of total talk in each language were examined in relation to the CLASS scores. The observations occurred in the last half of the school year and many of the programs may have been focused on helping children prepare for the transition to the English-only kindergarten context; therefore, observers noted limited talk in Spanish or another language in the spring. With limited talk, there was not enough variance in the observations to construct reliable scales for the Spanish or Other Language category. "Lead Teacher Talk in English" (alpha [α] = 0.77) and "Other Adult Talk in English" (α = 0.72) included all the categories of talk except singing and elaboration. Singing was not related to the other categories of talk, and elaboration of child language in the 2007 pilot was noted only four times (once per child) by observers in the pilot sample.

The strongest correlations between the CLASS and LISn were "Lead Teacher Talk in English" with the CLASS Instructional Support scale and dimensions. In the UPCOS sample of 14 classrooms with complete data, moderate correlations were found between CLASS Instructional Support and Total Talk in English (r = .55) and "Gives Information in Context" (r = .63), although not all of the dimensions of the CLASS Instructional Support scale were related to the LISn variables. The LISn variables showed no correlation with the CLASS dimension Concept Development. The strongest relationships were found between the CLASS Quality of Feedback and the LISn variables about requests for language, giving both contextualized and decontextualized information, repeating or confirming child language, and the total talk (r = .64 to .72). The LISn variables for elaborating, requesting language from children, and giving information showed moderate relationships with CLASS Language Modeling (r = .52 to .69). Singing, giving directions, and other talk were not related to the Instructional Support scale or its dimensions. Surprisingly, the frequency of reading detected with the time sampling also did not show a significant relationship to the Instructional Support scale or its dimensions. It may be due to the low frequency of this activity or to differences in how teachers share books with children. It could also be a function of the time sampling alternating the CLASS and the LISn. This was one of the findings that led the researchers to question whether the number of time samples was sufficient to represent the classroom instruction.

With limited variance on most Spanish variables, only "Lead Teacher Giving Directions" in Spanish showed significant relationships with the Instructional Support scale and dimensions.

The pilot sample was small, and only 45 minutes of classroom inter-action was coded (three children times 5 minutes per snapshot, times three snapshots per child). In addition, in classrooms in which the structure in-cluded more center-based or child-choice time, the adults in the room might be interacting with children other than the focus child. The sam-pling included outside time and transitions when there is often less inter-action between the teacher and the child. Only 6 out of 40 children (15%) had observations that included large-group time, whereas 17 out of 40 chil-dren (43%) had observations that included snack time, and more than half (55%) of the children had observations during outside time. Because some differences were observed by the context, particularly related to which in-dividual spoke, the limited number of snapshots per child likely influenced the estimates. In the current study, two observers are in classrooms, with one observer using the CLASS and the other observer using the LISn, and they will have the opportunity to look again at the relationships between these measures of the classroom.

Limitations

The pilot work in UPCOS looked at the use of Spanish and English in classrooms where Spanish was reported as the first language for 56% of the children in the sample and almost half of the teachers reported speak-ing at least some Spanish. When the LISn is used in other contexts and with other language groups, the differences and relationships found in the pilot studies may not replicate. In particular, when used with an Asian lan-guage group in classrooms that did not include much time in large or small group instruction, the relationships with the CLASS were not observed, and the frequency of talk observed was lower (the Preschool for All in San Francisco project also piloted the LISn). Only three snapshots per child were collected in those classrooms.

The LISn poses challenges to data collection. Although observers in the field are trained to be as unobtrusive as possible, the close observation of an individual child may alter the interactions of the child or the adult or both. For example, shy children may talk less when an unfamiliar adult is close by or may speak too quietly to be heard. Also, as previously noted, the number of codes needs to be limited to manage the cognitive demand of coding in real time. Three snapshots per child in the Spring 2007 pilot were not sufficient to sample enough activity settings to represent the overall language experiences of a child.

It is unclear how the observational process affects the adult interac-tions. The adults in the room may avoid the child being observed or they might use English more often if they do not realize that the observer is flu-ent in the other language. (Observers were told to be sure that the teacher knew that they understood both English and the other language and to ask the teacher to follow their typical day.) The teachers in the classroom may think that they should be modeling English and may do so more frequently than usual when being observed. Ensuring that the observer is unobtrusive while also staying close enough to the target child to hear interactions is a challenge.

Despite these concerns, the pilot results suggest that the LISn holds promise for examining how language environments may differ among children in classrooms serving DLLs.

CURRENT AND FUTURE WORK

The pilot work with the LISn indicated that individual children had limited overall exposure to language interactions and that the amount of English spoken versus the home language by different speakers differed by context. For example, Fall 2007 pilot results indicated that children talked more in Spanish during individual and center-based activities and seldom used Spanish during large-group activities, whereas observers noted the most teacher talk in English during individual time.

It is also not known if the use of English typically changes over the course of the year, as a reflection of a possible shift toward a greater emphasis on preparing children for entry into English-only kindergarten classrooms. The pilot results suggest greater use of Spanish in the fall, but these were different classrooms and a different group of children than those observed in the spring pilot. The change in language use over the course of the year is an area for future study.

The low incidence of decontextualized language in any language and very low incidence of sustained conversations was a concern after the Spring 2007 pilot, and the research team was not convinced that observers were recognizing it when it occurred. Training was strengthened to ensure that under-representation of codes was not a training issue. The training materials were revised and additional classroom video in bilingual classrooms was collected. Based on this video, it was noted that a lot of the decontextualized language was embedded in questions, and observers were coding this only as "requests language." The codes and training materials were then revised (see Appendix 5A) to include both questions and statements in the decontextualized category. Thus, the LISn captures whether the teacher uses or elicits language about things not present versus requesting language about things present and providing information about things that are present. Exercises were added to the training materials to ensure that observers would recognize the use of decontextualized language and questions, the use of contextualized language and questions, and giving directions. However, limited use of decontextualized talk was still observed.

The debriefing with observers in the Fall 2009 pilot confirms the data and suggests that there are real differences in the amount of adult–child language interactions experienced by individual children in some classrooms. The impression of the observers as they left the field is that the LISn captures the average language experiences of the children in the classrooms. Observers noted that, overall, the level of adult talk was low, particularly in the types of talk that go beyond classroom management, but they did note that classrooms varied in the amount of talk. Observers reported seeing very few sustained conversations, and they believe that that was because it was happening so seldom, rather than because it was difficult to identify. Adult interactions with children are often brief, and in many classrooms adults spend a lot of the time in supervision of children and managing materials. One observer also noted that children who spoke less frequently were spoken to less frequently by adults as well as by other children. Half of the observers reported that the children who were Spanish speakers interacted more frequently with peers (in English as well as in Spanish) than with adults.

Hart and Risley (1995) found that the amount of language that children hear from adults is related to the children's language development and that children from lower income homes hear far fewer words than children in more advantaged homes. In a 2002 preface that appears in later printings of their book, Hart and Risley wrote that the "most important aspect to evaluate in child care settings for very young children is the amount of talk actually going on, moment by moment, between children and their caregivers" (p. xxi). If the incidence of language experienced by individual children is as low as suggested by the pilot data from this small sample of classrooms, it calls for strong professional development focused on encouraging teachers to talk more frequently with children overall. Similar to the work of Hart and Risley, UPCOS found that teachers who used the less frequent and more challenging categories of talk (e.g., as decontextualized talk) were also the teachers who talked more overall. The LISn could help in measuring change in classroom interaction as a result of targeted interventions. With reliable estimates of the different categories of talk used in the classroom, the LISn can look at relationships between specific types of talk and child outcomes, particularly for DLLs, and help to inform interventions. The addition of the EVR will extend our knowledge about what teachers do to support children's language development in preschool.

STUDY QUESTIONS

1. The authors state that almost all learning in school is dependent on language. Give some examples from the chapter that support this claim.

2. Give a brief description of the LISn. How does it work? What methods does it use?

3. What kinds of results did the authors obtain in their pilot study using the LISn?

REFERENCES

Atkins-Burnett, S., Sprachman, S., & Caspe, M. (2010). *Language Interaction Snapshot + End of Visit Ratings (LISn + EVR)*. Princeton, NJ: Mathematica Policy Research.

Boller, K., Sprachman, S., & the Early Head Start Research Consortium. (1998). *Child–Caregiver Observation System*. Princeton, NJ: Mathematica Policy Research.

Capps, R., Fix, M., Murray, J., Ost, J., Passel, J.S., & Herwantoro, S. (2005). *The new demography of America's schools: Immigration and the No Child Left Behind Act.* Washington, DC: The Urban Institute

Chall, J.S., Jacobs, V.A., & Baldwin, L.E. (1990). *The reading crisis: Why poor children fall behind.* Cambridge, MA: Harvard University Press.

Cheung, A., & Slavin, R.E. (2005). Effective reading programs for English language learners and other language minority students. Bilingual Research *Journal, 29*(2), 241–267.

Cosentino de Cohen, C., & Clewell, B.C. (2007, May). *Putting English language learners on the educational map. Education in focus* (Urban Institute Policy Brief). Washington, DC: The Urban Institute.

Dickinson, D.K., McCabe, A., Anastasopoulos, L., Peisner-Feinberg, E.S., Poe., M.D. (2003). The comprehensive language approach to early literacy: the interrelationships among vocabulary, phonological sensitivity, and print knowledge among preschoolers. *Journal of Educational Psychology, 95*(3), 465–481.

Dickinson, D.K., & Sprague, K.E. (2001). The nature and impact of early childhood care environments on the language and early literacy development of children from low-income families. In S.B. Neuman & D.K. Dickinson (Eds.), *Handbook of early literacy research* (pp. 263–280). New York: Guilford Press.

Dickinson, D.K., & Tabors, P.O. (1992, April). Continuity and change in oral language and print skills between kindergarten and first grade. In R. Gallimore (Chair), *Pathways to literacy: Home and school factors affecting kindergarten and first grade achievement.* Symposium conducted at the annual meeting of the American Educational Research Association, San Francisco.

Dickinson, D.K., Tabors, P.O., & Roach, K.A. (1996, August). Predicting children's fourth grade reading comprehension using individual growth trajectories in vocabulary, decoding, and decontextualized language. In A. Spinillo & J. Oakhill (Chairs), *Thinking about texts: Comprehension and metalinguistic awareness.* Symposium conducted at the XIVth Biennial Meetings of the International Society for the Study of Behavioral Development, Quebec City, Quebec, Canada.

Federal Interagency Forum on Child and Family Statistics. *America's children: Key national indicators of well-being, 2007.* Washington, DC: U.S. Government Printing Office.

Gormley, W., & Gayer, T. (2005). Promoting school readiness in Oklahoma: An evaluation of Tulsa's pre-K program, *Journal of Human Resources, 40*, 533–558.

Gormley, Jr., W.T., Gayer, T., Phillips, D., & Dawson, B. (2005). The effects of universal pre-K on cognitive development, *Developmental Psychology, 41*(6), 872–884.

Hart, B., & Risley, T.R. (1995). *Meaningful differences in the everyday lives of young American children.* Baltimore: Paul H. Brookes Publishing Co.

Lee, V. E., & Burkam. D.T. (2002). *Inequality at the starting gate: Social background differences in achievement as children begin school.* Washington, DC: Economic Policy Institute.

Loeb, S., Fuller, B., Kagan, S.L., & Carrol, B. (2004). Child care in poor communities: Early learning effects of type, quality, and stability. *Child Development, 75,* 47–65.

Love, J.M., Atkins-Burnett, S., Vogel, C., Aikens, N., Xue, Y., Mabutas, M., et al. (2009). *Los Angeles Universal Preschool programs, children served, and children's progress in the preschool year: Final report of the First 5 LA Universal Preschool Child Outcomes Study.* Princeton, NJ: Mathematica Policy Research.

Neuman, S.B., & Dwyer, J. (2009). Missing in action: Vocabulary instruction in pre-K. *The Reading Teacher, 62*(5), 384–392.

Pianta, R.C., LaParo, K., & Hamre, B. (2008). *Classroom Assessment Scoring System^{TM} (CLASS)^{TM} manual, pre-K.* Baltimore: Paul H. Brookes Publishing Co.

Portes, A., & Rumbaut, R.G. (2001). *Legacies: The story of the immigrant second generation.* Berkeley: University of California Press.

Slavin, R., & Cheung, A. (2005). A synthesis of research on language of reading instruction for English language learners. *Review of Educational Research, 75*(2), 247–284.

Snow, C., Dickinson, D., & Tabors, P.O. (n.d.). *The home-school study of language and literacy development.* Retrieved October 3, 2009, from http://gseweb.harvard.edu/~pild/homeschoolstudy.htm

Sprachman, S., Caspe, M., & Atkins-Burnett, S. (2007). *Language Interaction Snapshot (LISn) field procedures and coding guide.* Princeton, NJ: Mathematica Policy Research.

Sprachman, S., Caspe, M., & Atkins-Burnett, S. (2009). *Language Interaction Snapshot (LISn) field procedures and coding guide.* Princeton, NJ: Mathematica Policy Research.

Appendix 5A

Language Interaction Snapshot Codes for Teacher or Other Adult Verbal Communication (LISn Codes in 2007)

Code	Definition
Response to child language	
Repeats or confirms	This code is used to represent occasions in which the teacher repeats or confirms the focus child's utterance (for example, when the child says, "milk" and the teacher says, "Yes, it's milk.").
Elaborates or builds	This code is used when the teacher responds to what the focus child says by building on the child's comment (for example, if the child says, "milk" and the teacher says, "You opened the carton of milk yourself."). *Note: This code must be used with one of the four codes below to indicate how the teacher elaborates.*
Types of teacher language	
Requests language	This code is used to capture a teacher's eliciting a response from a child, usually in the form of a question (for example, "What is this called?").
Gives directions	This code is used to capture a teacher's making a statement that prompts the child to do something that does not require a verbal response (for example, "Jump up and down like a frog." "Come over here." "Put your crayons away.").
Provides information (contextualized—objects present)	This code is used when the teacher provides information to the child that is connected to a visual or physical cue in the environment, a facial expression, or physical movement. The teacher is providing information about things or events that are present at that time and giving the child contextual cues about what he or she is talking about (for example, "The apple and the banana [in the child's snack] are both fruits." "This is a cotton ball. I am gluing it to the construction paper.").
Provides information (decontextualized—objects not present)	This code is used when the teacher provides information in which the meaning is conveyed solely by language. This code is most clearly recognized in the form of telling a story, recounting past events (for example, "This weekend I went to McDonalds. First I waited in line. Then, I ate a salad"), or anticipating future events ("Next week we will go to the zoo").

(continued)

Appendix 5A   *(continued)*

	This information might also be about a feeling or preference when the object is not present (for example, "I love cold days," without any contextual cues).
Other classroom talk	
Reading	This code is used when the teacher is reading a book with the focus child either individually or in a group (including whole group).
Singing	This code is used when the teacher sings with the focus child either individually or in a group.
Other	This code is used to capture any type of language the teacher might use that falls outside one of the codes already discussed (for example, "please," "thank you," or "wow").

From *Language Interaction Snapshot (LISn) Field Procedures and Coding Guide,* by S. Sprachman, M. Caspe, and S. Atkins-Burnett, 2007, Princeton, NJ: Mathematica Policy Research; reprinted by permission. © Developed by Mathematica Policy Research under contract with First 5 LA.

Appendix 5B

End of Visit Ratings (EVR)
Part I

The adults:

a. Effectively use pictures and objects to help children understand what is being said.

b. Effectively use gestures and facial expressions to help children understand what is being communicated (gestures and expressions match the meaning).

c. Intentionally teach more sophisticated words to children.

d. Intentionally teach basic concept words to children (*top, bottom, under, between…*).

e. Repeat phrases or sentences for children (allowing a wait time in between).

f. Repeat information when children struggle with understanding.

g. Effectively use vocal emphasis of key words when communicating.

h. Elicit elaborate responses from children (e.g., frequently ask open-ended questions like "How did that happen?" and "Tell me more about that," "And then what happened?").

i. Ask many questions that can be answered with a single word.

j. Engage children in meaningful conversations about a topic (sustained conversations with a child or group of children).

k. Models correct use of English.

☐ Do not code and check here if Spanish/Other Language Only.

l. Use routines and picture schedules to support children in knowing what to do.

m. Provide clear instructions for tasks and activities.

n. Read to children at different points throughout the day.

o. Talk meaningfully with children about books that are read.

p. Vocabulary words are taught or reviewed prior to book reading.

q. Listen attentively to children.

r. Help children learn to read by teaching them about sounds (e.g., by rhyming, teaching the sounds that each letter makes, and modeling how to put sounds together).

s. Encourage peer interactions that support language development.

(continued)

Appendix 5B *(continued)*

Part 2

Code based on what you observed over the entire visit. Consider the experiences of *all* of the children:

a. Children are cooperative and attentive.

b. Teachers spend a lot of time managing behavior.

c. Child behavior disrupts the classroom.

d. Instruction continues without disruption from children's problem behaviors.

e. Children are perfectly behaved.

f. Teachers utilize nonverbal methods to manage behavior.

g. Teachers use praise to maintain positive behavior.

h. Children are off task.

i. Children are passively engaged (watching and listening, but not doing or talking).

j. Children are actively engaged.

k. Children appear excited by the lesson.

l. Lead teacher and children have a warm, positive relationship.

m. Assistant teacher(s) and children have a warm, positive relationship.

n. Teachers encourage children to help one another.

o. Peer-to-peer interaction (including some nonverbal interaction) about activities occurs.

p. Teachers have techniques for gaining class attention in less than 10 seconds.

q. Children spend a lot of time waiting.

r. Transitions are smooth, and children quickly engage in activities.

s. Teachers spend a lot of time giving directions.

t. Teachers are fluid in the presentation of lessons.

u. Children appear familiar with the routines and procedures used.

v. Children are given the opportunity to think and respond (wait time).

From *Language Interaction Snapshot (LISn) Field Procedures and Coding Guide*, by S. Sprachman, M. Caspe, and S. Atkins-Burnett, 2007, Princeton NJ: Mathematica Policy Research; reprinted by permission. © Developed by Mathematica Policy Research under contract with First 5 LA.

6

Using the Observation Measures of Language and Literacy Instruction (OMLIT) to Characterize Early Literacy Classrooms—Focus on Dual Language Learners

Carolyn Layzer and Kenyon R. Maree

In this chapter, data collected are used in an intervention study in early childhood classrooms to describe language use across classroom activities and congruence or incongruence between the languages used by children and adults in the classrooms. Although the data were originally collected for evaluating an intervention, the focus of the analyses conducted here is on the linguistic context of instruction and classroom practices, rather than on specific interventions or structural elements of the classroom. (The

---

The research reported here was supported by the Institute of Education Sciences, U.S. Department of Education, through Grant R305G04145 to the University of Iowa, Abt Associates, Inc., subcontractor. The opinions expressed are those of authors and do not represent views of the funding agency (Institute of Education Sciences, U.S. Department of Education). Partial support for development of this chapter was provided by the National Center for Research on Early Childhood Education (NCRECE). It was supported by Grant R305A060021, administered by the Institute of Education Sciences, U.S. Department of Education. However, the contents do not necessarily represent the positions or policies of the U.S. Department of Education or NCRECE, and endorsement by the federal government or NCRECE should not be assumed.

intervention study was nicknamed CLIMBERs [Chicago Literacy Initiative: Making Better Early Readers] and was a large-scale effectiveness study of the early literacy curriculum Breakthrough to Literacy [BTL; Brown, 2004]. The study is described in greater detail next.) Broadly, the purpose of this chapter is to explore the capabilities of the instruments used in the study and to determine whether they could also be used to help answer questions about patterns of language use in classrooms and outcomes associated with those patterns. More specifically, classrooms are categorized by linguistic composition and quality ratings of instruction are compared as measured by the Observation Measures of Language and Literacy Instruction (OMLIT) across classrooms (Goodson, Layzer, Smith, & Rimdzius, 2004). Second, the relationship between instructional context and child outcomes is explored, using the classroom quality ratings and linguistic composition categories, as well as individual assessments of children's early language and literacy conducted at the end of each year. Finally, the properties of the variables yielded by the instruments to measure the extent to which they might help us predict child outcomes are examined.

BACKGROUND

The OMLIT measures were designed for use in documenting practices in early language and literacy instruction for purposes of research and evaluation. All of the OMLIT measures include some procedure for documenting aspects of language used in the setting, but the measures were not designed to look specifically at language use, although it is possible to capture some aspect of language use with each measure. Next, some of the assumptions on which the dual language learner (DLL)–specific aspects of the measures were based are briefly presented to provide some context for the research questions that are pursued in this paper.

A first assumption is that classroom language use is of central importance in understanding instruction of DLL children (i.e., children whose primary home language is not English), because for many DLLs, the classroom may be their only source of access to English language. Because all young learners—DLLs and non-DLLs—are developing their language and preliteracy skills and knowledge, knowing more about classroom language use could be of broader value. For DLLs, the OMLIT measures themselves were developed based on the scant empirical research literature on dual language learning, nearly all of which involved older subjects.

A second assumption is that although much of the same knowledge base upon which instructional decisions are made in classrooms with native English speakers may apply to teaching and learning in classrooms with DLLs, there is so little research in the specifics of what occurs in instructional contexts with DLLs that even exploratory research is valuable.

In 1996, the National Association for the Education of Young Children (NAEYC) modified their guidelines to support what researchers and advocates had been saying and writing for years—namely, that teachers and programs should support the continued development of children's home languages. Studies show that a strong basis in the primary language (L1) promotes academic achievement in the second language (August & Hakuta, 1997; Cummins, 1979; Greene, 1997; Lanauze & Snow, 1989; Willig, 1985) and that DLLs are more likely to become readers and writers of English when they are already familiar with the vocabulary and concepts in their L1 (see, e.g., research on linguistic interdependence, or transfer; cf. California State Department of Education, 1985; Cummins, Harley, Swain, & Allen, 1990; Geva & Ryan, 1993; Hakuta & Diaz, 1985; Kemp, 1984; McLaughlin, 1986; Medina & Escamilla, 1992; Ramirez, 1985; Ricciardelli, 1992). Studies also show that bilingualism does not impede academic achievement (Yeung, Marsh, & Suliman, 2000). In addition, maintenance of children's home language facilitates home/family nurturing and support of the child's education and development (Fillmore, 1991, 2000; Snow, Burns, & Griffin, 1998). Although there is no evidence that delaying exposure to English helps children maintain their L1 nor that exposure to English hinders L1 maintenance, there is no evidence that delaying exposure to English harms development of English language and literacy skills *in the long term*. One should not expect to see marked improvement in students' English proficiency after just 1–2 years of exposure to English; there is general agreement in the field that it takes between 5 and 7 years, on average, for learners to gain proficiency. All in all, there is a great deal of agreement among researchers that it is important for programs and teachers to plan classroom approaches that encourage L1 maintenance and development to the greatest extent possible, and this is one reason for examining the prevalence of the use of L1 in the classroom.

For instructional practices identified as being associated with supporting later reading achievement in native-English-speaking children, the approaches for DLLs would be the same in principle but with some modifications to ensure that material is presented in a way that is comprehensible to the learners. Tabors (1997) provided some guidelines for effective instruction of DLLs, which are operationalized in the OMLIT instruments (see Appendix 6.1). These modifications would presumably benefit all students but are especially crucial for students whose exclusive source of information about English may be the preschool or kindergarten classroom. One would expect that teachers would modify their classroom interactions based on the composition of the classroom. And, in classrooms with greater proportions of DLLs, one might expect to see more DLL-specific practices. Associations between practices believed to be "higher quality" and better outcomes for DLLs would strengthen confidence in the efficacy of these practices. However, weaker associations would still leave doubt as to whether the weakness of the statistical relationship was due to imprecision in measurement, lack of efficacy of practices, or unmeasured characteristics of the instructional context.

In this chapter, relationships among the following types of measures are explored and described:

- *Classroom linguistic composition:* Classes were grouped into five categories that ranged from classes in which 100% of students were DLLs to classrooms in which English was the L1 of 100% of the students.

- *Percentage of class activity time where:*

  - English is spoken by children—This is a measure of the percentage of activity time when children are speaking in English during activities.

  - Spanish or other language is spoken by children—This is a measure of the percentage of activity time when children are speaking in Spanish or another non-English language during activities.

  - Children are not speaking—This is a measure of the percentage of activity time when children are not speaking during activities.

- *Student–adult language match:* This is a measure of the match or mismatch between the language used by teachers and the primary or home language of children in the class.

- *Quality of instruction—general:* This is a measure of quality of literacy instruction and support for language and literacy development in the classroom.

- *Quality of instruction—DLL specific:* This measure focuses on the inclusion of DLL children in class activities, dual support for English and the home language of DLL children, integration of DLL children's native language in language and literacy activities, and availability of appropriate material and instructional methods for DLL children.

- *Child outcomes:* This is a measure of language development and emergent literacy skills. Measures were obtained from assessments using the Test of Preschool Emergent Literacy (TOPEL) (Lonigan, Wagner, & Torgesen, 2007), the Peabody Picture Vocabulary Test 3rd Edition, Revised (PPVT-III, R) (Dunn & Dunn, 1997), and the Print Knowledge subtest of the Pre-CTOPPP (Preschool Comprehensive Test of Phonological & Print Processing) (Lonigan, Wagner, Torgesen, & Rashotte, 2002), the prestandardization version of TOPEL (Test of Preschool Emergent Literacy) (Lonigan, Wagner, & Torgesen, 2007), the Expressive One-Word Picture Vocabulary Test–Third Edition

(EOWPVT) (Brownell, 2000), and the Woodcock Reading Mastery Test–Revised/Normative Update (WRMT-R/NU) (Woodcock, 1996).

Although the data used for this analysis were originally collected in an experimental design framework for evaluating an early literacy intervention, the investigations reported in the current report are from exploratory analyses and do not support causal inferences. Provided next is a brief summary of results. The remainder of the chapter describes the research questions, study design, data sources, measures, and results in more detail. A discussion and implications are provided at the end of the section.

Findings from the study included the following:

- There was more non-English L1 support in classrooms having a greater proportion of DLLs than in those with a smaller proportion, and teachers' use of non-English L1 was more prevalent in preschool classrooms than in kindergarten classrooms. Classrooms that were composed entirely of DLLs sharing a home language were much more likely to have at least one adult who spoke the children's language during instruction.

- The linguistic composition of the classroom is strongly related to the percentage of classroom activity time in which adults spoke in English versus Spanish or another language, and it is related to child outcomes at the end of the year; that is, classes with greater proportions of DLLs had lower scores on outcome assessments, even after controlling for pretest scores.

- Preschool DLLs whose teachers used the L1 in instruction performed worse on all four measures of early language and literacy (at the end of one year) than DLLs whose teacher did not use their L1.

- The measures of quality of instruction, both general and DLL-specific, did not have strong or consistent relationships to either classroom linguistic composition or student outcome measures.

RESEARCH QUESTIONS

As noted previously, the base study for this investigation was a study of the effectiveness of a literacy curriculum. Next, the study is briefly described, and then the research questions for this chapter are detailed.

Background of the CLIMBERs Study

Data for this study were drawn from the CLIMBERs study, a 5-year, large-scale study designed to test the effectiveness of BTL in preschool and kindergarten in the Chicago Public Schools system. BTL is a comprehensive curriculum designed to be implemented across all developmental centers throughout the day, with instruction organized around thematic units anchored in daily shared book read-alouds by the teacher. This shared book reading is the central activity and with related activities is aimed at developing children's oral language. The Breakthrough to Literacy (BTL) curriculum (Brown, 2004) carries its own set of books (from the Wright Group/ McGraw-Hill); includes interactive software (computers were provided as part of the experiment), one part of which consists of the weekly book read-aloud for the child; and recommends book-related small-group activities.

In the study, 44 schools were recruited and randomly assigned to either a treatment condition or a "business as usual" control condition. Overall, 67 preschool classrooms and 108 kindergarten classrooms participated. Teachers in the sample were all certified. The preschool program day was 2.5 hours long, with children typically eating one meal and one snack but not taking a nap during the program day. Kindergarten programs were roughly evenly divided between full-day (4 hours) and half-day (2.5 hours) programs. Classrooms in treatment and control groups in both preschool and kindergarten were observed at baseline in the first year and in the following two springs. Two waves of children in both grade levels were assessed at baseline and at the end of the school year.

The Chicago Public Schools policy does support bilingual education, but the developers did not advocate recruiting bilingual classrooms for the study, maintaining that although they provided some materials in Spanish, the curriculum was not designed to support bilingual language acquisition, just English, and the aim of the experiment was not to test the effectiveness of BTL in bilingual settings. Nevertheless, some bilingual classrooms did enroll in the study. Those classrooms are located in schools in which bilingual education is supported at all grade levels. In the vast majority of study schools, however, instruction was expected to take place in English from first grade on, and in nearly all study schools, kindergarten teachers were expected (by their school administrators) to be teaching in English. In addition to the few bilingual classrooms, many classrooms in the district include DLLs.

Data describing teachers, students, and classroom instructional practices were collected using the OMLIT, a battery of classroom observation measures originally developed as part of the Even Start Classroom Literacy Interventions and Outcomes Study. (The Even Start Classroom Literacy Intervention and Outcomes [CLIO] study was the third randomized study of Even Start [U.S. Department of Education, 2008]). Children were assessed at pretest and posttest (fall of their first year in the study and spring at the end of 1 year).

What are the capabilities of the instruments used in the CLIMBERs evaluation study, and could they also be used to help answer questions about patterns of language use in classrooms and outcomes associated with those patterns? Analyses can be generalized to only the populations from which the samples used in the study are drawn, and they address the following research questions:

1. What are the relationships between linguistic composition of early childhood classrooms and classroom language use (language used by children and adults, the match or mismatch between adult and child language use)?

2. What are the relationships between linguistic composition of early childhood classrooms and classroom instructional quality—both general quality and quality specifically related to appropriateness of instruction for DLLs?

3. After controlling for pretest differences, is there a relationship between any of the classroom variables and children's early literacy end-of-year outcomes? Specifically, is there a relationship between children's outcomes and the following:

   • Classroom linguistic composition: One might hypothesize at least that the mean outcomes on measures of English early language and literacy would be different in a classroom comprising only DLLs from the mean in a classroom comprising only native-English-speaking children (i.e., means in homogeneous DLL classrooms would be lower than those in homogeneous non-DLL classrooms), but are there other patterns associated with different configurations of composition?

   • Match or mismatch between adult and children language: Many people believe that it is important to have in the classroom at least one adult who speaks the L1 of children in the classroom to support children's academic and emotional development. Is there an association between language match and children's end-of-year outcomes?

   • Quality of instruction: It would seem that general quality of instruction (with a focus on language and literacy) would be related to children's language and literacy outcomes, but does this hold true for all groupings?

One aim of this study is to learn more about the relationships between different types of classroom practices (or quality of language and literacy instruction) and classroom linguistic composition. Do teachers' practices depend on linguistic composition of the classroom? What is the nature of that variation?

The hypothesis was that linguistic composition might make a difference in teachers' choice of instructional language. For example, if a class is composed primarily of children whose dominant language is Spanish and whose English proficiency is extremely limited, it would seem that the teacher might intentionally use more Spanish in instruction to increase comprehensibility of the content. This would be called "language match"—the teacher's instructional language matches the L1 of the students. What kind of outcomes would be associated with classrooms where this pattern is observed? How would outcomes vary depending on the composition of the classroom (e.g., all students share a non-English L1 as compared with a classroom composed of children with several different L1s, with no majority sharing an L1)?

Does general quality of language and literacy instruction vary by classroom linguistic composition? It is possible that teachers providing literacy instruction in both languages actually provided more language and literacy instruction overall, and this would increase the quality rating. Or it would also be possible for a teacher with DLLs to "dumb down" the instructional level, lowering the general language and literacy quality rating. Which of these patterns occurred, and was there any trend according to classroom linguistic composition?

Finally, the OMLIT's DLL-specific items were based on consensus in the field rather than on empirical research on instructional practices associated with language and literacy development of DLLs (because such a research literature base did not exist or at least did not exist in sufficient heft to support building items for an observational measure). It is thus interesting to explore whether the items are actually associated with any differences in practices in classrooms with quite different contexts and compositions.

Classroom Observation Instruments

Classroom observations were conducted using the OMLIT battery. In this chapter, four particular instruments within that battery are examined—the Classroom Description, the Snapshot of Classroom Activities (OMLIT-SNAP), the Read-Aloud Profile (OMLIT-RAP), and the Quality of Language and Literacy Instruction (OMLIT-QUILL). Examples of each instrument and reliability statistics are provided in Appendixes 6.1 and 6.2, respectively.

The Classroom Description is a record of certain aspects of the classroom context, including number and ages of children enrolled and present on the day of the observation, home languages of children enrolled, staff present on the day of observation, and languages used by staff for instruction on the day of observation.

The OMLIT-SNAP provides a measure of language use by children and adults in the classroom. It is a time-sampled description of classroom activities and groupings, integration of literacy in other activities, and language use in the classroom. A record, or snapshot, of what is happening in the classroom is recorded every 15 minutes throughout an observation. During each snapshot, the number of children and adults speaking English, another language, or not speaking is recorded. These numbers are converted to percentages of the total children and adults in the classroom for each category, and the percentages are averaged across all snapshots to provide a measure of the proportion of children and adults speaking English, another language, or not speaking during a typical snapshot of classroom activities.

The OMLIT-RAP is an event-sampled measure coded during shared book readings that records instructional practices used by teachers while reading aloud to children, including the language or languages used by the teacher.

The OMLIT-QUILL is a rating of the frequency and quality of literacy instruction and support for language and literacy development in the classroom. In these studies, the QUILL consisted of nine items rated on a five-point Likert scale (see Appendix 6.1.). (A 10th item, Opportunities for Print Motivation, was added after data collection for the preschool samples and was included in the kindergarten data.)

The first five QUILL items focus on key aspects of early language and literacy instruction:

- Opportunities to engage in writing

- Attention to and/or promotion of letter/word knowledge

- Opportunities and encouragement of oral language to communicate ideas and thoughts

- Attention to the functions and features of print

- Attention to the sounds in words throughout the day

Each item is rated in terms of quality/authenticity, variety of activities, integration into non–literacy-focused activities, group size for activities (e.g., individual, small group, large/whole group), and proportion of the class with which staff worked in activities; scores are then averaged across these features to arrive at a single score for each item. Further, for the analysis in this chapter, scores on these five items were averaged to arrive at a rating of overall language and literacy instruction across domains.

The remaining four QUILL items focus on practices with children who are DLLs. The content of these items is based on what is generally accepted in the field as best practices with children who are learning English, although there is not the same level of evidence to support their predictive significance for the development of children's English language skills. These items focus on *inclusion* of DLL children in class activities, *dual support* for English and for the home languages of DLL children, *integration* of DLL children's native language in language and literacy activities, and *availability* of appropriate materials and instructional methods with DLL children. They are also scored on a five-point Likert scale. As with the general quality items, for the analysis in this chapter, scores on these four items were averaged to arrive at a rating of overall support and appropriateness of instruction for DLLs. The items on this subscale were only administered in classrooms with at least one DLL enrolled and present.

Child Assessment Instruments

Assessments of children's early language and literacy skills were conducted at baseline both in preschool and kindergarten using the PPVT-III, R and the Print Knowledge subtest of the Pre-CTOPPP (Lonigan, Wagner, Torgesen, & Rashotte, 2002).

Preschool children's language development and emergent literacy skills were assessed at the end of the school year using the TOPEL, a standardized assessment of the aspects of language development and preliteracy skills that research has shown to predict later reading success. (Note that it is the skills that have been associated with children's later reading success, not the particular instrument [TOPEL], for which predictive validity has not been established independently of the instrument's authors' own publications.) At posttest, three subtests from the TOPEL were used: Definitional Vocabulary, Phonological Awareness, and Print Knowledge. They are described in greater detail subsequently in the Measures section.

Kindergarten children were assessed using the Expressive One-Word Picture Vocabulary Test–Third Edition (EOWPVT; Brownell, 2000) and Woodcock Reading Mastery Test–Revised/Normative Update (WRMT-R/NU; Woodcock, 1996). The EOWPVT is a standardized, norm-referenced measure of an individual's English speaking vocabulary. WRMT-R/NU measures several important aspects of reading ability, and three subtests were used from this battery: Letter Identification, Word Identification, and Word Attack. They are described in greater detail subsequently in the Measures section.

Measures

To answer the research questions, constructs were developed to measure the characteristics of interest—classroom linguistic composition, match between children's L1s and language of adults in the classroom (language match), language used by adults and children during instructional activities, and quality of instruction. Next are descriptions of how each of these measures was constructed.

Classroom Linguistic Composition   The Classroom Description instrument within the OMLIT collects information on the distribution of primary or home language of students in the classroom. From these data, and based on substantively interesting or useful definitions, five categories of the linguistic composition of classrooms were established based on students' L1: homogeneous dual-language learner (DLL), heterogeneous DLL, heterogeneous non-DLL, nearly homogeneous non-DLL, and homogeneous non-DLL.

Homogeneous DLL classrooms were defined as classrooms in which all students spoke the same non-English L1, the most common example being classrooms where all students primarily spoke Spanish. *Heterogeneous DLL classrooms* were defined as classrooms with a majority (50%–100%) of DLLs, but no single L1 shared among all students. To contrast with homogeneous DLL classrooms, a heterogeneous DLL classroom could have had 75% of students who spoke Spanish and 25% of students who spoke Urdu; although the classroom was entirely composed of DLLs, the language use in the classroom was not homogeneous. Most commonly, heterogeneous DLL classrooms had a majority of students who spoke Spanish, some students who spoke English, and possibly a few students who spoke another language. *Heterogeneous non-DLL classrooms* mark the shift in categories to where more than half (51%–90%) of the students spoke English as their L1. *Nearly homogeneous non-DLL classrooms* were defined as those where 90%–99% of students primarily spoke English, essentially identifying those classrooms with only one or two DLL students (sometimes referred to as "low-incidence ELL"). *Homogeneous non-DLL classrooms* were defined as classrooms with no DLLs.

Student–Adult Language Match   In addition to capturing the distribution of students' L1s, the OMLIT Classroom Description also records language used for instruction by teachers or other staff in the classroom. (The text that follows describes a classroom-level measure of language match between teachers and students, based on observation data. In the student achievement analysis, an individual student-level language match variable was used; the creation of that variable is described next.) For each of up to four adult staff in a classroom, observers recorded at the end of an observation session whether the adult spoke English, Spanish, or other languages for instruction and the approximate proportion of time spent speaking each language. Combined with the distribution of student L1, a continuous measure of language match was created first: the percentage of students in a classroom whose L1 was used, during at least some of the instructional time, by at least one teacher. From this continuous measure, four categories also were created: classrooms where teachers spoke the languages of all (100%) students, most (50%–99%) students, some (1%–49%) students, and no (0%) students.

In addition to these classroom-level measures, the following student-level language match indicators, measuring the language match between students and their teachers also were created:

- *English match indicator:* This indicator equals 1 if the student and at least one of the teachers in the classroom spoke English and 0 otherwise.

- *Non-English match indicator:* This indicator equals 1 if the student and at least one of the teachers in the classroom spoke the same non-English language.

- *Nonmatch indicator:* This indicator is set to 1 if the language of the student did not match to any of the teachers in the classroom. This indicator was omitted from the regressions.

Classroom Language Use   Using the OMLIT-SNAP, on which observers document languages spoken by children and adults during a minute-long period at 15-minute intervals across the 2.5-hour observation period, a percentage of the class activity time during which various languages were spoken by children and adults was computed, yielding the following variables:

- *Percentage of class activity time when English is spoken by children:* This variable indicates how much of activity time (not including management routines and gross motor play) children were observed to be speaking English.

- *Percentage of class activity time when Spanish or other [language] is spoken by children.* This variable indicates how much of activity time (not including management routines and gross motor play) children were observed to be speaking Spanish or another non-English language.

- *Percentage of class activity time when children are not speaking.* This variable indicates how much of activity time (not including management routines and gross motor play) children were observed to be not speaking at all.

In addition to these measures, data from the OMLIT-RAP—an instrument used to record interactions, including language use—was implemented during teacher-led shared book reading. Observers would have recorded data on the OMLIT-RAP whenever the teacher or paraprofessional read a book aloud with more than one child and would have recorded which language the teacher used during the reading and any book-related discussion or other book-related activities.

Instructional Practice and Quality   Using OMLIT measures of instructional practice and of instructional quality, three measures were constructed: a measure of time spent in various types of activities and two measures of quality of instruction. The first measure was created from OMLIT-SNAP variables that indicated the proportion of time spent by children in four categories of activity: Language and Literacy Activities, Developmental Activities, Circle Time; and Management Routines, Gross Motor Play, other. Language and Literacy Activities included reading (read-aloud, shared reading, child reading alone), letters, letter–sound correspondence, writing (emergent writing, tracing/copying), and computer language programs. Developmental Activities included math, science, dramatic play, creative play, sensory play, blocks, fine motor play, and playing rule-based games. Circle Time included instructional activities conducted in whole or large group, excluding gross motor play, structured physical development, and classroom management routines. Routines included management routines such as lining up and health and hygiene (handwashing, toileting); "other" was used to capture activities not listed in the protocol (such as graduation practice, holiday assembly, picture day, or a visit from a guest speaker). Gross Motor Play was included in this category in part because all of these activities involved limited linguistic interactions between adults and children other than for management purposes.

To construct the measure of instructional practice and quality, OMLIT-QUILL, which rates the frequency and quality of literacy instruction and support for children's language and literacy development, was used. Indicators are coded on a five-point scale (1 = *minimal*, 5 = *high*) at the end of an observation session for a classroom. Five indicators represent general quality measures: opportunities to engage in writing; attention to/promotion of letter/word knowledge, opportunities/encouragement of oral language to communicate ideas and thoughts, attention to the functions and features of print, and attention to sounds in words throughout the day. The mean values of these indicators are summed and averaged to form a composite mean of General Quality Indicators.

An additional four indicators represent measures of quality of instruction specifically for DLL students: DLL children intentionally included in activities and conversations (QUILL Item 7), development of both home language(s) and English supported for DLL children (QUILL Item 8), home language(s) of DLL children integrated into language and literacy activities (QUILL Item 9), and use of language and literacy materials/ methods appropriate for DLL children (QUILL Item 8). The means of these indicators were used individually and also summed and averaged to form a composite, the mean of DLL Quality Indicators.

Child Outcome Measures

For prekindergarten, TOPEL subtests were used at posttest. Standard scores are used in the analysis:

- *Definitional Vocabulary:* This is a test of vocabulary in which the child is asked to identify a pictured item (target word) and produce an entailment (i.e., answer questions such as, What is it for? What does it do? Where is it found?) in which associated verbs, adjectives, and nouns are elicited.

- *Phonological Awareness:* This test of phonemic sensitivity combines blending, specifically the ability to blend sounds (put sounds together— e.g., *hay* + *stack* is . . . *haystack*) and elision, specifically the ability to remove sounds from words (e.g., what word is left when you take *stack* away from *haystack*?). The test moves from word level, to syllable level, to subsyllable level and from receptive (multiple choice, identification) to productive (free response) skills.

- *Print Knowledge:* This subtest measures early print knowledge (print concepts, letter discrimination, word discrimination, letter–name identification and production, letter–sound identification and production).

- *Early Literacy Index:* Scores from the three subtests were combined to produce an index of early literacy.

For kindergarten children, WRMT-R/NU subtests were used at posttest. Again, standard scores were used in analysis:

- *Letter Identification:* This subtest measures the child's ability to identify uppercase and lowercase letters. The letter forms presented include roman, italic, bold type, serif and sans serif type styles, cursive characters, and special-type styles. The child is shown the letter and asked to provide the name of the letter.

- *Word Identification:* This subtest measures the child's ability to identify isolated words that appear in large type on the stimulus pages. To get credit, the child must produce a natural reading of the word within 5 seconds.

- *Word Attack:* This subtest requires the child to read either nonsense words or words with extremely low frequency. Nearly all phonemes in the English language are represented in at least one of their major spelling patterns in the items. The test measures the child's ability to apply phonic and structural analysis skills in order to pronounce words with which he or she may be unfamiliar.

In addition, the EOWPVT was used to measure kindergarten children's vocabulary at posttest; standard scores were used in analysis.

Samples

As discussed in subsequent detail, classroom-level data are used to address the first two research questions, whereas student-level data are employed for the third research question. Panel 1 of Exhibit 6.1 shows the data collection cycles and the total number of classrooms used for the first two research questions. In particular, dividing all classrooms observed by study and grade level yields two samples of classrooms: prekindergarten ($n = 130$) and kindergarten ($n = 211$) classrooms. The observations are not independent after combining across years; many of the classrooms in the first year of data collection for each sample remained in the study and were observed again during the second year. In both samples, some additional teachers joined the study in a second cohort in the second year. Some teachers in the study dropped out of the study after the first year and were only observed during the first year. Panel 2 of Exhibit 6.1, in turn, presents the number of classrooms and students employed for the third research question. Note that students in two kindergarten classroom in Spring 2007 could not be tested and had to be excluded from corresponding analyses.

Analytic Approach

A primary motivation for this study was to determine whether there were associations between the linguistic composition of classrooms, instructional practices, and student outcomes. To that end, the first task was to create a measure of linguistic composition within classrooms and then categorize the study classrooms using that measure. The categories are then used as the frame for each research question.

Linguistic Composition and Language Use

To address our first research question, patterns of classroom language use within each category are described. In particular, cross-tabulations of linguistic composition categories are presented with 1) classroom language use measures, 2) percentage of students speaking a non-English L1, 3) classroom-level measures of language match between teachers and students, and 4) measures of language used by teachers during shared book readings. These analyses were conducted separately for the prekindergarten and kindergarten samples.

Exhibit 6.1. Classroom linguistic composition, by sample (grade level)

Panel 1: Percentage and count of classrooms by group

Sample	Total classrooms	Homogeneous DLL		Heterogeneous DLL		Heterogeneous non-DLL		Nearly homogeneous non-DLL		Homogeneous non-DLL	
		%	n	%	n	%	n	%	n	%	n
Pre-K	130	16	21	39	51	11	14	4	5	30	39
Kindergarten	211	20	42	32	68	15	31	6	12	27	58

Panel 2: Mean percentage of students speaking a non-English primary language by group

Sample		Homogeneous DLL		Heterogeneous DLL		Heterogeneous non-DLL		Nearly homogeneous non-DLL		Homogeneous non-DLL	
		Mean %	SD	Mean %	SD	Mean %	SD	Mean %	SD	Mean %	SD
Pre-K		100	0	84	13	29	12	4	2	0	0
Kindergarten		100	0	79	15	33	11	6	1	0	0

Key: DLL, dual language learner; *SD*, standard deviation; *n*, number of subjects.
Note: Classrooms categorized as homogeneous DLL had all students speaking the same non-English primary/home language, heterogeneous DLL had 50% or more DLL students but no single primary language common to all students, heterogeneous non-DLL had 51%–90% non-DLL students, nearly homogeneous non-DLL had 91%–99% non-DLL students, and homogeneous non-DLL classrooms had all students speaking English as their primary language.

Linguistic Composition and Instructional Practice and Quality

The second research question inquires whether classroom instructional practices and quality are related to linguistic composition. To address this, box-and-whisker plots were created depicting minimum, lower quartile, median, mean, upper quartile, and maximum values of general and DLL-specific quality of instruction measures (individual measures and the composite) for each linguistic composition category. Correlations between quality of instruction measures (separately for general and DLL-specific measures) were also computed. Finally, the distribution of time spent on various classroom activities across the linguistic composition groups was examined.

Predicting Child Outcomes from Classroom Measures

To address the third research question—whether the classroom measures examined could predict child outcomes—regression analyses were conducted that utilized child test scores as outcomes and the classroom measures as independent variables (or predictors). In particular, separate regressions were estimated for each of the following predictors:

- Linguistic composition categories: Regressions included indicator variables for the first four categories (homogeneous DLL, heterogeneous DLL, heterogeneous non-DLL, and nearly homogeneous non-DLL), comparing the outcomes of students in these categories to those in the homogeneous non-DLL category.

- Student–adult language match: Regressions included two of the three student-level adult–student language match indicators (English match indicator and non-English match indicator), omitting the nonmatch indicator as the reference. Note that these measures are confounded with the composition categories. Hence, the regressions also included the four linguistic composition indicators listed previously to control for the association between linguistic composition and child outcomes when estimating the relationship between match indicators and child outcomes. (Also investigated, by including interactions of the two sets of measures, was whether the relationships between student–adults language match indicators and child outcomes differ across the linguistic composition categories. These models, however, did not yield sufficient precision and were excluded from this chapter.)

- A composite measure of the general quality of language and literacy instruction.

- Measures of the DLL-specific quality of language and literacy instruction: Regression models included the four QUILL indicators of DLL-specific quality of language and literacy instruction (DLL Items 7–10, described previously) as well as the composite measure.

The extent of the relationships between these predictors of interest and outcome measures were estimated using hierarchical models (Raudenbusch & Bryk, 2002) to account for the nested structure of the data. More specifically, two-level models were used where students (level 1) were nested within schools (level 2). (The process began with three-level models in which students [level 1] nested within classrooms [level 2] that were nested within schools [level 3]. In most cases, there was not enough variation in the outcomes to estimate separate classroom and school-level variances. Thus, a two-level model was used for all outcome measures.)

The regression analyses were conducted separately for the treatment and control groups in each respective sample to capture any potential effect of the treatment conditions on the relationship between the predictors and outcomes, and the control condition represents the "business as usual" better than the treatment conditions. To increase the precision of estimated relationships and to reduce the unexplained variation in the outcome measures, covariates were used to account for any factors that could confound the relationships between child outcomes and predictors of interest. These covariates included classroom-level baseline test scores (PPVT-III and Pre-CTOPPP: Print Knowledge), sampling stratifiers (locale [north and south] and schools' L1 of instruction [Spanish or English]), an indicator variable for Spring 2007 (latest posttest) observations and assessments, age, sex, and school-level percentage of minority students. Each outcome measure was standardized using the standard deviation of the control group of the corresponding sample so that coefficient estimates are represented in standard deviation units (SD, or effect sizes). More details on the regression models are presented in Appendix 6.2.

It is important to note that the estimated associations between the predictors and outcomes should not be interpreted as *causal* even though they were collected in two randomized control trial studies. In other words, the analyses described here are not experimental, because classrooms were not randomly assigned to different levels of the predictors. Hence, the presence of unobservable and/or uncontrolled for factors that affected the values of both predictors and outcomes could confound the estimated relationships between the predictors and outcomes. Nevertheless, these analyses describe such relationships and enable us to generate hypotheses that could later be tested more rigorously.

Results

In this section, results of the analyses described in the previous section are discussed. First, the distribution of prekindergarten and kindergarten classrooms across the five linguistic composition groups are presented. Then measures of classroom language use and quality ratings of instruction vary across these groups are depicted. Finally, results of the regressions assessing the relationships between these measures and child outcomes are presented.

Classroom Linguistic Composition

As shown in Exhibit 6.1, of the 130 classrooms in the prekindergarten sample, 16% were homogeneous DLL, 39% heterogeneous DLL, 11% heterogeneous non-DLL, 4% nearly homogeneous non-DLL, and 30% homogeneous non-DLL classrooms. In the prekindergarten sample, in homogeneous DLL classrooms, 100% of students, on average, spoke a non-English L1; in heterogeneous DLL, 84%; in heterogeneous non-DLL, 29%; in nearly homogeneous non-DLL, 4%; and in homogonous non-DLL, 0% of students spoke a non-English L1. Because the two samples are drawn from the same schools, it is not surprising that they nearly mirrored each other in the distribution of classrooms across linguistic composition categories. Although the distinction between heterogeneous non-DLL and nearly homogeneous non-DLL classrooms made for small numbers of classrooms in these categories across both samples, there was a substantive interest in whether there might be variations in classroom language use, instructional practice, or student achievement between classrooms with a substantial number of DLL students (heterogeneous non-DLL) and those with only one or two DLL students (nearly homogeneous non-DLL, or "low-incidence ELL"). Panel 2 of Exhibit 6.1 shows the average proportion of DLL students in a classroom for each category; the proportions decrease as expected moving along the linguistic composition continuum from homogeneous DLL to homogeneous non-DLL classrooms.

The vast majority of DLL students in the samples considered in this chapter spoke Spanish as their L1. Of all the homogeneous DLL classrooms, only one had students speaking a language other than Spanish: In the prekindergarten sample, one classroom had students who all spoke Chinese (Cantonese). Among the heterogeneous DLL classrooms, *all but* 12 (24%) in the pre-K sample and 18 (26%) in the kindergarten sample had a majority of DLL students who spoke Spanish as their L1.

Research Question 1: What Is the Relationship Between Classroom Linguistic Composition and Language Use?

As shown in Exhibit 6.2, the distribution of classrooms across the four categories of language use for each sample panned out as follows: In the prekindergarten sample, teachers spoke the L1s of all students in 75% of classrooms, of most students in 21% of classrooms, of some students in 3% of classrooms, and of none of the students in 1% of classrooms. (The four categories are classrooms where teachers spoke the languages of all [100%] students, most [50%–99%] students, some [1%–49%] students, and no [0%] students.) Comparing the distribution of the kindergarten sample to that of the prekindergarten, in the latter sample there was a smaller proportion of classrooms in which teachers used the language of all students and a larger proportion in which teachers used the language of only some students in instruction.

The language match categories with the classroom linguistic composition categories panned out as follows: In the prekindergarten sample, teachers spoke the L1s of all students in 95%, of most students in 0%, of some students in 0%, and of none of the students in 5% of homogeneous DLL classrooms (please see Exhibit 6.3). The observed difference between the pre-K and kindergarten samples is driven primarily by the difference in the language match distribution within heterogeneous DLL classrooms. Language match appears much greater in homogeneous classrooms, where nearly all classrooms have teachers who speak the L1 of all students. The few cases in homogeneous DLL classrooms in which there is no match in teacher and student language indicate classrooms in which teachers spoke only English. Average percentages of students in a classroom with their L1 spoken by a teacher (from the original continuous measure) were reported as follows: In the prekindergarten sample, on average,

Exhibit 6.2. Language match between teachers and students, by sample

Teacher(s) spoke the primary/home language(s) of ...	All students (100% of students)		Most students (50%–99% of students)		Some students (1%–49% of students)		No students (0% of students)	
	%	n						
Pre-K	75	98	21	27	3	4	1	1
Kindergarten	56	119	23	49	18	39	2	4

Key: n, number of subjects.

Exhibit 6.3. Language match between teachers and students, by sample and classroom linguistic composition

Panel 1: Distribution of classrooms on categorical measure of language match

Teacher(s) spoke the primary/home language(s) of …	Homogeneous DLL	Heterogeneous DLL	Heterogeneous non-DLL	Nearly homogeneous non-DLL	Homogeneous non-DLL
Pre-K n =	21	51	14	5	39
All students	95	59	43	60	100
Most students	0	33	57	40	0
Some students	0	8	0	0	0
No students	5	0	0	0	0
Kindergarten n =	42	68	31	12	58
All students	93	22	23	100	100
Most students	0	19	77	0	0
Some students	0	57	0	0	0
No students	7	1	0	0	0

Panel 2: Mean percentage of students with primary language spoken by teacher(s)

	Homogeneous DLL		Heterogeneous DLL		Heterogeneous non-DLL		Nearly homogeneous non-DLL		Homogeneous non-DLL	
	Mean %	SD	Mean %	SD	Mean %	SD	Mean %	SD	Mean %	SD
Pre-K	95	22	86	23	90	11	98	3	100	0
Kindergarten	93	26	50	37	75	18	95	1	100	0

Key: DLL, dual language learner; *SD*, standard deviation; *n*, number of subjects.
Note: Classrooms categorized as homogeneous DLL had all students speaking the same non-English primary/home language, heterogeneous DLL had 50% or more DLL students but no single primary language common to all students, heterogeneous non-DLL had 51%–90% non-DLL students' nearly homogeneous non-DLL had 91%–99% non-DLL students, and homogeneous non-DLL classrooms had all students speaking English as their primary language. Cells (sample by column) may not total to 100% due to rounding.

167

95% of students in homogeneous DLL, 86% of students in heterogeneous DLL, 90% of students in heterogeneous non-DLL, 98% of students in nearly homogeneous non-DLL, and 100% of students in homogeneous non-DLL classrooms had their L1 spoken by at least one teacher in the classroom. Kindergarten heterogeneous DLL classrooms remained the most outstanding group, with only half of the students on average having any teacher who spoke their L1.

The OMLIT-SNAP was used to examine, albeit superficially, the prevalence of spoken languages in classrooms. The language use by children and adults based on the OMLIT-SNAP measure, by the classroom linguistic composition categories, were reported as follows (see Exhibit 6.4): In homogeneous DLL classrooms in the prekindergarten sample, during an average snapshot of classroom activities, 35% of students were speaking English, 21% were speaking Spanish or another language, and 44% were not speaking. In homogeneous DLL classrooms in the prekindergarten sample, during an average snapshot of classroom activities, 51% of teachers were speaking English, 14% were speaking Spanish or another language, and 35% were not speaking.

Looking at language use by children, among prekindergarten classrooms, a shift in the distribution of language use (the proportion of children speaking English, Spanish or other, or not speaking) is seen between the homogeneous DLL and heterogeneous DLL classrooms, and then a smaller shift is seen from heterogeneous DLL to heterogeneous non-DLL classrooms. The distribution of children's language use appears relatively consistent between heterogeneous non-DLL and homogeneous non-DLL classrooms. In classrooms in which all children shared a non-English L1, a much greater proportion of the children were speaking that shared language (with each other and with adults in the classroom) than in classrooms in which children did not all share the same non-English L1. In classrooms in which a large proportion of children had a non-English L1 but didn't share an L1, the shift was to greater use of English (which becomes their shared language), with only a small increase in the proportion of children not speaking at all. As the proportion of the class whose L1 is English increases, there are fewer children not speaking at all, more speaking English, and fewer speaking a non-English language. The kindergarten sample shows only the first shift in language use, with a consistent pattern from heterogeneous DLL out to homogeneous non-DLL classrooms.

Similar overall trends are evident in the distributions of language use by teachers. Additionally noteworthy in examining teacher language use is the much lower proportion of teachers "not speaking" across all linguistic composition categories in kindergarten classrooms as opposed to prekindergarten classrooms.

Exhibit 6.4. Language use by children and adults, by sample and classroom linguistic composition

Panel 1: During an average snapshot of classroom activities, proportion of children speaking

	Homogeneous DLL		Heterogeneous DLL		Heterogeneous non-DLL		Nearly homogeneous non-DLL		Homogeneous non-DLL	
Pre-K $n =$	21		51		14		5		39	
	Mean %	SD	Mean %	SD	Mean %	SD	Mean %	SD	Mean %	SD
English	35	28	48	24	61	20	67	23	59	23
Spanish or other	21	22	6	9	1	2	0	0	1	4
Not speaking	44	25	46	22	38	20	33	23	40	22
Kindergarten $n =$	42		68		31		12		58	
English	24	31	66	23	74	20	66	19	66	23
Spanish or other	50	30	1	4	0	0	0	0	0	0
Not speaking	26	17	32	23	26	20	34	19	34	23

Panel 2: During an average snapshot of classroom activities, proportion of adults speaking

	Homogeneous DLL		Heterogeneous DLL		Heterogeneous non-DLL		Nearly homogeneous non-DLL		Homogeneous non-DLL	
Pre-K $n =$	21		51		14		5		39	
English	51	32	61	28	71	22	63	25	70	27
Spanish or other	14	21	5	10	2	5	0	0	0	0
Not speaking	35	32	33	28	27	22	37	25	30	27
Kindergarten $n =$	42		68		31		12		58	
English	42	32	83	16	88	17	85	13	85	15
Spanish or other	47	30	1	3	0	0	0	0	0	0
Not speaking	11	11	16	16	12	17	15	13	15	15

Key: DLL, dual language learner; SD, standard deviation; n, number of subjects.

Note: Classrooms categorized as homogeneous DLL had all students speaking the same non-English primary/home language, heterogeneous DLL had 50% or more DLL students but no single primary language common to all students, heterogeneous non-DLL had 51%–90% non-DLL students, nearly homogeneous non-DLL had 91%–99% non-DLL students, and homogeneous non-DLL classrooms had all students speaking English as their primary language. Classroom observers recorded languages being spoken by children and adults during a snapshot recorded every 15 minutes throughout an observation session. Counts were converted to proportions for each snapshot, and these proportions were averaged across the observation to provide one set of classroom-level proportions. Presented values are the mean of these classroom-level proportions within the sample and column category. Cells (sample by column) may not total to 100% due to rounding.

169

A final look at teacher language use is provided by the OMLIT-RAP. The proportion of teachers, within each linguistic composition category, speaking English or Spanish at any point during a shared book reading were reported as follows: In the prekindergarten sample, 100% of teachers in homogeneous DLL classrooms spoke English, and 38% spoke Spanish at any point during a shared book reading. (In the kindergarten sample in the heterogeneous DLL group, one teacher [1%] used another language [Gujarati] during book reading.) Note that the percentages total more than 100, indicating that in the homogeneous DLL classrooms, teachers often read books aloud in both English and Spanish. There is a shift in language use similar to the observations on adult language use from the OMLIT-SNAP, with a much greater proportion of English use and lower proportion of Spanish use between homogeneous DLL and heterogeneous DLL classrooms across the board. This makes sense, as the children with non-Spanish L1s would have been left out if the teacher read the book in Spanish and in English (as seems to be the case).

Once again, there appears to be a smaller secondary shift in language use between heterogeneous DLL and heterogeneous non-DLL prekindergarten classrooms, with no strong secondary shift in the kindergarten sample. In classrooms with a mix of languages, teachers tended to conduct shared book reading in English. It is interesting to note that in homogeneous DLL prekindergarten classrooms, where 100% of teachers used English and 38% used Spanish in read-alouds, this means that 38% of the teachers used both English and Spanish in shared book reading.

Research Question 2: What Is the Relationship Between Classroom Linguistic Composition and Instructional Practice and Quality?

Exhibit 6.5 reports on these summary measures of instructional practice and quality for each linguistic composition category in each sample. (The DLL-specific quality ratings were only conducted in classrooms with DLLs, so the fifth linguistic composition category, homogeneous non-DLL, is absent, leaving only four categories.) The most immediate observation is that, across all linguistic composition groups, the DLL-specific instructional quality ratings appear to be consistently higher than the general quality ratings, but the criteria for the DLL-specific and general quality ratings are distinct, so this is not a meaningful difference. Focusing on the DLL-specific instructional quality measure, classrooms with lower proportions of DLL students in the kindergarten sample had lower average ratings than those with higher proportions of DLL

Exhibit 6.5. Means and distributions of summary measures of the quality of instruction in language and literacy, by sample and classroom linguistic composition

	Pre-K				Kindergarten			
	Homogeneous DLL	Heterogeneous DLL	Heterogeneous non-DLL	Nearly Homogeneous non-DLL	Homogeneous DLL	Heterogeneous DLL	Heterogeneous non-DLL	Nearly Homogeneous non-DLL
$n =$	20	49	13	4	41	67	25	11
Mean of DLL Quality Indicators[a]								
$M =$	3.84	3.39	3.42	3.56	4.35	3.12	2.82	2.59
$SD =$	0.77	0.65	0.64	0.52	0.70	0.70	0.64	0.53

(continued)

Exhibit 6.5. (continued)

	DLL Homogeneous	DLL Heterogeneous	non-DLL Heterogeneous	Nearly Homogeneous non-DLL	Homogeneous non-DLL	DLL Homogeneous	DLL Heterogeneous	non-DLL Heterogeneous	Nearly Homogeneous non-DLL	Homogeneous non-DLL
$n =$	21	51	14	5	39	42	68	31	12	58
Mean of general quality indicators[b]										
$M =$	1.98	2.14	2.23	2.76	1.96	2.43	2.49	2.39	2.23	2.31
$SD =$	0.60	0.61	0.59	0.55	0.58	0.43	0.57	0.44	0.53	0.52

Key: DLL, dual language learner; *SD*, standard deviation; *M*, mean; *n*, number of subjects.

Note: Classrooms categorized as homogeneous DLL had all students speaking the same non-English primary/home language, heterogeneous DLL had 50% or more DLL students but no single primary language common to all students, heterogeneous non-DLL had 51%–90% non-DLL students, nearly homogeneous had non-DLL 91%–99% non-DLL students, and homogeneous non-DLL classrooms had all students speaking English as their primary language.

All plots use matching scales. The vertical axis is from 1 (*minimal*) to 5 (*high*). Means and standard deviations are presented in the same order; dots identify the mean on the plots.

[a]Mean of 4 indicator ratings on quality of language and literacy instruction for DLL students, including DLL children intentionally included in activities and conversations, development of both home language(s) and English supported for DLL children, home language(s) of DLL children integrated into language and literacy activities, and use of language and literacy materials/methods appropriate for DLL children. Homogeneous DLL classrooms, with no DLL students, were not rated on these indicators.

[b]Mean of 5 indicator ratings on general quality of language and literacy instruction, including opportunities to engage in writing, attention to/promotion of letter/word knowledge, opportunities/encouragement of oral language to communicate ideas and thoughts, attention to the functions and features of print, and attention to sounds in words throughout the day.

Individual indicators were each rated on a five-point scale: 1 = *minimal*, 5 = *high*. Summary measures (means of indicators) were first calculated for each classroom; the distributions, means, and standard deviations shown were calculated from the classroom-level means.

Exhibit 6.6. Correlations for summary measures of the quality of language and literacy instruction

Indicator	Mean of DLL quality indicators[a]	Mean of general quality indicators[b]
Mean of General Quality Indicators	0.12	1
Percentage of students with primary language spoken by teacher(s)	0.34	−0.19
Proportion of DLL students in class	0.35	0.01

Note: Correlations calculated from pooled sample (pre-K and kindergarten combined), from all observations with no missing values for any of the variables, $n = 231$.

[a]Mean of four indicator ratings on quality of language and literacy instruction for dual language learner (DLL) students, including DLL children intentionally included in activities and conversations, development of both home language(s) and English supported for DLL children, home language(s) of DLL children integrated into language and literacy activities, and use of language and literacy materials/methods appropriate for DLL children. Homogeneous DLL classrooms, with no DLL students, were not rated on these indicators.

[b]Mean of five indicator ratings on general quality of language and literacy instruction, including opportunities to engage in writing, attention to/promotion of letter/word knowledge, opportunities/ encouragement of oral language to communicate ideas and thoughts, attention to the functions and features of print, and attention to sounds in words throughout the day.

Individual indicators were each rated on a five-point scale: 1 = *minimal,* 5 = *high.*

students. The prekindergarten sample showed no such trend. Generally, one might expect it to be more difficult to provide support for children's L1 in more heterogeneous classrooms, so the prekindergarten ratings are more surprising, but the differences are not great. Looking at the general quality ratings, there was no systematic variation in average ratings across the linguistic composition groups—the quality of language and literacy instruction (excluding questions of appropriateness for DLLs) did not vary by linguistic composition of the classroom. These observations are generally consistent with the correlations presented in Exhibit 6.6.

Looking at the four individual indicators of quality of instruction in language and literacy for DLL students in Exhibit 6.7, one first observes that nearly all classrooms were rated highly on the inclusion of DLL children in activities and conversations, although there was less inclusion in the kindergarten classrooms with fewer DLLs. That is, in classrooms with fewer DLLs, less effort was made to include DLLs in activities with their native English-speaking peers, the very kind of integration that provides DLLs with opportunities to practice using English and reduces social isolation. Average ratings also tended to be higher on the development of both home language and English support for DLL students across all groups, in contrast with the remaining two indicators (integration of home languages of DLL children into language and literacy activities

Exhibit 6.7. Means and distributions of indicators of the quality of instruction in language and literacy for DLL students, by sample and classroom linguistic composition

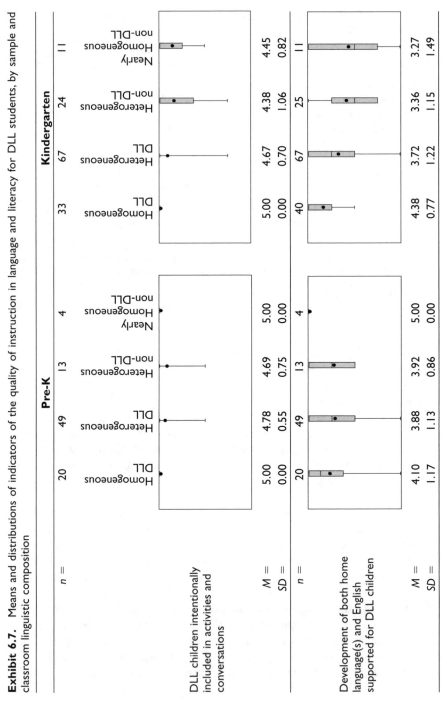

Home language(s) of DLL children integrated into language and literacy activities

n =	20	49	13	4		34	67	25	11
M =	3.30	2.59	2.77	2.50		4.38	1.82	1.48	1.00
SD =	1.26	1.06	1.09	1.00		1.07	0.98	0.51	0.00

Use of language and literacy materials and methods appropriate for DLL children

n =	20	49	13	4		36	67	24	11
M =	2.95	2.31	2.31	1.75		4.19	2.28	2.08	1.64
SD =	1.10	1.16	0.85	1.50		0.95	0.98	0.93	0.67

Key: DLL, dual language learner; *SD*, standard deviation; *M*, median; *n*, number of subjects.

Note: Classrooms categorized as homogeneous DLL had all students speaking the same non-English primary/home language, heterogeneous DLL had 50% or more DLL students but no single primary language common to all students, heterogeneous non-DLL had 51%–90% non-DLL students, nearly homogeneous non-DLL had 91%–99% non-DLL students, and homogeneous non-DLL classrooms had all students speaking English as their primary language.

All plots use matching scales. The vertical axis is from 1 (*minimal*) to 5 (*high*). Means and standard deviations are presented in the same order; dots identify the mean on the plots.

Individual indicators were rated on a five-point scale at the conclusion of a classroom observation session: 1 = *minimal*, 5 = *high*.

Homogeneous DLL classrooms, with no DLL students, were not rated on these indicators. Homogeneous DLL classrooms were automatically rated at 5 on the first item ("DLL children intentionally included in activities and conversations") unless there was clear isolation of children based on linguistic proficiency.

and the use of materials and methods appropriate for DLL students), which were generally rated low except in homogeneous DLL classrooms. This essentially means that teachers did not openly express a negative disposition toward having DLLs in their class, nor did they tend to overtly push children not to use their L1 (e.g., by saying things like, "English only in school!" or reprimanding children for using languages other than English), but they did not actively support maintenance or development of the children's L1 (e.g., by including activities and materials in non-English L1) or using appropriate methods (e.g., contextualizing new vocabulary).

As reflected in the summary measure discussed previously, the indicators in the kindergarten sample showed an apparent trend in the average ratings by linguistic composition categories, with generally much higher average ratings in homogeneous DLL classrooms than all other groups and lower average ratings as the proportion of DLL students declined. Again reflecting the overall measure, there were few between-group differences across the prekindergarten classrooms. Exhibit 6.8 shows the correlations between each of the four indicators. Perhaps due to a ceiling effect with nearly all classrooms rated at the highest value on the scale, the inclusion of DLL children in activities and conversations had the weakest association with the overall measure (mean of the four indicators).

As with the composite quality indicator, the individual indicators of general classroom quality in language and literacy instruction show no systematic variation, and little overall variation, across classroom linguistic composition groups or individual indicators (Exhibit 6.9). Within the two samples, it was observed that 75% of classrooms in every linguistic composition group fall at or below the midpoint of the rating scale on every indicator (with the exception of the first indicator in nearly homogeneous non-DLL classrooms). The distributions also indicate, however, that the concentration of ratings for kindergarten classrooms was generally between 2 and 3, whereas more prekindergarten classrooms were concentrated at ratings of 1 (the lowest possible rating). This feature of the distributions is also reflected in comparing the means across the two grade levels, where the mean ratings in the kindergarten sample are nearly always greater than the comparable mean rating in the prekindergarten sample for the same indicator and classroom linguistic composition group: Generally, the quality of language and literacy instruction in prekindergarten was rated lower than that of kindergarten.

Correlations between the general quality indicators are presented in Exhibit 6.10; again one notes essentially no association between the proportion of DLL students or the level of language match between teachers

Exhibit 6.8. Correlations for indicators of the quality of language and literacy instruction for DLL students

Indicator	Mean of DLL quality indicators	DLL children intentionally included in activities and conversations	Development of both home language(s) and English supported for DLL children	Home language(s) of DLL children integrated into language and literacy activities	Use of language and literacy materials and methods appropriate for DLL children
DLL children intentionally included in activities and conversations	.41	1			
Development of both home language(s) and English supported for DLL children	.75	.35	1		
Home language(s) of DLL children integrated into language and literacy activities	.84	.22	.49	1	
Use of language and literacy materials and methods appropriate for DLL children	.82	.12	.46	.70	1
Percentage of students with primary language spoken by teacher(s)	.35	.11	.15	.48	.28
Proportion of DLL students in class	.35	.24	.22	.41	.38

Key: DLL, dual language learner; n, number of subjects.
Note: Correlations calculated from pooled sample (pre-K and kindergarten combined), from all observations with no missing values for any of the variables, n = 221.
Individual indicators were each rated on a five-point scale: 1 = minimal, 5 = high.
Cronbach's alpha = 0.72 for the four quality of instruction for DLLs indicators; with "DLL children intentionally included" deleted, alpha = 0.77.

Exhibit 6.9. Means and distributions of general indicators of the quality of instruction in language and literacy, by sample and classroom linguistic composition

Pre-K

	Homogeneous DLL	Heterogeneous DLL	Heterogeneous non-DLL	Nearly Homogeneous non-DLL	Homogeneous non-DLL
n =	21	51	14	5	39
Opportunities to engage in writing					
M =	2.24	2.45	2.43	2.80	2.31
SD =	1.18	0.97	1.09	1.30	1.00
Attention to/promotion of letter and word knowledge					
M =	2.14	2.33	2.36	3.20	1.95
SD =	1.11	0.95	0.84	0.45	0.89

Kindergarten

	Homogeneous DLL	Heterogeneous DLL	Heterogeneous non-DLL	Nearly Homogeneous non-DLL	Homogeneous non-DLL
n =	42	68	31	12	58
Opportunities to engage in writing					
M =	2.93	2.68	2.77	2.58	2.48
SD =	0.78	0.84	0.92	0.79	0.84
Attention to/promotion of letter and word knowledge					
M =	2.45	2.57	2.45	2.50	2.34
SD =	0.94	0.85	0.85	0.67	0.69

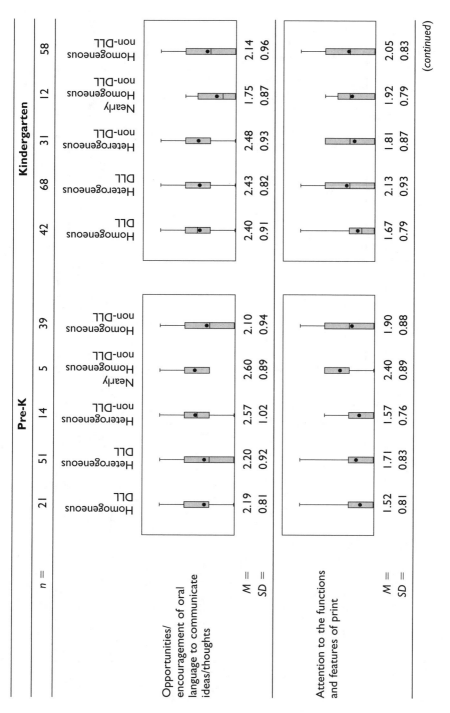

(continued)

Exhibit 6.9. (*continued*)

	Pre-K					Kindergarten				
	Homogeneous DLL	Heterogeneous DLL	Heterogeneous non-DLL	Nearly Homogeneous non-DLL	Homogeneous non-DLL	Homogeneous DLL	Heterogeneous DLL	Heterogeneous non-DLL	Nearly Homogeneous non-DLL	Homogeneous non-DLL
$n =$	21	51	14	5	39	42	68	31	12	58
Attention to sounds in words throughout the day										
$M =$	1.80	2.02	2.21	2.80	1.56	2.71	2.62	2.45	2.42	2.52
$SD =$	0.89	0.95	1.05	0.45	0.85	0.83	0.88	0.81	0.79	0.98

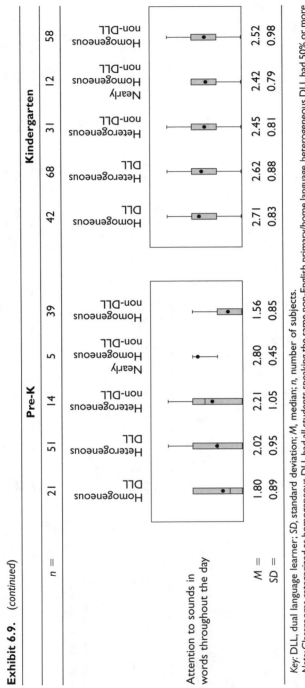

Key: DLL, dual language learner; *SD*, standard deviation; *M*, median; *n*, number of subjects.

Note: Classrooms categorized as homogeneous DLL had all students speaking the same non-English primary/home language, heterogeneous DLL had 50% or more DLL students but no single primary language common to all students, heterogeneous non-DLL had 51%–90% non-DLL students, nearly homogeneous non-DLL had 91%–99% non-DLL students, and homogeneous non-DLL classrooms had all students speaking English as their primary language.

All plots use matching scales. The vertical axis is from 1 (*minimal*) to 5 (*high*). Means are presented in the same order; dots identify the mean on the plots. Individual indicators were rated on a five-point scale at the conclusion of a classroom observation session: 1 = *minimal*, 5 = *high*. Presented values are the mean rating within the sample and column category.

Exhibit 6.10. Correlations for indicators of the general quality of language and literacy instruction

Indicator	Mean of general quality indicators	Opportunities to engage in writing	Attention to/promotion of letter and word knowledge	Opportunities/ encouragement of oral language to communicate ideas/thoughts	Attention to the functions and features of print	Attention to sounds in words througout the day	Percentage of students with primary language spoken by teacher(s)
Opportunities to engage in writing	.61	1					
Attention to/promotion of letter and word knowledge	.66	.24	1				
Opportunities/ encouragement of oral language to communicate ideas/thoughts	.59	.29	.15	1			
Attention to the functions and features of print	.59	.13	.30	.20	1		
Attention to sounds in words throughout the day	.68	.22	.38	.21	.26	1	
Percentage of students with primary language spoken by teacher(s)	-.18	-.09	-.12	-.11	-.05	-.19	1
Proportion of DLL students in class	.09	.11	.10	.08	-.09	.08	-.30

Key: DLL, dual language learner; *n*, number of subjects.

Note: Correlations calculated from pooled sample (pre-K and kindergarten combined), from all observations with no missing values for any of the variables, *n* = 340.

Individual indicators were each rated on a five-point scale: 1 = *minimal*, 5 = *high*.

Cronbach's alpha = 0.61 for the five general quality indicators; this is reduced if any variable is deleted.

and students in the classroom and the individual indicators of general quality of language and literacy instruction.

Another series of quality measures available come from the OMLIT-RAP. Three quality indicators are rated on a five-point scale (1 = *minimal*, 5 = *high*) for each shared book reading that occurs during the observation session; these values are averaged to obtain one overall rating for each observation. As with the general quality indicators from the QUILL, there was no systematic variation in quality ratings between the linguistic composition groups (Exhibit 6.11), and the ratings were generally low for all three indicators.

In addition to examining instructional quality, the study explored whether there were differences in the distribution of time spent on various classroom activities across the linguistic composition groups. Information on classroom activities is recorded on the OMLIT-SNAP, described previously. Exhibit 6.12 indicates the average proportions of time spent on language and literacy activities; developmental activities; circle time; and routines, gross motor play, or other (noninstructional) activities. There was noticeably little variation in the distribution of activities by linguistic composition group. There do appear to be substantial differences by grade level, however, with kindergarten classrooms showing much greater proportions of time on language and literacy activities than prekindergarten classrooms. This is in line with current expectations of more academically focused kindergarten.

Research Question 3: Predictors of Child Outcome Measures (Student Achievement): Do These Classroom Variables Predict Children's Early Literacy Outcomes?

Exhibits 6.13–6.16 and 6.17–6.20 present the estimated associations between predictors and each outcome measure and their *p*-values for the kindergarten and prekindergarten samples, respectively. These results are discussed in detail next. All assessments were conducted in English, but instructions were provided in Spanish for children whose L1 was Spanish and who were not able to understand the instructions in English.

Kindergarten   In the kindergarten sample, students (both treatment and control) in homogeneous DLL classrooms were performing significantly worse than their peers in homogeneous non-DLL classrooms (reference group) in Expressive Vocabulary and Letter Identification. As Exhibits 6.14 and 6.15 show, the range of the score differences between the two groups was between −0.34 and −0.99 of a standard deviation (*SD*). In addition, Letter Identification scores of the treatment students in heterogeneous DLL classrooms were also significantly lower (Exhibit 6.15; 0.25 *SD*) than

Exhibit 6.11. Means and distributions of ratings on indicators for the quality of shared book readings, by sample and classroom linguistic composition

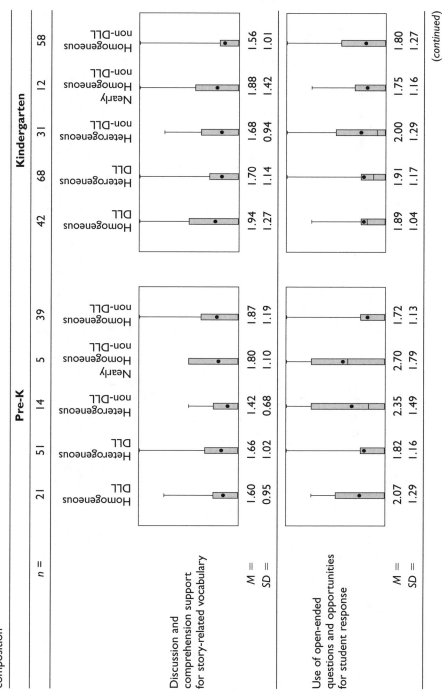

(continued)

Exhibit 6.11. (continued)

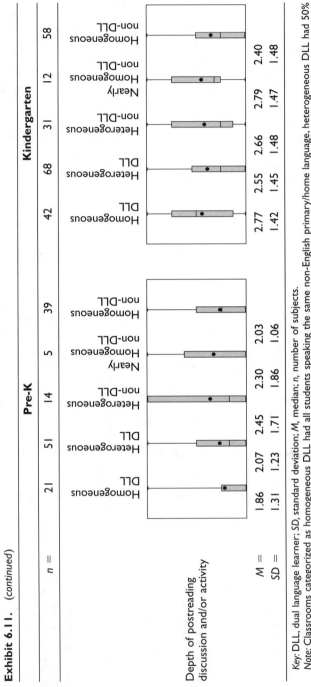

Key: DLL, dual language learner; SD, standard deviation; M, median; n, number of subjects.

Note: Classrooms categorized as homogeneous DLL had all students speaking the same non-English primary/home language, heterogeneous DLL had 50% or more DLL students but no single primary language common to all students, heterogeneous non-DLL had 51%–90% non-DLL students, nearly homogeneous non-DLL had 91%–99% non-DLL students, and homogeneous non-DLL classrooms had all students speaking English as their primary language. Means are presented in the same order; dots identify the mean on the plots. The vertical axis is from 1 (minimal) to 5 (high). All plots use matching scales.

Exhibit 6.12. Distribution of time spent on various classroom activities, by sample and classroom linguistic composition

Mean proportion of time on:	Homogeneous DLL		Heterogeneous DLL		Heterogeneous non-DLL		Nearly homogeneous non-DLL		Homogeneous non-DLL	
Pre-K n =	21		51		14		5		39	
	Mean %	SD	Mean %	SD	Mean %	SD	Mean %	SD	Mean %	SD
Language and literacy activities[a]	21	11	21	12	19	11	15	13	22	14
Developmental activities[b]	19	11	21	10	18	10	18	12	21	11
Circle time	13	11	8	8	10	11	18	15	8	9
Routines, gross motor play, other	48	14	50	12	53	15	50	16	50	14
Kindergarten n =	42		68		31		12		58	
Language and literacy activities[a]	40	13	39	14	45	18	39	14	40	14
Developmental activities[b]	17	14	14	10	15	12	15	12	11	14
Circle time	6	9	8	9	6	10	5	6	6	8
Routines, gross motor play, other	38	11	39	13	34	14	41	14	43	15

Key: DLL, dual language learner; SD, standard deviation; n, number of subjects.

Note: Classrooms categorized as homogeneous DLL had all students speaking the same non-English primary/home language, heterogeneous DLL had 50% or more DLL students but no single primary language common to all students, heterogeneous non-DLL had 51%–90% non-DLL students, nearly homogeneous non-DLL had 91%–99% non-DLL students, and homogeneous non-DLL classrooms had all students speaking English as their primary language.

[a]Language and literacy activities include reading (read-aloud, shared reading, child reading alone), letters, letter–sound correspondence, and writing (emergent writing, tracing/copying,) and computer language programs.

[b]Developmental activities include math and science activities, dramatic play, creative play, sensory play, blocks, fine motor play, and playing rule-based games.

Exhibit 6.13. CLIMBERs kindergarten relational analyses, Expressive Vocabulary

Variables	(1) Treatment	(2) CTRL	(3) Treatment	(4) CTRL	(5) Treatment	(6) CTRL	(7) Treatment	(8) CTRL	(9) Treatment	(10) CTRL
Homogenous DLL	-0.34* (.012)	-0.99** (<.001)	-0.15 (.313)	-0.52** (.009)						
Heterogeneous DLL	0.01 (.927)	-0.26 (.104)	0.20 (.080)	0.01 (.925)						
Heterogeneous non-DLL	0.02 (.875)	-0.08 (.589)	0.10 (.393)	0.05 (.750)						
Nearly homogenous non-DLL	-0.00 (.976)	-0.26 (.168)	0.02 (.836)	-0.28 (.131)						
Student–adult language match: English			0.25** (<.001)	0.48** (<.001)						
Student–adult language match: Non-English			-0.00 (.967)	-0.15 (.118)						
General quality of language and literacy instruction: Composite					0.12** (.002)	0.08 (.162)				
DLL-specific quality of language and literacy instruction: Composite							-0.02 (.693)	-0.25** (<.001)		

QUILL Item 7	0.06	-0.08
	(.232)	(.107)
QUILL Item 8	-0.01	0.01
	(.695)	(.857)
QUILL Item 9	-0.07*	-0.21**
	(.040)	(<.001)
QUILL Item 10	-0.02	-0.05
	(.549)	(.271)

Note: Classrooms categorized as homogeneous DLL (dual language learner) had all students speaking the same non-English primary/home language, heterogeneous DLL had 50% or more DLL students but no single primary language common to all students, heterogeneous non-DLL had 51%–90% non-DLL students, nearly homogeneous non-DLL 91%–99% non-DLL students, and homogeneous non-DLL classrooms had all students speaking English as their primary language. QUILL Item 7 focuses on *inclusion* of DLL children in class activities, while QUILL Item 8 measures the extent of *dual support* for English and for the home languages of DLL children. QUILL Item 9 reflects the *integration* of DLL children's native language in language and literacy activities, and QUILL Item 10 measures *availability* of appropriate materials and instructional methods with DLL children.

Each column corresponds to a separate regression, which is estimated in the treatment or the control group (as specified in the column header) using the predictors for which parameter estimates are provided; *p*-values are presented in parentheses (*p < .05, **p < .01).

Exhibit 6.14. CLIMBERs kindergarten relational analyses, Letter Identification

Variables	(1) Treatment	(2) CTRL	(3) Treatment	(4) CTRL	(5) Treatment	(6) CTRL	(7) Treatment	(8) CTRL	(9) Treatment	(10) CTRL
Homogenous DLL	−0.69* (<.001)	−0.87* (<.001)	−0.51* (.001)	−0.85* (<.001)						
Heterogeneous DLL	−0.25** (.042)	−0.14 (.345)	−0.16 (.238)	−0.13 (.410)						
Heterogeneous non-DLL	−0.20 (.147)	−0.10 (.500)	−0.17 (.227)	−0.10 (.529)						
Nearly homogenous non-DLL	0.01 (.923)	−0.21 (.241)	0.01 (.905)	−0.20 (.270)						
Student–adult language match: English			0.08 (.259)	0.03 (.669)						
Student–adult language match: Non-English			−0.13 (.084)	0.04 (.661)						
General quality of language and literacy instruction: Composite					0.02 (.568)	−0.01 (.859)				
DLL-specific quality of language and literacy instruction: Composite							−0.11* (.007)	0.03 (.618)		

188

QUILL Item 7	−0.01	−0.06
	(.882)	(.217)
QUILL Item 8	0.02	0.07
	(.500)	(.085)
QUILL Item 9	−0.08**	−0.05
	(.013)	(.225)
QUILL Item 10	−0.04	0.02
	(.386)	(.620)

Note: Classrooms categorized as homogeneous DLL (dual language learner) had all students speaking the same non-English primary/home language, heterogeneous DLL had 50% or more DLL students but no single primary language common to all students, heterogeneous non-DLL had 51%–90% non-DLL students, nearly homogeneous non-DLL had 91%–99% non-DLL students, and homogeneous non-DLL classrooms had all students speaking English as their primary language. QUILL Item 7 focuses on *inclusion* of DLL children in class activities, while QUILL Item 8 measures the extent of *dual support* for English and for the home languages of DLL children. QUILL Item 9 reflects the *integration* of DLL children's native language in language and literacy activities, and QUILL Item 10 measures *availability* of appropriate materials and instructional methods with DLL children.

Each column corresponds to a separate regression, which is estimated in the treatment or the control group (as specified in the column header) using the predictors for which parameter estimates are provided; *p*-values are presented in parentheses (**p* < .01, ***p* < .05).

Exhibit 6.15. CLIMBERs kindergarten relational analyses, Word Attack

Variables	(1) Treatment	(2) CTRL	(3) Treatment	(4) CTRL	(5) Treatment	(6) CTRL	(7) Treatment	(8) CTRL	(9) Treatment	(10) CTRL
Homogenous DLL	0.04 (.799)	0.10 (.664)	0.09 (.580)	0.13 (.581)						
Heterogeneous DLL	-0.03 (.830)	0.13 (.464)	-0.03 (.825)	0.16 (.369)						
Heterogeneous non-DLL	-0.24 (.107)	0.17 (.338)	-0.25 (.114)	0.18 (.331)						
Nearly homogenous non-DLL	0.11 (.373)	-0.35 (.107)	0.12 (.339)	-0.35 (.103)						
Student–adult language match: English			-0.06 (.441)	0.06 (.492)						
Student–adult language match: Non-English			-0.12 (.152)	0.02 (.839)						
General quality of language and literacy instruction: Composite					0.09* (.032)	-0.02 (.717)				
DLL-specific quality of language and literacy instruction: Composite							0.06 (.148)	-0.11 (.060)		

QUILL Item 7	0.05	−0.08
	(.425)	(.126)
QUILL Item 8	0.08*	−0.13**
	(.018)	(.004)
QUILL Item 9	0.06	−0.03
	(.064)	(.475)
QUILL Item 10	−0.07	0.16**
	(.113)	(.004)

Note: Classrooms categorized as homogeneous DLL (dual language learner) had all students speaking the same non-English primary/home language, heterogeneous DLL had 50% or more DLL students but no single primary language common to all students, heterogeneous non-DLL had 51%–90% non-DLL students, nearly homogeneous non-DLL had 91%–99% non-DLL students, and homogeneous non-DLL classrooms had all students speaking English as their primary language. QUILL Item 7 focuses on *inclusion* of DLL children in class activities, while QUILL Item 8 measures the extent of *dual support* for English and for the home languages of DLL children. QUILL Item 9 reflects the *integration* of DLL children's native language in language and literacy activities, and QUILL Item 10 measures *availability* of appropriate materials and instructional methods with DLL children.

Each column corresponds to a separate regression, which is estimated in the treatment or the control group (as specified in the column header) using the predictors for which parameter estimates are provided; *p*-values are presented in parentheses (*p < .05, **p < .01).

Exhibit 6.16. CLIMBERs kindergarten relational analyses, Word Identification

Variables	(1) Treatment	(2) CTRL	(3) Treatment	(4) CTRL	(5) Treatment	(6) CTRL	(7) Treatment	(8) CTRL	(9) Treatment	(10) CTRL
Homogenous DLL	-0.19 (.183)	-0.14 (.497)	-0.21 (.212)	-0.16 (.445)						
Heterogeneous DLL	0.03 (.818)	0.04 (.805)	-0.06 (.685)	0.02 (.927)						
Heterogeneous non-DLL	-0.16 (.289)	0.17 (.290)	-0.21 (.168)	0.16 (.349)						
Nearly homogenous non-DLL	0.11 (.385)	-0.29 (.128)	0.09 (.495)	-0.29 (.138)						
Student–adult language match: English			-0.13 (.066)	-0.06 (.467)						
Student–adult language match: Non-English			-0.16* (.050)	-0.05 (.635)						
General quality of language and literacy instruction: Composite					0.06 (.168)	-0.06 (.343)				
DLL-specific quality of language and literacy instruction: Composite							-0.06 (.119)	-0.03 (.550)		

192

QUILL Item 7	−0.06	−0.06
	(.320)	(.178)
QUILL Item 8	0.01	0.02
	(.655)	(.564)
QUILL Item 9	0.03	−0.05
	(.331)	(.248)
QUILL Item 10	−0.08	0.06
	(.058)	(.210)

Note: Classrooms categorized as homogeneous DLL (dual language learner) had all students speaking the same non-English primary/home language, heterogeneous DLL had 50% or more DLL students but no single primary language common to all students, heterogeneous non-DLL had 51%–90% non-DLL students, nearly homogeneous non-DLL had 91%–99% non-DLL students, and homogeneous non-DLL classrooms had all students speaking English as their primary language. QUILL Item 7 focuses on *inclusion* of DLL children in class activities, while QUILL Item 8 measures the extent of *dual support* for English and for the home languages of DLL children. QUILL Item 9 reflects the *integration* of DLL children's native language in language and literacy activities, and QUILL Item 10 measures *availability* of appropriate materials and instructional methods with DLL children.

Each column corresponds to a separate regression, which is estimated in the treatment or the control group (as specified in the column header) using the predictors for which parameter estimates are provided; *p*-values are presented in parentheses (*$p < .05$).

Exhibit 6.17. CLIMBERs preschool relational analyses, Definitional Vocabulary

Variables	(1) Treatment	(2) CTRL	(3) Treatment	(4) CTRL	(5) Treatment	(6) CTRL	(7) Treatment	(8) CTRL	(9) Treatment	(10) CTRL
Homogenous DLL	−0.41*	−0.09	−0.34*	0.29						
	(.018)	(.653)	(.039)	(.174)						
Heterogeneous DLL	−0.40*	0.04	−0.44**	0.32						
	(.020)	(.823)	(.008)	(.074)						
Heterogeneous non-DLL	−0.15	−0.10	−0.07	0.08						
	(.410)	(.614)	(.680)	(.690)						
Nearly homogenous non-DLL	−0.09	−0.49	−0.19	−0.47						
	(.647)	(.094)	(.301)	(.099)						
Student–adult language match: English			0.18	0.31**						
			(.279)	(.01)						
Student–adult language match: Non-English			−0.55**	−0.42**						
			(.001)	(.001)						
General quality of language and literacy instruction: Composite					−0.03	0.01				
					(.668)	(.811)				

194

DLL-specific quality of language and literacy instruction: Composite

			−0.13 (.067)	−0.18* (.044)
QUILL Item 7	−0.16 (.111)	−0.06 (.531)		
QUILL Item 8	0.05 (.271)	0.02 (.777)		
QUILL Item 9	−0.06 (.303)	−0.16** (.007)		
QUILL Item 10	−0.09 (.176)	0.04 (.582)		

Note: Classrooms categorized as homogeneous DLL (dual language learner) had all students speaking the same non-English primary/home language, heterogeneous DLL had 50% or more DLL students but no single primary language common to all students, heterogeneous non-DLL had 51%–90% non-DLL students, nearly homogeneous non-DLL had 91%–99% non-DLL students, and homogeneous non-DLL classrooms had all students speaking English as their primary language. QUILL Item 7 focuses on *inclusion* of DLL children in class activities, while QUILL Item 8 measures the extent of *dual support* for English and for the home languages of DLL children. QUILL Item 9 reflects the *integration* of DLL children's native language in language and literacy activities, and QUILL Item 10 measures *availability* of appropriate materials and instructional methods with DLL children.

Each column corresponds to a separate regression, which is estimated in the treatment or the control group (as specified in the column header) using the predictors for which parameter estimates are provided; *p*-values are presented in parentheses (*$p < .05$, **$p < .01$).

195

Exhibit 6.18. CLIMBERs preschool relational analyses, Phonemic Awareness

Variables	(1) Treatment	(2) CTRL	(3) Treatment	(4) CTRL	(5) Treatment	(6) CTRL	(7) Treatment	(8) CTRL	(9) Treatment	(10) CTRL
Homogenous DLL	−0.15 (.373)	0.14 (.616)	−0.07 (.661)	0.43 (.082)						
Heterogeneous DLL	−0.22 (.175)	0.04 (.883)	−0.18 (.253)	0.27 (.204)						
Heterogeneous non-DLL	−0.00 (.997)	0.03 (.904)	0.03 (.870)	0.21 (.373)						
Nearly homogenous non-DLL	0.13 (.507)	0.04 (.889)	0.04 (.844)	0.03 (.931)						
Student–adult language match: English			0.22 (.192)	0.15 (.217)						
Student–adult language match: Non–English			−0.39* (.023)	−0.45** (.001)						
General quality of language and literacy instruction: Composite					−0.01 (.857)	0.05 (.457)				

DLL-specific quality of language and literacy instruction: Composite

	−0.14**	−0.19*
	(.010)	(.036)
QUILL Item 7	−0.02	−0.05
	(.852)	(.578)
QUILL Item 8	−0.06	0.01
	(.218)	(.832)
QUILL Item 9	−0.04	−0.04
	(.507)	(.508)
QUILL Item 10	−0.01	−0.12*
	(.905)	(.046)

Note: Classrooms categorized as homogeneous DLL (dual language learner) had all students speaking the same non-English primary/home language, heterogeneous DLL had 50% or more DLL students but no single primary language common to all students, heterogeneous non-DLL had 51%–90% non-DLL students, nearly homogeneous non-DLL had 91%–99% non-DLL students, and homogeneous non-DLL classrooms had all students speaking English as their primary language. QUILL Item 7 focuses on *inclusion* of DLL children in class activities, while QUILL Item 8 measures the extent of *dual support* for English and for the home languages of DLL children. QUILL Item 9 reflects the *integration* of DLL children's native language in language and literacy activities, and QUILL Item 10 measures *availability* of appropriate materials and instructional methods with DLL children.

Each column corresponds to a separate regression, which is estimated in the treatment or the control group (as specified in the column header) using the predictors for which parameter estimates are provided; *p*-values are presented in parentheses (*p < .05, **p < .01).

197

Exhibit 6.19. CLIMBERs preschool relational analyses, Print Knowledge

Variables	(1) Treatment	(2) CTRL	(3) Treatment	(4) CTRL	(5) Treatment	(6) CTRL	(7) Treatment	(8) CTRL	(9) Treatment	(10) CTRL
Homogenous DLL	-0.12	-0.04	-0.09	0.17						
	(.493)	(.816)	(.597)	(.423)						
Heterogeneous DLL	-0.06	-0.09	-0.06	0.07						
	(.717)	(.569)	(.723)	(.722)						
Heterogeneous non-DLL	-0.12	-0.08	-0.07	0.04						
	(.502)	(.681)	(.704)	(.853)						
Nearly homogenous non-DLL	0.15	-0.33	0.11	-0.34						
	(.417)	(.242)	(.567)	(.231)						
Student–adult language match: English			-0.13	0.02						
			(.422)	(.871)						
Student–adult language match: Non-English			-0.52**	-0.34**						
			(.002)	(.006)						
General quality of language and literacy instruction: Composite					-0.02	0.03				
					(.749)	(.592)				

198

DLL-specific quality language and literacy instruction: Composite	−0.05 (.315)	−0.03 (.723)		
QUILL Item 7			0.03 (.724)	0.03 (.713)
QUILL Item 8			−0.01 (.839)	0.03 (.555)
QUILL Item 9			−0.01 (.829)	−0.07 (.161)
QUILL Item 10			−0.03 (.652)	0.02 (.665)

Note: Classrooms categorized as homogeneous DLL (dual language learner) had all students speaking the same non-English primary/home language, heterogeneous DLL had 50% or more DLL students but no single primary language common to all students, heterogeneous non-DLL had 51%–90% non-DLL students, nearly homogeneous non-DLL had 91%–99% non-DLL students, and homogeneous non-DLL classrooms had all students speaking English as their primary language. QUILL Item 7 focuses on *inclusion* of DLL children in class activities, while QUILL Item 8 measures the extent of *dual support* for English and for the home languages of DLL children. QUILL Item 9 reflects the *integration* of DLL children's native language in language and literacy activities, and QUILL Item 10 measures *availability* of appropriate materials and instructional methods with DLL children.

Each column corresponds to a separate regression, which is estimated in the treatment or the control group (as specified in the column header) using the predictors for which parameter estimates are provided; p-values are presented in parentheses (**$p < .01$).

Exhibit 6.20. CLIMBERs preschool relational analyses, Early Literacy Index

Variables	(1) Treatment	(2) CTRL	(3) Treatment	(4) CTRL	(5) Treatment	(6) CTRL	(7) Treatment	(8) CTRL	(9) Treatment	(10) CTRL
Homogenous DLL	−0.25 (.150)	−0.02 (.933)	−0.20 (.224)	0.34 (.141)						
Heterogeneous DLL	−0.30 (.081)	−0.03 (.898)	−0.31 (.060)	0.26 (.201)						
Heterogeneous non-DLL	−0.05 (.760)	−0.04 (.860)	−0.01 (.967)	0.14 (.503)						
Nearly homogenous non-DLL	0.08 (.677)	−0.16 (.596)	−0.02 (.899)	−0.19 (.514)						
Student–adult language match: English			0.09 (.592)	0.22 (.062)						
Student–adult language match: Non-English			−0.62** (<.001)	−0.48** (<.001)						
General quality of language and literacy instruction: Composite					−0.05 (.396)	0.03 (.607)				

200

DLL-specific quality of language and literacy instruction: Composite

	−0.17**	−0.16
	(.001)	(.069)
QUILL Item 7	−0.03	0.01
	(.747)	(.920)
QUILL Item 8	−0.04	0.01
	(.426)	(.815)
QUILL Item 9	−0.05	−0.09
	(.387)	(.097)
QUILL Item 10	−0.04	−0.04
	(.493)	(.484)

Note: Classrooms categorized as homogeneous DLL (dual language learner) had all students speaking the same non-English primary/home language, heterogeneous DLL had 50% or more DLL students but no single primary language common to all students, heterogeneous non-DLL had 51%–90% non-DLL students, nearly homogeneous non-DLL 91%–99% non-DLL students, and homogeneous non-DLL classrooms had all students speaking English as their primary language. QUILL Item 7 focuses on *inclusion* of DLL children in class activities, while QUILL Item 8 measures the extent of *dual support* for English and for the home languages of DLL children. QUILL Item 9 reflects the *integration* of DLL children's native language in language and literacy activities, and QUILL Item 10 measures *availability* of appropriate materials and instructional methods with DLL children.

Each column corresponds to a separate regression, which is estimated in the treatment or the control group (as specified in the column header) using the predictors for which parameter estimates are provided; *p*-values are presented in parentheses (**p < .01).

those of the reference group. On the other hand, there were no statistically significant differences between the four DLL categories and the reference group in Word Attack and Word Identification (Exhibits 6.15 and 6.16).

As seen in the third and fourth columns of Exhibits 6.13–6.16, inclusion of student–teacher language match indicators as additional predictors did not change the coefficient estimates on the language composition categories. The largest change occurred in the Expressive Vocabulary analyses (Exhibit 6.13), in which the coefficient estimate on the homogenous DLL indicator decreased (in absolute value) both in the treatment and control group (and became not significant in the treatment group), whereas the indicator capturing the student–adult language match in English emerged as a statistically significant predictor. More specifically, as seen in Exhibit 6.13, Expressive Vocabulary scores of the English-speaking students with at least one English-speaking teacher ("English match") were significantly *higher* than those whose language did not match with their teachers' (reference group): 0.25 and 0.48 of a *SD* for treatment and control students, respectively. It is important to note that we did not observe this pattern with the other outcome measures. Because the reference group consists of DLLs being taught by adults using English ("no language match"), it is not surprising that their native English-speaking peers outperformed them on measures of English language and literacy. As for the students who spoke the same non-English language with their teachers ("non-English match"), their scores were significantly different (0.27 of a *SD* lower) than their "no language match" peers only in the treatment group in Word Identification, showing that at least in the short term (at the end of 1 year), we do not see better early literacy outcomes for children simply because their teachers provide instruction in the L1.

The two composite measures of instructional quality were significantly related to the test scores in only 4 instances (out of the 16 that were tested). For example, one unit change in the composite measure of the general quality of language and literacy instruction measure (five-point scale) was *positively* associated with test scores in Expressive Vocabulary (Exhibit 6.13: 0.12 *SD*) and Word Attack (Exhibit 6.15: 0.09 *SD*) in treatment classrooms, whereas the composite measure of the DLL-specific language and literacy instruction was *negatively* associated with Expressive Vocabulary (control: −0.25 *SD*) and Letter ID scores (treatment: 0.11 *SD*).

As for the individual QUILL items measuring DLL-specific instructional quality, the relationship between Item 8 (teacher's positive disposition toward maintenance and development of L1) and Word Attack scores was positive (Exhibit 15: 0.08 *SD*) in treatment classrooms and negative (Exhibit 6.15: −0.13 *SD*) in control classrooms. Moreover, Item 9 (integration of L1 into language and literacy activities) was *negatively* associated with Expressive Vocabulary (Exhibit 6.13: -0.07 and -0.21 *SD* in the treatment and control group, respectively), and Letter Identification (Exhibit 6.14: -0.08 *SD* in treatment) scores, and Item 10 (appropriateness of methods for supporting DLLs' language and literacy acquisition) was *positively* related to Word Attack scores (Exhibit 6.15: 0.16 *SD*) of the control students. Based on these patterns (a mix of positive and negative relationships, all of very small magnitude), it is safe to conclude that neither composite nor individual measures of DLL-specific instruction quality were strong predictors of student test scores.

Prekindergarten   The differences between the test scores across the linguistic composition categories were less pronounced in the prekindergarten sample than in the kindergarten sample. There were only two statistically significant results: Definitional Vocabulary scores of the treatment students in homogeneous and heterogeneous DLL classrooms were significantly lower (Exhibit 6.17: -0.41 and -0.40 *SD*, respectively) than those in homogeneous non-DLL classrooms. In other words, DLLs as a group consistently scored lower than their non-DLL peers on measures of expressive vocabulary in the treatment group, and these differences persisted after 1 year. (See Exhibit 6.13 for kindergarten results.) These differences were not consistent across DLL groups, however. DLLs in heterogeneous groupings scored higher on these English outcome measures than their peers in homogeneous DLL settings. This is not surprising, as it was noted that teachers were more likely to use English and less likely to use children's L1 in heterogeneous DLL settings.

As with the kindergarten sample, addition of the student–adult language match indicators to the literacy composition indicators as predictors did not change the estimated coefficients on the latter at all. The non-English match indicator, however, came up as a strong and consistent predictor of all four test scores. In particular, as seen in Exhibits 6.17–6.20, both treatment and control DLLs with a matching non-English-speaking teacher ("non-English match") scored significantly *lower* than the reference group (DLL students whose language did not match with their teachers) in all tests at the $p < .01$ level (range: -0.62 and -0.34 of *SD*). A possible explanation for this is that teachers using students' non-English L1s for instruction provide less English input for DLLs. Another is that teachers who are using students' L1s in class do so to make input comprehensible for students with weaker second language (L2; English) skills, who would be expected to perform worse than their peers with better L2 (English) skills in tests that assess students' language and literacy skills in English. As for the "English match" students, their scores tended to be better than the reference group, but the test score difference was statistically significant only in Definitional Vocabulary in the control group (0.31 *SD*, Exhibit 6.17). (Because the "English match" students outperformed the reference students in all but one test, they outperformed the "non-English match" students as well.)

The composite measure of the general quality of language and literacy instruction was not statistically significantly related to any of the outcomes. The DLL-specific instruction quality composite, however, was significantly and negatively associated with three outcome measures: Definitional Vocabulary (control: -0.18 *SD*), Phonemic Awareness (treatment: -0.14 *SD*; control: -0.19 *SD*), and the Early Literacy Index (treatment: -0.17 *SD*). These negative associations were more likely to be driven by the negative associations between Item 9 and Definitional Vocabulary scores (Exhibit 6.17: -0.16 *SD*) and Item 10 and Phonemic Awareness scores (Exhibit 6.18: -0.12 *SD*). With no clear pattern and so many tests, no real finding can be extracted from these points other than that the QUILL items are not reliable strong predictors of children's outcomes.

DISCUSSION

When interpreting the results from these relational analyses, it is important to keep the "multiple comparisons" or "multiple-hypothesis testing" issue in mind (Schochet, 2008). Multiple-hypothesis testing is a problem because as the number of tests conducted increase, the probability of making a Type I error (i.e., finding a significant result when in fact there is none) increases. More specifically, when 20 hypothesis tests are performed in a setting where there are no true relationships between an outcome and a predictor at the usual $p < .05$ significance level, we expect to have one false significant relationship (i.e., one relationship by chance). For the relational analyses addressing the third research question, we conducted 256 hypotheses tests, which implies that finding 13 significant results can be explained by chance alone (we found 39 statistically significant results at the $p < .05$ level). Therefore, in this section, we focus on findings that were significant for more than one sample and one measure.

The descriptive analysis highlighted the fact that, in contrast with kindergarten classrooms, a larger proportion of preschool classrooms had teachers who spoke the language of all of the students and a smaller proportion of classrooms with teachers who spoke the language of only some of the students. It is not clear what the reason for this might be—school policy encouraging bilingual education for preschool but not kindergarten, assignment of bilingual teachers to classrooms with greater proportions of bilingual children, tendency to assign bilingual children to homogeneous-DLL classrooms—but clearly it would be more difficult to staff a more heterogeneous classroom to maximize the language match.

In terms of the language actually used in the classroom, children's language use was strongly associated with the linguistic composition. For example, the homogeneous-DLL classrooms had the lowest proportion of children speaking English during classroom activities (and the highest proportion of children speaking non-English languages), but the shift toward greater proportions of the class using English occurs as soon as we move to more than one L1 spoken by children. This pattern held across grade levels, across the samples, and was more or less mirrored by the teachers' language: Teachers used less English in homogeneous-DLL classrooms, both preschool and kindergarten.

One possible reason for this was that there were kindergartens that were designated as bilingual as part of the district's bilingual education policy, whereas the preschools were all part of the state preschool program that was not within the regular school bilingual policy. In kindergarten classrooms with different linguistic composition, far fewer (virtually no) teachers used non-English languages in classroom activities, and in the two preschool samples, use of non-English language dropped dramatically with the presence of more than one non-English L1 in the class. Use of more than one language in some language and literacy activities (e.g., shared book reading) was more common in preschool classrooms but was observed to some extent in kindergarten classrooms as well. As with all other activities, beyond the heterogeneous-DLL level, there was very little use of non-English languages.

Overall, the linguistic composition of the classroom seems to be strongly associated with the language use in the classrooms across all of these direct observation measures. However, the match or lack of match does not predict children's outcomes in the way that the literature would have predicted. Specifically, students whose non-English L1 matched with that of an adult tended to score significantly lower than their peers whose language did not match with adults in the classroom, at least not in the short term. However, it is likely that the timing of outcome measurement is one reason for this. It would not be expected that DLLs become proficient in English in such a short time, with such limited exposure. If anything, it should be expected that benefits appear later, when they have the language and literacy skills in their L1 that can be transferred to English, as well as when they have had more exposure to rich language and literacy experiences in English.

Looking at differences by linguistic composition group does highlight that the greater linguistic homogeneity (i.e., with respect to DLL L1), the greater the likelihood that the teacher is using DLLs' L1 in instruction, and the stronger the association with lower scores on assessments of English language and literacy, although no causal relationship is implied. We found this relationship at both grade levels.

Not surprisingly, DLLs fared worse than their non-DLL peers on their Definitional Vocabulary outcome, and the situation was most pronounced in the treatment group and with higher concentrations of DLLs (homogeneous DLL and heterogeneous DLL).

There is not a strong relationship between the QUILL measures and children's outcomes—nearly all impacts were small, and there was no consistent trend in either sign or association with treatment/control in any outcome. Moreover, neither composite nor individual measures of DLL-specific instructional quality were strong predictors of test scores in any of the groupings studied.

IMPLICATIONS

One key learning from this investigation is that the measures do help describe what is going on but do not necessarily yield insight into *why*. For that kind of understanding, one would need a more fine-grained observation looking at just the elements of interest, a better defined DLL-specific measure, and possibly a more qualitative description of the classroom context and interactions.

The findings about DLLs in homogeneous or near-homogeneous (DLL) settings are potentially interesting. In the field of bilingual education, it is known that language acquisition takes 5–7 years. The children in these studies have been learning at least one language for 4 or 5 years and have begun learning an additional language. They will go through a period of consolidating their knowledge, so their performance on standardized tests of language and literacy in the additional language at preschool or kindergarten does not necessarily predict their later proficiency or achievement. Perhaps with data on teachers' instructional use of children's L1s across intervening years, longitudinal achievement studies could help patterns of language development and achievement emerge.

The findings on teachers' instructional behaviors are interesting in two ways. First, the fact that teachers' general language and literacy practices were relatively unrelated to the classroom composition is an interesting topic for investigation. Does this reflect the teachers' intentions, or does it simply indicate that with limited time and resources, there are limits to what kinds of things teachers are able to do within their mandate to foster healthy development in the children in their care? The fact that neither the general nor the DLL-specific variables (nor their composites) showed meaningful associations is also curious: Is it just that the measure is not finely tuned enough to detect differences? Would pulling apart the components of each item help to tease out differences (or would it just increase the number of hypothesis tests, thus increasing the probability of findings just due to chance)? Or are these questions that the OMLIT is not suited to answer? One certain conclusion is that a more robust research basis for the DLL-specific items is needed to strengthen them for future investigations.

STUDY QUESTIONS

1. What are two assumptions about DLLs and their language use that underlie the research questions in this chapter?

2. What were the research questions posed by the authors?

3. Briefly summarize the findings of the intervention study discussed in this chapter.

REFERENCES

August, D., & Hakuta, K. (1997). *Improving schooling for language-minority children: A research agenda.* Washington, DC: National Academy Press.

Brown, C. (2004). *Breakthrough to Literacy.* Des Moines, IA: Wright Group/McGraw Hill.

Brownell, R. (Ed.). (2000). *Expressive One-Word Picture Vocabulary Test–Third Edition.* Novato, CA: Academic Therapy Publications.

California State Department of Education. (1985). *Case studies in bilingual education: First year report.* Sacramento: Author.

Cummins, J. (1979). Linguistic interdependence and the educational development of bilingual children. *Review of Educational Research, 49*(2), 222–251.

Cummins, J., Harley, B., Swain, M., & Allen, P.A. (1990). Social and individual factors in the development of bilingual proficiency. In J. Cummins, B. Harley, M. Swain, & P.A. Allen (Eds.), *The development of second language proficiency* (pp. 119–133). Cambridge, United Kingdom: Cambridge University Press.

Dunn, L.M., & Dunn, L.M. (1997). *Peabody Picture Vocabulary Test, 3rd Edition, Revised (PPVT-III, R).* Circle Pines, MN: American Guidance Service.

Fillmore, L.W. (1991). When learning a second language means losing the first. *Early Childhood Research Quarterly, 6,* 323–346.

Fillmore, L.W. (2000). Loss of family languages: Should educators be concerned? *Theory into Practice, 39*(4), 203–210.

Geva, E., & Ryan, E.B. (1993). Linguistic and cognitive correlates of academic skills in first and second languages. *Language Learning, 43,* 5–42.

Goodson, B.D., Layzer, C., Smith, W.C., & Rimdzius, T. (2004). *Observation Measures of Language and Literacy Instruction (OMLIT).* Washington, DC: U.S. Department of Education, Institute of Education Sciences.

Greene, J.P. (1997). A meta-analysis of the Rossell and Baker review of bilingual education research. *Bilingual Research Journal, 21*(2/3), 1–22.

Hakuta, K., & Diaz, R.M. (1985). The relationship between degree of bilingualism and cognitive ability: A critical discussion and some new longitudinal data. In K.E. Nelson (Ed.), *Children's language* (Vol. V). Hillsdale, NJ: Lawrence Erlbaum Associates.

Kemp, J. (1984). *Native language knowledge as a predictor of success in learning a foreign language with special reference to a disadvantaged population.* Unpublished master's thesis, Tel-Aviv University.

Lanauze, M., & Snow, C.E. (1989). The relation between first- and second-language skills: Evidence from Puerto Rican elementary school children in bilingual programs. *Linguistics and Education, 1,* 323–340.

Lonigan, C., Wagner, R. Torgesen, J., & Rashotte, C. (2002). *Preschool Comprehensive Test of Phonological & Print Processing (Pre-CTOPPP).* Unpublished assessment.

Lonigan, C., Wagner, R., & Torgesen, J. (2007). *Test of Preschool Early Literacy (TOPEL).* Austin, TX: Pro-Ed.

McLaughlin, B. (1986). Multilingual education: Theory east and west. In B. Spolsky (Ed.), *Language and education in multilingual settings.* Clevedon, United Kingdom: Multilingual Matters.

Medina, M.J., & Escamilla, K. (1992). Evaluation of transitional and maintenance bilingual programs. *Urban Education, 27,* 263–290.

National Association for the Education of Young Children. (1996). NAEYC position statement: Responding to linguistic and cultural diversity—Recommendations for effective early childhood education. *Young Children, 51,* 4–12.

Ramirez, C.M. (1985). *Bilingual education and language interdependence: Cummins and beyond.* Unpublished doctoral dissertation, Yeshiva University, New York.

Raudenbusch, S.W., & Bryk, A.S. (2002). *Hierarchical linear models.* Thousand Oaks, CA: Sage.

Ricciardelli, L.A. (1992). Bilingualism and cognitive development in relation to threshold theory. *Journal of Psycholinguistic Research, 21,* 301–316.

Schochet, P.Z. (2008). *Technical methods report: Guidelines for multiple testing in impact evaluations* (NCEE 2008-4018). Washington, DC: National Center for Education Evaluation and Regional Assistance, Institute of Education Sciences, U.S. Department of Education.

Snow, C.E., Burns, M.S., & Griffin, P. (Eds.). (1998). *Preventing reading difficulties in young children.* Washington, DC: National Academies Press.

Tabors, P.O. (2008). *One child, two languages: A guide for preschool educators of children learning English as a second language* (2nd ed.). Baltimore: Paul H. Brookes Publishing Co.

U.S. Department of Education, Institute of Education Sciences (2008). *A Study of Classroom Literacy Interventions and Outcomes in Even Start (CLIO).* Washington, DC: Author.

Willig, A. (1985). A meta-analysis of selected studies on the effectiveness of bilingual education. *Review of Educational Research, 55*(3), 269–317.

Woodcock, R.W. (1996). *Woodcock Reading Mastery Test–Revised/Normative Update (WRMT-R/NU).* Circle Pines, MN: American Guidance Services.

Yeung, A.E., Marsh, H.W., & Suliman, R. (2000). Can two tongues live in harmony? Analysis of the National Education Longitudinal Study of 1988 (NELS88) longitudinal data on the maintenance of home language. *American Educational Research Journal, 37*(4), 1001–1002.

Appendix 6.1

**Observation Measures of
Language and Literacy Instruction (OMLIT)**

Early Childhood Education Classroom Description

OMLIT

Part 1: Identifying Information

	Name	ID#	Date of Observation ___/___/___ mm dd yyyy
Observer:			Time Observation Began _____ : _____ : am pm
Project/Classroom:			Time Observation Ended _____ : _____ : am pm

Part 2: Staff List (teachers/assistants/regular staff)

Staff Name	Staff Role	Staff ID#
(1) _____	(1) _____	(1) _____
(2) _____	(2) _____	(2) _____
(3) _____	(3) _____	(3) _____
(4) _____	(4) _____	(4) _____

From Goodson, Layzer, Smith, & Rimdzius (2004). *Observation Measures of Language and Literacy Instruction (OMLIT)*. Developed under contract ED-01-CO-0120, as administered by the Institute of Education Sciences, U.S. Department of Education, with Westat as prime contractor.

In *Dual Language Learners in the Early Childhood Classroom*, edited by Carollee Howes and Robert C. Pianta (2011, Baltimore: Paul H. Brookes Publishing Co.)

Part 3: Classroom Context

Number of Children Enrolled (by age group)

_____ Infants & toddlers (under 3 yrs)

_____ Preschool (3–5 yrs) [_____ / _____ Even Start]
                              (#)   (%)

_____ School Age (6+ yrs)

_____ Total

Primary Home Language of the Children (% should add to 100)

_____ % English only

_____ % Spanish only/bilingual Spanish/English

_____ % Other language (1) only/bilingual other
         language-English
         Specify language (1): _____

_____ % Other language (2) only/bilingual other
         language-English
         Specify language (2): _____

Any Children with Diagnosed Special Needs?

☐ Yes   ☐ No   ☐ Don't know

Classroom Theme: Any theme, topic, unit (for day, for week, for month) that class is focusing on?

☐ No theme

Describe theme _____

From Goodson, Layzer, Smith, & Rimdzius (2004). *Observation Measures of Language and Literacy Instruction (OMLIT)*. Developed under contract ED-01-CO-0120, as administered by the Institute of Education Sciences, U.S. Department of Education, with Westat as prime contractor.

In *Dual Language Learners in the Early Childhood Classroom*, edited by Carollee Howes and Robert C. Pianta (2011, Baltimore: Paul H. Brookes Publishing Co.)

Part 4: Post-Observation Summary

Language of Instruction of Staff: Select one response for each staff member present during observation

Staff (1) ID#___	Staff (2) ID#___	Staff (3) ID#___	Staff (4) ID#___	
☐	☐	☐	☐	English only
☐	☐	☐	☐	Spanish Only
☐	☐	☐	☐	Primary English, some Spanish
☐	☐	☐	☐	Primary Spanish, some English
☐	☐	☐	☐	English and Spanish equally
☐	☐	☐	☐	Primarily English, another language (specify:____)
☐	☐	☐	☐	Primarily another language, some English (specify:____)
☐	☐	☐	☐	English and another language (specify:____)
☐	☐	☐	☐	English and multiple other languages (specify:____)
☐	☐	☐	☐	Other combination of languages (specify:____)
☐	☐	☐	☐	NA—not in classroom on day of observation

Language of Other Adults in Classroom: Select one response for the other adults that were present

N/A:	Other adults in classroom speak additional language(s)
☐ No other adults in classroom	☐ Adults speak language(s) of *all* ELL groups in classroom
☐ No ELL children in the class	☐ Adults speak language(s) of *some* but not all ELL groups in classroom
☐ Other adults in classroom speak only English	☐ Adults speak language(s) of *none* of ELL groups in classroom

Other adults include adults who are not regular staff but who work with the children, such as parent volunteers and other center staff such as director. Do NOT include special visiting musicians, health care professionals, etc.

From Goodson, Layzer, Smith, & Rimdzius (2004). *Observation Measures of Language and Literacy Instruction (OMLIT)*. Developed under contract ED-01-CO-0120, as administered by the Institute of Education Sciences, U.S. Department of Education, with Westat as prime contractor.

In *Dual Language Learners in the Early Childhood Classroom*, edited by Carollee Howes and Robert C. Pianta (2011, Baltimore: Paul H. Brookes Publishing Co.)

Indication that Observation Day Was Not Typical:

Describe any special events or unusual circumstances that indicate that the day was not typical _____

No RAPs:

☐ No RAPs coded because no read alouds occurred

---

1. Reading/text/vocabulary (with print)

Looking at books or pictures, adult reading aloud, children reading together without adult, emergent reading (pretending to read), shared reading activities. Listening to stories on audiotape or CD. Teaching children new vocabulary words **with print support** for vocabulary (e.g., printed word).

1a. Alphabet/numerals

Recognizing letter/numeral forms, letter/sound correspondence. **Always involves print.**

1b. Sounds/singing

Sounds of words with no print. All singing (may or may not have print, e.g., words of song displayed).

1c. Oral language/vocabulary

Discussions, new concepts and vocabulary with either **no print or no print emphasis.**

2. Emergent writing/copying/tracing

Child(ren) writing, includes pretend writing, scribbling, invented spelling. Child dictation to teacher. Tracing letter or number templates. Practice in correctly writing numerals/ distinguishing numerals. **Always involves print.**

3. Science/nature

Formal and informal communication of science or nature. Science examples: astronomy, working with pets, collecting leaves, feeding pets, magnets, health & safety.

4. Math concepts/attributes/colors

Formal and informal communication of math concepts, attributes, or colors. Shapes, counting, measuring, patterns, amount. Identifying and matching non-geometric shapes (animals, familiar objects). Identifying and matching colors and color names.

5. Dramatic play

Pretend or make-believe play; dress-up, playing with dolls; assigning roles; zooming cars and trucks.

Note: Includes acting out stories/playing with puppets, figures of people/animals, and stuffed animals in pretend environments.

From Goodson, Layzer, Smith, & Rimdzius (2004). *Observation Measures of Language and Literacy Instruction (OMLIT)*. Developed under contract ED-01-CO-0120, as administered by the Institute of Education Sciences, U.S. Department of Education, with Westat as prime contractor.

In *Dual Language Learners in the Early Childhood Classroom*, edited by Carollee Howes and Robert C. Pianta (2011, Baltimore: Paul H. Brookes Publishing Co.)

6. Creative play

Arts and crafts – creating visual art (painting, drawing, sculpting clay & play dough, cutting and pasting). **Note:** Always code Play-Doh as "*Creative play.*"

Music – instruments, formal and informal movement/dance activities.

7. Block play

All building with blocks and other large building materials.

Note: Once construction is done, and blocks are part of a completed pretend environment with cars, trucks, figures of people, code as "*Dramatic play.*"

8. Fine motor play

Manipulation of materials, such as puzzles, stringing beads, sewing cards, woodworking, LEGOs, Lincoln Logs, interconnecting building pieces.

9. Sensory play

Manipulating sand, water, and textured materials such as beans, rice, shaving cream, where objective is learning about qualities of materials and not constructing a particular object.

10. Meeting time

Routines or daily rituals as part of group or circle time. Includes activities such as calendar, day of the week, weather, the day's activities, etc. Also includes discussions, such as sharing by children with questions from teacher, peers.

11. Games with rules

Playing board games, card games, and video games (e.g., Nintendo, Game Boy, Play Station) that are **not** explicitly educational.

12. TV/video/computer

Watching commercial television programs, video tapes/DVDs or computer programs may or may not be educational.

Note: If activity involves computer, circle "Computer" in description box.

13. Gross motor play

Large muscle play–active outdoor play and indoor physical activity (tunnels, gymnastics). Include outdoor walks here (e.g., walking to and from a destination such as the library).

Note: Code organized dance/movement activity as "*Creative play.*"

14. Other activity

Special activities that are not part of the regular activities on list, such as special events/destinations, field trips, student assessments (e.g., school assembly, library, fire station, ice cream store).

Note: The activity should be specified in the description box.

15. Meals/Routines/Transitions/Conversation/Management/No activity

Meals/snacks: Engaged in the act of eating a meal/snack, and/or meal/snack preparation and clean up.

Routines/transitions: Arriving/departing, napping/sleeping, physical care/hygiene (including first aid, toileting), setting-up or cleaning-up of activities/materials, lining-up.

Conversation/management: Any talking or interaction between adult and child, between children, or between adults outside of a listed activity. Conversation may be positive or negative. Examples: adult managing a child's behavior; comforting a child, or chatting. Children may be interacting in nonproductive ways.

Uninvolved/administration: Not involved in any activity listed above and not interacting with another person. Child roaming aimlessly around classroom, having a tantrum, otherwise unengaged. Teacher/other adult doing administrative work, monitoring overall classroom activity from a distance.

Not in class

List children and staff who have left classroom and, if known, where they have gone. Do **NOT** include these children or staff in counts at top of form.

From Goodson, Layzer, Smith, & Rimdzius (2004). *Observation Measures of Language and Literacy Instruction (OMLIT).* Developed under contract ED-01-CO-0120, as administered by the Institute of Education Sciences, U.S. Department of Education, with Westat as prime contractor.

In *Dual Language Learners in the Early Childhood Classroom,* edited by Carollee Howes and Robert C. Pianta (2011, Baltimore: Paul H. Brookes Publishing Co.)

Snapshot of Classroom Activities

Number	Children Present in Classroom
	Infants & toddlers (under 3 yrs old)
	Preschool (3–5 yrs old)
	School Age (5+ yrs old)
	Total Children (all ages)
☐	**Whole Group Activity (1–14)**

Number	Staff Present in Classroom
	Teacher
	Assistant teacher/Aide
Number	**Other Adults Present in Classroom**
	Parent dropping off/picking up/visiting
	Volunteer (parent or other)
	Other adult (visitor, other center staff)
	Total Adults (staff and other adults)

Snapshot # 1

Time: ____:____ am pm

No Snapshot Coded:
- ☐ RAP
- ☐ Gross motor group activity
- ☐ Other reason

Talk	E	S	O	None
Ad/C	☐	☐	☐	☐
C/C	☐			☐

Left Activity Table

	# of Children and Adults in Activity				L	Literary Resources/Activities Describe
Activity	Children	Teachers	Aides	Other Adults		
1 Reading/texts/alphabet/vocabulary (w/print)					L	
1a Alphabet/numerals					L	
1b Sounds/singing						
1c Oral language/vocabulary (no print)					L	
2 Emergent writing/copying/tracing						
3 Science/nature						
4 Math concepts/Attributes/colors						
5 Dramatic play						
6 Creative play						

Right Activity Table

	# of Children and Adults in Activity				L	Literary Resources/Activities Describe
Activity	Children	Teachers	Aides	Other Adults		
7 Block play						
8 Fine motor play						
9 Sensory play					L	
10 Meeting time					L	
11 Games with rules						
12 TV/video/computer						
13 Gross motor play					L	
14 Other activity						
15 Meals/routines/management						
Not in class						

Notes:

From Goodson, Layzer, Smith, & Rimdzius (2004). *Observation Measures of Language and Literacy Instruction (OMLIT)*. Developed under contract ED-01-CO-0120, as administered by the Institute of Education Sciences, U.S. Department of Education, with Westat as prime contractor.

In *Dual Language Learners in the Early Childhood Classroom*, edited by Carollee Howes and Robert C. Pianta (2011, Baltimore: Paul H. Brookes Publishing Co.)

A. PRE-Reading

1. **Guides book choice; discusses children's book choice(s):** Adult encourages children to choose the book; talks about their choice with them. Helps them make appropriate choice.

2. **Points to features of the book such as the title, illustrator, author:** Points to title, author, illustrator, or illustration on front of book (or points to chapter title in a chapter book)

2a. **Discusses concepts of print such as the title, illustrator, author:** Defines, describe meaning of concepts of print such as title, author, illustrator, or illustration.

3. **Reminds children of similar books they have read or that they have read same book before:** Calls attention to books children have read by the same author, same illustrator, same topic, etc. OR reminds children they've already read same book before. Ex: "What was another book that we read about ducks?" or "... by Eric Carle?"

4. **Comments on sounds, letters, and/or sound-letter links to listen, look for in the story/book:** Talks about sounds they will hear in the story, especially sounds they may have been learning about in class. Or talks about letters they will see in the story, especially letters they have been learning about. Ex: "During the story, when you hear the 'buh' sound, raise your hand." Or "This story has a lot of words that begin with the letter 'g.' Let me know when you see one."

5. **Introduces story-related vocabulary:** Highlights or explains new vocabulary. Ex: "This book is about a fish called a 'sunfish.' Sunfish have fins. Fins are what they use to move around in the water. When we read the book, you will see pictures of sunfish and we can pick out their fins."

6. **Relates the story/book to other activities in class, class theme:** Calls attention to book's relation to class activities or theme. Ex: "This duck likes to eat fish. What does our pet turtle like to eat?" Or, "Remember last week when we went to the fire station? This story is about firemen like the ones we met."

7. **Talks about events and/or features for listen, look for in the story/book:** Helps children anticipate things that will happen in the book. Ex: "At the end we'll talk about all the different things that the caterpillar likes to eat. What do we think his favorite food is?"

8. **Introduces background information related to the story/book (with or without child input):** Describes what the book is about. Ex: "This book is about a birthday party that Little Bear has with all his forest friends." May or may not invite child discussion.

9. **Narrates/tells the story in advance of reading:** Recites all or major parts of book (e.g., nursery rhyme in book based on rhyme) before actually reading story.

10. **Relates the story/book to children's own experiences outside of classroom activities:** Links book to children's experiences outside of class. For example: "Have you ever fed the ducks in the park before? What sound did they make?" or "What kinds of things do you like to do on a rainy day?"

11. **No pre-reading experiences or activities (without any codes 1–10):** The adult may alert children to the reading activity but does not provide any of the above listed experiences or activities.

B. Reading

1. **Tracks print:** Adult moves her finger along the page below the line of print or points sequentially to words in text as she reads.

2. **Uses props/dramatic voices/gestures:** Uses props (e.g., hand puppets, stuffed animals, items in the story), gestures, or different voices to tell story.

3. **Directs children's attention to illustrations/text/story. (i.e., asks questions about; discusses/expands on meaning; offers new information):** Points to, or in some way calls children's attention to the book's illustrations, details of the illustrations. Engages children in (brief) discussion about the meaning of text or illustrations and/or offers new information about the story that may not be written in the text or depicted in illustration (e.g., explaining about something unfamiliar in the text or pictures).

4. **Comments on sounds, letters, and/or sound-letter links in the story/book:** Calls children's attention to sounds, letters, or sounds and their corresponding letters in the story text.

5. **Highlights new story-related vocabulary:** Calls attention to, defines, and/or gives examples to help children understand unfamiliar words in story.

6. **Relates the story/book to other activities in class, class theme:** Places the story in context by mentioning the class theme and/or how the book fits into the class activities.

7. **Expands on children's comments about the story/book:** When child makes a comment, adult extends by asking child for elaboration or restating child's comment.

From Goodson, Layzer, Smith, & Rimdzius (2004). *Observation Measures of Language and Literacy Instruction (OMLIT)*. Developed under contract ED-01-CO-0120, as administered by the Institute of Education Sciences, U.S. Department of Education, with Westat as prime contractor.

In *Dual Language Learners in the Early Childhood Classroom*, edited by Carollee Howes and Robert C. Pianta (2011, Baltimore: Paul H. Brookes Publishing Co.)

8. **Answers children's questions about the story/book or related topics:** Allows children to ask questions about the story and then responds to those questions.

9. **Has children join in reading/completing text on their own or as a group (choral reading):** Pauses and/or indicates to children in some way that they should recite words/numbers, phrases, or longer chunks of the text aloud with her.

10. **Asks recall questions about earlier parts of the story/book:** Asks children to recall events, characters, attributes from earlier in the story.

11. **Relates the story/book to children's experiences/Asks the story/book-related questions about children's experiences outside of classroom activities:** Extends children's understanding by tapping into their own experiences to help them comprehend the story.

12. **Asks the story/book-related open-ended questions (requires prediction, expanded response, thinking, and/or analysis):** Probes children's comprehension by asking questions about the story that require children to predict (e.g., "What do you think will happen next? What if . . ."), elaborate responses; engage in more thought or analysis of the story.

13. **Picture walk:** "Walks through" the book without reading text; turns pages and describes aspects of the illustrations, and/or asks children about the illustrations. May or may not "tell" the story.

14. **Reads text straight through (without any codes 1-13):** The adult does not engage children in any of the activities or behaviors listed above while reading the story.

C. POST-Reading

1. **Answers children's questions about the story/book or related topics:** Teacher reads, speaks, without expecting response from children at that time.

2. **Expands on children's comments about the story/book or illustrations:** Allows children to ask questions about the story and then responds to those questions.

3. **Comments on sounds, letters, and/or sound-letter links in the story/book:** Calls children's attention to sounds, letters, or sounds and their corresponding letters in the story text.

4. **Reviews/reinforces story-related vocabulary with or without print reference:** The teacher suggests ways of extending activities (e.g., to include or extend literacy activity) or offers materials (e.g., literacy materials).

5. **Summarizes/retells the story without child involvement:** Re-tells plot of story to remind children; help children who didn't understand what the story meant.

6. **Summarizes/retells the story with child involvement:** Involves children in retelling plot of story.

7. **Asks for recall of information about the story/book:** Asks children to recall events, characters, attributes from the story she just read aloud.

8. **Asks story/book-related questions about children's experiences outside of classroom activities:** Extends children's understanding by tapping into their own experiences to help them comprehend the story.

9. **Asks story/book-related open-ended questions (requires speculation, expanded response, thinking, and/or analysis):** Probes children's comprehension by asking questions about the story that require speculation, longer or more elaborated responses, more thought, or analysis of the story. Ex: "What do you think would have happened if . . . ?"

10. **Organizes post-reading story/book-related activity (beyond oral discussion):** The teacher suggests ways of extending activities (e.g., to include or extend literacy activity) or offers materials (e.g., literacy materials).

11. **No post-reading activity or extension occurs (without any codes 1-10):** The adult does none of the above listed extensions or activities after reading the book.

Note: Discussion of concepts of print during post-reading should be coded as A-2a.

From Goodson, Layzer, Smith, & Rimdzius (2004). *Observation Measures of Language and Literacy Instruction (OMLIT)*. Developed under contract ED-01-CO-0120, as administered by the Institute of Education Sciences, U.S. Department of Education, with Westat as prime contractor.

In *Dual Language Learners in the Early Childhood Classroom*, edited by Carollee Howes and Robert C. Pianta (2011, Baltimore: Paul H. Brookes Publishing Co.)

Read-Aloud Profile OMLIT-RAP

| Start Time ___ : ___ am pm | Title of Book: | Staff ID# | RAP #1 |
| End Time ___ : ___ am pm | Author: | ☐ Read-Aloud ends before book is complete | |

A. PRE-Reading (set-up) (circle all that apply)

1. Guides book choice; discusses children's book choice(s)
2. Points to features of the book such as the title, illustrations, author
2a. Discusses/defines concepts of print such as the title, illustrator, author
3. Reminds children of similar books they have read or that they have read same book before
4. Comments on sounds, letters, sound/letter links, or tells children to listen and look for them in the story
5. Introduces story-related vocabulary
6. Relates the story/book to other activities in class, class theme
7. Talks about events and/or features to listen, look for in the story/book
8. Introduces background information related to the story/book (with or without child input)
9. Narrates/tells the story in advance of reading
10. Relates the story/book to children's experiences outside of classroom activities
11. No pre-reading experiences or activities (without any codes 1-10)

B. Reading (circle all that apply)

1. Tracks print
2. Uses props/dramatic voices/gestures
3. Directs Children's attention to illustrations/text/story (i.e., asks questions about; discusses/expands on meaning; offers new information
4. Comments on sounds, letters, and/or sound letter links in the story/book
5. Highlights new story-related vocabulary
6. Relates the story/book to other activities in class, class theme
7. Expands on children's comments about the story/book
8. Answers all children's questions about the story/book or related topic
9. Has children join in reading/completing text on their own or as a group (choral reading)
10. Asks recall question about earlier parts of the story/book
11. Relates the story/book to children's experiences/Asks story/book-related questions about children's experiences outside of classroom activities
12. Asks story-related open-ended questions (requires prediction, expanded response, thinking, and/or analysis
13. Picture Walk
14. Reads text straight through (without any codes 1-13)

C. POST-Reading (extension) (circle all that apply)

1. Answers children's question about the story/book or related topics
2. Expands on children's comments about the story/book or illustrations
3. Comments on sounds, letters, and/or sound-letter links in the story/book
4. Reviews/reinforces story-related vocabulary with or without print reference
5. Summarizes/retells the story without child involvement
6. Summarizes/retells the story with child involvement
7. Asks for recall of information about the story/book
8. Asks story/book-related questions about the children's experiences outside of classroom activities
9. Asks story/book-related open-ended questions (requires speculation, expanded response, thinking, analysis)
10. Organizes post-reading story/book-related activity (beyond oral discussion)
11. No post-reading activities or extension occurs (without any codes 1-10)

D. Adult Reading Book (circle all that apply)

1. Teacher
2. Assistant/Aide
3. Other Adult

Vocabulary & Supports:

Open-ended Questions:

E. Adult Language with Children (circle all that apply)

1. English
2. Spanish
3. Other language

F. Number of Children Reading (circle one if F1-4, also F5 if applies)

1. One child
2. Two children
3. Small group (3-5 children)
4. Large group (6+ children)
5. Whole class

G. Book Characteristics (circle one for each)

Type of book
1a Picture book
1b Alphabet book
1c Counting book
1d Chapter book
1e Reference book

Big Book
2a Yes
2b No

Language
3a English only
3b Spanish only
3c Eng & Spanish
3d Other language
3e Eng & other language
☐ Book is read in different language

Words/page
4a 0 words
4b 1 word
4c 2-10 words
4d >10 words

Book on tape
5a Yes
5b No

Related to class theme
6a Yes
6b No
6c Don't know

From Goodson, Layzer, Smith, & Rimdzius (2004). *Observation Measures of Language and Literacy Instruction (OMLIT)*. Developed under contract ED-01-CO-0120, as administered by the Institute of Education Sciences, U.S. Department of Education, with Westat as prime contractor.

In *Dual Language Learners in the Early Childhood Classroom*, edited by Carollee Howes and Robert C. Pianta (2011, Baltimore: Paul H. Brookes Publishing Co.)

Quality of Language and Literacy Instruction
OMLIT-QUILL

Item	Frequency Rating	Overall Quality Rating					Item Score
		1 = Minimal	2	3 = Moderate	4	5 = High	
1. Opportunities to engage in language and literacy activities	☐ No opportunities ☐ Minimal (one) opportunity ☐ Moderate number of (a few) opportunities ☐ Extensive number of (many) opportunities	Language and literacy activities **rarely/never** higher-quality; typically lower-quality, such as worksheets, tracing/copying, recitation, lecture	☐	Language and literacy activities **sometimes** higher-quality and **sometimes** lower-quality (about 50% of each)	☐	Language and literacy activities **often/consistently** higher-quality, such as songs, rhymes, reading aloud, games, extended 1-1 discussions/dialogue, journals	Scores on these features are the average from Items 2–6.
		Little/no variety in language and literacy activities provided (only 1 domain of activities)[a]		**Some variety** in language and literacy activities provided (3 domains of activities)[a]		**Wide variety** in language and literacy activities provided (5 domains of activities)[a]	
[a]Domain = writing, letter/word knowledge, oral language, functions/features of print, sound in words		Language and literacy (not solely oral language) **rarely/never** integrated into activities with goal other than literacy		Language and literacy (not solely oral language) **sometimes** integrated into activities with goals other than literacy		Language and literacy (not solely oral language) **often** integrated into activities with goals other than literacy	
		Language and literacy activities **rarely/never** conducted with children in small groups/individual children[b]		Language and literacy activities **sometimes** conducted with small groups/individual children and sometimes with large groups[b]		Language and literacy activities are **often/consistently** conducted with small groups/individual children[b]	
[b]Small groups = 3–5 children; large groups = 6+ children		Staff work with **only a few/a small percentage** of the children in language and literacy activities over the day		Staff work with **up to half** of the children in language and literacy activities over the day		Staff work with **most/all** of the children in language and literacy activities over the day	
[c]Rich language = rare vocabulary, extended sentences, new words		Staff **rarely/never** use rich language with children, talk about abstract concepts, or talk about language itself[c]		Staff **sometimes** use rich language with children, **sometimes** talk about abstract concepts, and **sometimes** talk about language itself[c]		Staff **often/consistently** use rich language with children, talk about abstract concepts, and talk about language itself[c]	
Abstract concepts = non-present topics (prediction, analysis)		Staff **rarely/never** positive, enthusiastic engaged in language and literacy activities		Staff **sometimes** positive, enthusiastic, engaged in language and literacy activities and **sometimes** not		Staff **often/consistently** positive, enthusiastic, engaged in language and literacy activities	

Snapshots	CLIPs/RAPs		Other Language and Literacy Activities
		ALL LANGUAGE AND LITERACY	

From Goodson, Layzer, Smith, & Rimdzius (2004). *Observation Measures of Language and Literacy Instruction (OMLIT)*. Developed under contract ED-01-CO-0120, as administered by the Institute of Education Sciences, U.S. Department of Education, with Westat as prime contractor.

In *Dual Language Learners in the Early Childhood Classroom*, edited by Carollee Howes and Robert C. Pianta (2011, Baltimore: Paul H. Brookes Publishing Co.)

Quality of Language and Literacy Instruction
OMLIT-QUILL

Overall Quality Rating

Item	Frequency Rating	☐ 1 = Minimal	☐ 2	☐ 3 = Moderate	☐ 4	☐ 5 = High	Item Score
2. Opportunities to engage in writing [a]Children writing on their own = using invented or phonetic spelling and irregular letter forms Note: Writing can include writing numerals, not just letters	☐ No opportunities ☐ Minimal (one) opportunity ☐ Moderate number of (a few) opportunities ☐ Extensive number of (many) opportunities	Writing activities *rarely/never* higher quality; usually lower quality, such as worksheets, tracing/copying		Writing activities *sometimes* higher quality and *sometimes* lower-quality (about 50% of each)		Writing activities *often/consistently* higher-quality, such as emergent writing, captioning, dictation with teacher, writing own name on work, book-making, journals	
		Little/no variety in writing activities provided (either only 1 activity or only 1 type of activity)		*Some* variety in writing activities provided (3 different types of activities)		*Wide* variety in writing activities provided (5+ different types of activities)	
		Writing *rarely/not* integrated into activities with goals other than literacy		Writing *sometimes* integrated into activities with goals other than literacy		Writing *often* integrated into activities with goals other than literacy	
		Writing activities *rarely/never* conducted with children in small groups/individual children		Writing activities *sometimes* conducted with small groups/individual children and sometimes with children in large groups		Writing activities are *often/ consistently* conducted with small groups/individual children	
		Staff work with *only a few/a small percentage* of the children in writing activities over the day		Staff work with *some/up to half* of the children in writing activities over the day		Staff work with *most/all* of the children in writing activities over the day	
		In *few/no* writing activities, writing is done by children themselves rather than by adults		In *some* writing activities, writing is done by children themselves rather than by adults		In *most/all* writing activities, writing is done by children themselves rather than by adults	
		Staff *rarely/never* allow or encourage children to write on their own; *usually* insist on conventional letter formation/ spelling		Staff *sometimes* allow or encourage children to write on their own and *sometimes* insist on conventional letter formation/spelling		Staff *often/consistently* allow or encourage children to write on their own[a] rather than insisting on conventional letter formation/spelling	
Snapshots		**CLIPs/RAPs**				**Other Writing Activities**	

WRITING

From Goodson, Layzer, Smith, & Rimdzius (2004). *Observation Measures of Language and Literacy Instruction (OMLIT)*. Developed under contract ED-01-CO-0120, as administered by the Institute of Education Sciences, U.S. Department of Education, with Westat as prime contractor.

In *Dual Language Learners in the Early Childhood Classroom*, edited by Carollee Howes and Robert C. Pianta (2011, Baltimore: Paul H. Brookes Publishing Co.)

Quality of Language and Literacy Instruction
OMLIT-QUILL

Item	Frequency Rating	Overall Quality Rating					Item Score
		☐ 1 = Minimal	☐ 2	☐ 3 = Moderate	☐ 4	☐ 5 = High	
3. Attention to/promotion of letter/word knowledge[a]	☐ No opportunities ☐ Minimal (one) opportunity ☐ Moderate number of (a few) opportunities ☐ Extensive number of (many) opportunities	Activities promoting letter/word knowledge *rarely/never* higher-quality; usually lower quality, such as drills, flashcards, worksheets		Activities promoting letter/word knowledge *sometimes* higher-quality and *sometimes* lower-quality (about 50% of each)		Activities promoting letter/word knowledge *often/consistently* higher quality, such as reading alphabet books, having children write own name, helping child locate classroom job by calling attention to key letters, games such as letter bingo, letter wall	
		Little/no variety in activities to promote letter/word knowledge (either only 1 activity or only 1 type of activity)		*Some variety* in activities to promote letter/word knowledge (3 different types of activities)		*Wide variety* in activities to promote letter/word knowledge (5+ different types of activities)	
[a]**Letter/word knowledge:** attention to same/different in letters, names, words; associating letter names and letter shapes; letter-sound matches		Letter/word knowledge *rarely/not* integrated into activities with goals other than literacy		Letter/word knowledge *sometimes* integrated into activities with goals other than literacy		Letter/word knowledge *often* integrated into activities with goals other than literacy	
		Activities to promote letter/word knowledge *rarely/never* conducted with children in small groups/individual children		Activities to promote letter/word knowledge *sometimes* conducted with small groups/individual children and sometimes with children in large groups		Activities to promote letter/word knowledge are *often/consistently* conducted with small groups/individual children	
		Staff promote letter/word knowledge with *only a few/a small percentage* over the day		Staff promote letter/word knowledge with *some/up to half* of the children over the day		Staff promote letter/word knowledge with *most/all* of the children over the day	

Snapshots	CLIPs/RAPs	Other Examples of Attention to Letter/Word Knowledge

LETTER/WORD KNOWLEDGE

From Goodson, Layzer, Smith, & Rimdzius (2004). *Observation Measures of Language and Literacy Instruction (OMLIT)*. Developed under contract ED-01-CO-0120, as administered by the Institute of Education Sciences, U.S. Department of Education, with Westat as prime contractor.

In *Dual Language Learners in the Early Childhood Classroom*, edited by Carollee Howes and Robert C. Pianta (2011, Baltimore: Paul H. Brookes Publishing Co.)

Quality of Language and Literacy Instruction
OMLIT-QUILL

Item	Frequency Rating	Overall Quality Rating					Item Score
		☐ 1 = Minimal	☐ 2	☐ 3 = Moderate	☐ 4	☐ 5 = High	
4. Opportunities/ encouragement of oral language to communicate ideas and thoughts	☐ No opportunities ☐ Minimal (one) opportunity ☐ Moderate number of (a few) opportunities ☐ Extensive number of (many) opportunities	Oral language activities are **rarely/never** higher-quality; usually lower-quality, such as recitation, short dialogues, topics that don't promote thinking, lecture—adult talk predominates		Oral language activities **sometimes** higher-quality and **sometimes** lower-quality (about 50% of each)		Oral language activities **often/ consistently** higher-quality, such as in-depth conversations, dialogues, oral presentations by children, rich symbolic play	
		Little/no variety in oral language activities provided (either only 1 activity or only 1 type of activity)		**Some variety** in oral language activities provided (3 different types of activities)		**Wide variety** in oral language activities provided (5+ different types of activities)	
[a]"One "turn" refers to a back-and-forth verbal exchange. Multiple turns means at least 3 back-and-forth exchanges.		Oral language opportunities **rarely/not** integrated into activities with goals other than literacy		Oral language opportunities **sometimes** integrated into activities with goals other than literacy		Oral language opportunities **often** integrated into activities with goals other than literacy	
		Oral language activities **rarely/never** conducted with children in small groups/individual children		Oral language activities **sometimes** conducted with small groups/individual children and **sometimes** with children in large groups		Oral language activities **often/ consistently** conducted with small groups/individual children	
		Staff work with **only a few/a small percentage** of the children in oral language activities over the day		Staff work with **some/up to half** of the children in oral language activities over the day		Staff work with **most/all** of the children in oral language activities over the day	
		Staff **rarely/never** encourage/provide opportunities for children to use oral language in higher-level cognitive operations		Staff **sometimes** encourage/provide opportunities for children to use oral language in higher-level cognitive operations		Staff **often/consistently** encourage/provide opportunities for children to use oral language in higher-level cognitive operations	
		Verbal interactions between staff and children **rarely/never** involve multiple turns[a] and topics other than management issues		Verbal interactions between staff and children **sometimes** involve multiple turns[a] and non-management topics and **sometimes** involve short, involve mainly management issues		Verbal interactions between staff and children **often/consistently** involve multiple turns[a] and topics other than management	
		Staff **rarely/never** extend or scaffold children's oral language by adding new words or concepts, elaborating on child ideas or descriptions		Staff **sometimes** extend or scaffold children's oral language by adding new words or concepts, elaborating on child ideas or descriptions		Staff **often/consistently** extend or scaffold children's oral language by adding new words or concepts, elaborating on child ideas or descriptions	
Snapshots		**CLIPs/RAPs**				**Other Oral Language Activities**	
				ORAL LANGUAGE			

From Goodson, Layzer, Smith, & Rimdzius (2004). *Observation Measures of Language and Literacy Instruction (OMLIT)*. Developed under contract ED-01-CO-0120, as administered by the Institute of Education Sciences, U.S. Department of Education, with Westat as prime contractor.

In *Dual Language Learners in the Early Childhood Classroom*, edited by Carollee Howes and Robert C. Pianta (2011, Baltimore: Paul H. Brookes Publishing Co.)

Quality of Language and Literacy Instruction
OMLIT-QUILL

Item	Frequency Rating	1 = Minimal	2	3 = Moderate	4	5 = High	Item Score
5. Attention to functions and features of print ᵃ **Functions** of print: labeling, naming, categorizing, describing **Features** of print: directionality (i.e., print goes from left to right, top to bottom) Note: functional print on display in the classroom is not sufficient; staff must engage in active behaviors to draw children's attention to the functions/features of print	☐ No opportunities ☐ Minimal (one) opportunity ☐ Moderate number of (a few) opportunities ☐ Extensive number of (many) opportunities	Activities that draw attention to the functions/features of print *rarely/never* higher-quality; usually lower quality, such as direct instruction in absence of authentic, meaningful text *Little/no variety* in activities that draw attention to the functions/features of print (either only I activity or only I type of activity) Attention to the functions/features of print is *rarely/not* integrated into activities with goals other than literacy Activities that draw attention to functions/features of print *rarely/never* conducted with children in small groups/individual children Staff work with *only a few/a small percentage* of the children in activities that draw attention to the functions/features of print	☐	Activities that draw attention to the functions/features of print *sometimes* higher-quality and *sometimes* lower-quality (about 50% of each) *Some variety* in activities to draw attention to the functions/features of print (3 different types of activities) Attention to functions/features of print is *sometimes* integrated into activities with goals other than literacy Activities that draw attention to functions/features of print *sometimes* conducted with small groups/individual children and sometimes with children in large groups Staff work with *some/up to half* of the children in activities that draw attention to the functions/features of print	☐	Activities that draw attention to the functions/features of print are *often/consistently* higher-quality, such as being part of reading aloud, working with authentic print materials. *Wide variety* in activities to draw attention to the functions/features of print (5+ different types of activities) Attention to functions/features of print is *often* integrated into activities with goals other than literacy Activities that draw attention to functions/features of print *often/consistently* conducted with small groups/individual children Staff work with *most/all* of the children in activities that draw attention to the functions/features of print	

Snapshots	CLIPs/RAPs	Other Examples of Attention to Features/Functions of Print

FUNCTIONS/FEATURES OF PRINT

From Goodson, Layzer, Smith, & Rimdzius (2004). *Observation Measures of Language and Literacy Instruction (OMLIT)*. Developed under contract ED-01-CO-0120, as administered by the Institute of Education Sciences, U.S. Department of Education, with Westat as prime contractor.

In *Dual Language Learners in the Early Childhood Classroom*, edited by Carollee Howes and Robert C. Pianta (2011, Baltimore: Paul H. Brookes Publishing Co.)

Quality of Language and Literacy Instruction
OMLIT-QUILL

Item	Frequency Rating	Overall Quality Rating					Item Score
		☐ 1 = Minimal	☐ 2	☐ 3 = Moderate	☐ 4	☐ 5 = High	
6. Attention to sounds in words[a] **throughout the day**	☐ No opportunities ☐ Minimal (one) opportunity ☐ Moderate number of (a few) opportunities ☐ Extensive number of (many) opportunities	Activities that call attention to sounds in words *rarely/never* higher-quality; usually lower quality, such as drills, practice on isolated sounds		Activities that call attention to sounds in words *sometimes* higher-quality and *sometimes* lower-quality (about 50% of each)		Activities that call attention to sounds of words *often/consistently* higher-quality; higher-quality, such as reading text that has rhymes/alliteration; singing songs or playing games that emphasize rhyming, syllables in words (clapping out syllables)	
[a]Rhyming; alliteration; sentence segmenting; syllable blending/segmenting; onset-rime blending/segmenting; phoneme blending/segmenting; phoneme manipulation		*Little/no variety* in activities that draw attention to sounds in words (either only 1 activity or only 1 type of activity)		*Some variety* in activities that draw attention to sounds in words (3 different types of activities)		*Wide variety* in activities that draw attention to sounds in words (5+ different types of activities)	
		Attention to sounds in words *rarely/not* integrated into activities with goals other than literacy		Attention to sounds in words *sometimes* integrated into activities with goals other than literacy		Attention to sounds in words *often* integrated into activities with goals other than literacy	
		Activities that draw attention to sounds in words *rarely/never* conducted with children in small groups/individual children		Activities that draw attention to sounds in words *sometimes* conducted with small groups/individual children and sometimes with children in large groups		Activities that draw attention to sounds in words are *often/consistently* conducted with small groups/individual children	
		Staff work with *only a few/a small percentage* of the children in activities that draw attention to sounds in words over the day		Staff work with *some/up to half* of the children in activities that draw attention to sounds in words over the day		Staff work with *most/all* of the children in activities that draw attention to sounds in words over the day	
		Staff explain sounds in words incorrectly[b] *more than twice* (Note: regional/societal accents, variants not counted as incorrect)		Staff *usually* explain sounds in words correctly but explain sounds incorrectly[b] once or twice		Staff *always* explain sounds in words correctly (regional/societal accents, variants not counted as incorrect[b])	

[b] Types of possible errors in explaining sounds in words include: giving the wrong sound for a letter; indicating that a letter has only one correct sound when it has more than one; asking children to name or identify things that start with a particular letter when no printed text is referenced, rather than a particular sound (e.g., "Look around and tell me all the things that start with the letter 'r.'" Adult should ask about things that start with the /r/ sound).

Snapshots		CLIPs/RAPs				Other Examples of Attention to Sounds in Words	
				SOUNDS IN WORDS			

From Goodson, Layzer, Smith, & Rimdzius (2004). *Observation Measures of Language and Literacy Instruction (OMLIT)*. Developed under contract ED-01-CO-0120, as administered by the Institute of Education Sciences, U.S. Department of Education, with Westat as prime contractor.

In *Dual Language Learners in the Early Childhood Classroom*, edited by Carollee Howes and Robert C. Pianta (2011, Baltimore: Paul H. Brookes Publishing Co.)

Quality of Language and Literacy Instruction
OMLIT-QUILL

Language and Literacy Strategies with English-Language Learners (ELLs) ☐ No ELL children in classroom

Item	Frequency	Overall Quality Rating					Item Score
		☐ 1 = Minimal	☐ 2	☐ 3 = Moderate	☐ 4	☐ 5 = High	
7. ELL children intentionally included in activities, conversations	☐ Check and skip item if *all* children in class are ELLs.	ELL children *rarely/never* integrated with English-speaking children in activities		ELL children *sometimes* integrated with English-speaking children in activities and *sometimes* segregated		ELL children *often/regularly* integrated with English-speaking children in activities	
		ELL children *rarely/never* encouraged/supported to join conversations with English-speaking children		ELL children *sometimes* encouraged/supported to join conversations with English-speaking children and *sometimes* not		ELL children *often/regularly* encouraged/supported to join conversations with English-speaking children	

Item	Frequency						Item Score
		☐ 1 = Minimal	☐ 2	☐ 3 = Moderate	☐ 4	☐ 5 = High	
8. Development of both home language(s) and English supported for ELL children		Staff *rarely/never* positive about having ELL children in the classroom		Staff *sometimes* positive about having ELL children in the classroom (or only some staff appear positive)		All staff *consistently* positive about having ELL children in the classroom	
		ELL children *never* encouraged OR sometimes forced to try using English		ELL children *sometimes* encouraged but never forced to try using English		ELL children *regularly* encouraged but never forced to try using English	
		➤ Code only if >1 ELL child in class or >2 ELLs with same home language ELL children *rarely/never* encouraged to use their home language with each other; are *actively* discouraged		➤ Code only if >1 ELL child in class or >2 ELLs with same home language ELL children *rarely* encouraged to use their home language with each other but *not discouraged*		➤ Code only if >1 ELL child in class or >2 ELLs with same home language ELL children *often/consistently* encouraged to use their home language with each other	

Snapshots	CLIPs/RAPs	Other Examples

ELL INSTRUCTION: INCLUSION AND SUPPORT FOR HOME LANGUAGE

From Goodson, Layzer, Smith, & Rimdzius (2004). *Observation Measures of Language and Literacy Instruction (OMLIT)*. Developed under contract ED-01-CO-0120, as administered by the Institute of Education Sciences, U.S. Department of Education, with Westat as prime contractor.

In *Dual Language Learners in the Early Childhood Classroom*, edited by Carollee Howes and Robert C. Pianta (2011, Baltimore: Paul H. Brookes Publishing Co.)

Quality of Language and Literacy Instruction
OMLIT-QUILL

Language and Literacy Strategies with English-Language Learners (ELLs)						☐ No ELL children in classroom	
				Overall Quality Rating			
Item	Language	☐ 1 = Minimal	☐ 2	☐ 3 = Moderate	☐ 4	☐ 5 = High	Item Score
9. Home language(s) of ELL children integrated into language and literacy activities	☐ No English used (only ELL children's home language used). **[Skip item.]**	**No** staff members speak ELL children's home language(s) AND **no** other adults used as translators		**No** staff members speak ELL children's home language(s) AND other adults only **sometimes** used as translators		**At least one** staff member speaks ELL children's home language(s) OR other adults **often/regularly** used as translators	
		ELL children's home language(s) **rarely/never** integrated with English in print-based language and literacy activities		ELL children's home language(s) **sometimes** integrated with English in print-based language and literacy activities		English/ELL children's home language(s) **often/regularly** integrated in print-based language and literacy activities	
		English and ELL children's home language(s) **rarely/never** integrated in oral language activities (songs, rhymes, language games)		English and ELL children's home language(s) **sometimes** integrated in oral language activities (songs, rhymes, language games)		English/ELL children's home language(s) **often/regularly** integrated in oral language activities (songs, rhymes, language games)	
Item	Language	☐ 1 = Minimal	☐ 2	☐ 3 = Moderate	☐ 4	☐ 5 = High	Item Score
10. Language and literacy materials/methods appropriate for ELL children	☐ No English used (only ELL children's home language used). **[Code features.]**	**Few/no** text materials in language and literacy activities in English and in ELL children's home language(s)		**Some** text materials in language and literacy activities in English and in ELL children's home language(s)		**Most/all** text materials in language and literacy activities in English and in ELL children's home language(s)	
		Few/no other print materials in classroom (labels, posters, charts) include both English and home language(s) of ELL children		**Some** other print materials in classroom (labels, posters, charts) include both English and home language(s) of ELL children		**Many/most** print materials in classroom (labels, posters, charts) include English and home language(s) of ELL children	
		Methods used to teach English to ELL children **rarely/never** explicit and contextualized[a]		Methods used to teach English to ELL children **sometimes** explicit and contextualized[a] and **sometimes** not		Methods used to teach English to ELL children **usually/consistently** explicit and contextualized	
		Few/no books available to children/read aloud are appropriate for English language learners[b]		**Some** books available to children/read aloud are appropriate for English language learners[b]		**Many/most** books available to children/read aloud are appropriate for English language learners[b]	

[a] Explicit = emphasis on key words, oral description of actions, events Contextualized = use of gestures, images, objects
[b] Predictable, clearly illustrated; clear, repetitive themes, plots

Snapshots	CLIPs/RAPs	Other Examples

ELL INSTRUCTION: INTERGRATION INTO LITERACY ACTIVITIES/MATERIALS

From Goodson, Layzer, Smith, & Rimdzius (2004). *Observation Measures of Language and Literacy Instruction (OMLIT)*. Developed under contract ED-01-CO-0120, as administered by the Institute of Education Sciences, U.S. Department of Education, with Westat as prime contractor.

In *Dual Language Learners in the Early Childhood Classroom*, edited by Carollee Howes and Robert C. Pianta (2011, Baltimore: Paul H. Brookes Publishing Co.)

Appendix 6.2

Regression Models for Analysis

Relationships between predictors and student outcomes are estimated using a two-level hierarchical linear model (students nested within classrooms/schools or centers) that employs predictor(s) and covariates (e.g., student-, classroom-, and school-level covariates as well as randomization stratifiers or blocking indicators). For simplicity, classroom-level variables (e.g., pretest and predictors) are represented in the second level. As an example, the following is a model for a typical outcome for the kindergarten sample; the model for the preschool sample is similar to this one:

Level 1 (student):

$$Y_{ik} = \pi_{0k} + \pi_{1k}\,Year_{jk} + \pi_{2k}\,Age_{jk} + \pi_{3k}\,Male_{jk} + \varepsilon_{jk}$$

where:

Y_{ik} is the outcome measure for student i in school k,

$Year_{ik}$ is the observation year indicator of the outcome measure, Y_{ik}. In particular, it equals 1 if the measure is from Spring 07 and zero otherwise.

Age_{ik} is the age of student i in school k,

$Male_{ik}$ is the indicator variable, which equals 1 if student i in school k is male and zero, otherwise,

π_{0k} is the mean of the outcome measure in school k, and

ε_{jk} is the residual associated with student i in school k. All error terms are assumed to be normally distributed and independent of one another.

Level 2 (classroom/school):

$$\pi_{0k} = \gamma_{00} + \gamma_{01}\,Predictor_k + \gamma_{02}\,north_k + \gamma_{03}\,Spanish_k + \gamma_{04}\,N_k * S_k$$
$$+ \gamma_{05}\,Minority_k + \gamma_{06}\,Y_k^{pre}\,u_k$$

$$\pi_{1k} = \gamma_{10}$$

$$\pi_{21k} = \gamma_{20}$$

$$\pi_{3k} = \gamma_{30}$$

where:

$Predictor_k$ is the predictor variable. Note that we used multiple predictor variables in some models (e.g., literacy category indicators). Also note that without loss of generality, this prototypical model includes a classroom-level predictor; student–teacher language match indicators, which are student-level variables, should be entered to the model in Level 1.

$Minority_k$ is the school level percentage of minority students,

Y_k^{pre} is the baseline value of the outcome measure in school k. Note that this covariate is only used for Arnett outcomes,

γ_{00} is the grand mean of the outcome measure for the average control school,

γ_{01} is the estimated relationship between the predictor and the outcome,

γ_{02}, γ_{03}, and γ_{04} are the effects associated with the stratification indicators used during the random assignment process, and their interaction, to control for the study design,

γ_{05} is the effect associated with school-level percentage of minority students,

γ_{10} is the estimated overall difference in the outcome measure in Spring 06 and Spring 07,

γ_{06} is the effect associated with the baseline measure, and

u_k is the residual associated with school k.

Appendix 6.3

Early Childhood Education (ECE) Classroom Outcomes and Component Observation Measures of Language and Literacy Instruction (OMLIT, Goodson, Layzer, Smith, & Rimdzius, 2004) Variables

Outcome construct	Instructional behaviors (OMLIT variables) in each construct	Field reliability of behavior percentage[a]
	Read-Aloud Profile (OMLIT-RAP)	
	• Time in reading across observation period	74
	• Number of books read in observation period	99
	• Percent read-alouds with different supports for comprehension of text	87
	• Percent read-alouds with open-ended questions	83
Support for oral language	• Quality of open-ended questions, vocabulary supports, postreading	92
	Literacy activities (OMLIT-CLIP)	
	• Time on oral language activities	88
	• Percent oral language activities with small groups	79
	• Quality of teacher–child discussion	93
	Rating of frequency/quality of support for oral language development (OMLIT-QUILL)	
	• Frequency of oral language activities	67
	• Quality of oral language activities	87
	Read-Aloud Profile (OMLIT-RAP):	
	• Reads-alouds with discussion of sounds	91
Support for phonological awareness	**Literacy activities (OMLIT-CLIP)**	
	• Time on sounds	90
	• Percent activities on sounds with small groups	89
	Classroom activities (OMLIT-SNAP)	
	• Proportion classroom time on sounds, singing	77

(continued)

229

Appendix 6.3   *(continued)*

Outcome construct	Instructional behaviors (OMLIT variables) in each construct	Field reliability of behavior percentage[a]
Support for phonological awareness	**Rating of frequency and quality of support for phonological awareness (OMLIT-QUILL)**	
	• Frequency of activities to support phonological awareness	71
	• Quality of activities to support phonological awareness	69
Support for print knowledge	**Read Aloud Profile (OMLIT-RAP):**	
	• Percent read-alouds with discussion of print concepts	83
	Classroom activities (OMLIT-SNAP)	
	• Proportion classroom time in activities with text, letters	80
	• Proportion classroom time in activities with writing (copying, emergent)	78
	• Percent text, writing activities in small groups	76
	• Percent activities with print involved	89
	Literacy activities (OMLIT-CLIP)	
	• Time on print knowledge activities	92
	• Percent print knowledge activities with small groups	87
	• Time on emergent writing activities	80
	• Time on copying/tracing activities	82
	• Percent print knowledge activities with small groups	88
	Rating of frequency and quality of support for print knowledge (OMLIT-QUILL)	
	• Frequency of activities to support writing	88
	• Quality of activities to support writing	85
	• Frequency of print knowledge activities to support print knowledge	82
	• Quality of activities to support print knowledge	85
	• Frequency of activities to support understanding functions/features of print	67
	• Quality of activities to support understanding functions/features of print	68

Outcome construct	Instructional behaviors (OMLIT variables) in each construct	Field reliability of behavior percentage[a]
Support for print motivation	**Read-Aloud Profile (OMLIT-RAP):**	
	• Percent read-alouds with support for print motivation	95
	• Number of RAPs	99
	• Number of minutes of reading aloud	75
	Literacy activities (OMLIT-CLIP)	
	• Time on activities involving print motivation	94
	• Percent activities on print motivation with small groups	93
Adequacy of literacy resources	**Literacy resources in the classroom (OMLIT-CLOC)**	
	• Environmental print	77
	• Text materials	78
	• Writing resources	81
	• Rich, integrated theme	76
	• Literacy manipulative	82
	• Integration of print in other centers	71

Key: ECE, Early Childhood Education; OMLIT, Observation Measures of Language and Literacy Instruction (Goodson, Layzer, Smith, & Rimdzius, 2004); OMLIT measurements include RAP, Read-Aloud Profile; CLIP, Classroom Literacy Instruction Profile; QUILL, Quality of Language and Literacy Instruction; SNAP, Snapshot of Classroom Activities; CLOC, Classroom Literacy Opportunities Checklist; CLIO, Classroom Literacy Interventions and Outcomes Study (U.S. Department of Education, Institute of Education Sciences, 2008).

[a]Based on exact agreement between paired observers in 90 paired observations conducted over the three waves of data collection—Spring 2004 (baseline), Spring 2005, and Spring 2006.

Internal consistency interrater reliability of early childhood education outcome constructs, Spring 2004

Construct	Number of items in construct	Cronbach's alpha		CLIO interrater reliability[c] ($n = 33$ paired observations)
		CLIO[a] ($n = 199$ classrooms)	Miami[b] ($n = 162$ classrooms)	
Support for oral language	14	.84	.80	.87
Support for print knowledge	16	.84	.82	.89
Support for phonological awareness	4	.58	.61	.83
Support for print motivation	5	.73	.72	.89
Adequacy of literacy resources in class	7	.75	.73	.80

Key: ECE, Early Childhood Education; *n,* 199 Even Start projects; CLIO, Classroom Literacy Interventions and Outcomes Study (U.S. Department of Education, Institute of Education Sciences, 2008); OMLIT, Observation Measures of Language and Literacy Instruction (Goodson et al., 2004).

[a]Data from observation conducted in Spring 2004 in CLIO classrooms.

[b]In Miami child care center data, Cronbach's alpha derived from same set of OMLIT variables that are included in the final version of constructs derived from the CLIO data.

[c]Based on exact agreement between coding from paired observations.

Correlations among early childhood education outcome constructs, Spring 2004

	Support for print knowledge	Support for phonological awareness	Support for print motivation	Adequacy of literacy resources
Support for oral language	.15*	.12	.37***	.10
Support for print knowledge		.39***	.32***	.25***
Support for phonological awareness			.19**	.13
Support for print motivation				.10

*p < .05, **p < .001, ***p < .01.

7

The Classroom Assessment of Supports for Emergent Bilingual Acquisition

Psychometric Properties and Key Initial Findings from New Jersey's Abbott Preschool Program

Margaret Freedson, Alexandra Figueras-Daniel,
Ellen Frede, Kwanghee Jung, and John Sideris

Preschool programs have expanded greatly in recent years. Since 2002, when the National Institute for Early Education Research (NIEER) first began reporting on state-funded preschool, enrollment has increased 64%, with over 1.2 million children served in state-funded general education prekindergarten programs in 2008–2009 (Barnett, Epstein, Friedman, Sansanelli, & Hustedt, 2009). Head Start served over 900,000 children in 2009. At the same time as these marked increases in preschool provision, the U.S. population of families who do not speak English at home has also grown rapidly (Hernandez, 2010), with one in nine children under age 5 now coming from a home where one or both parents do not speak English well. Because many of the state-funded preschool programs are either targeted to income-eligible populations or actually use home language as an eligibility criterion (Barnett et al., 2009), the proportion of children whose home language is not English served in Head Start or state preschool is actually larger than that of the population as a whole.

Recent analyses of national data sets have shown that young children who start kindergarten without knowing English begin with an ability gap that schools have thus far failed to help close (Galindo, 2010). However, other recent research indicates that being bilingual may not only be socially and economically advantageous but may also enhance cognitive abilities (Frede & Garcia, 2010). Taken together, this rise in dual language learners (DLLs) in preschool, their unpromising academic trajectory, and the potential benefits of capitalizing on their bilingual abilities clearly indicates that determining how best to educate DLL children prior to school entry is an imperative of education reform.

This chapter examines the Classroom Assessment of Supports for Emergent Bilingual Acquisition (CASEBA; Freedson, Figueras-Daniel, & Frede, 2009), a newly developed, research-based classroom observation tool designed to assess the quality of preschool classroom supports for DLLs, with a focus on language and literacy development in both the home language and English. The CASEBA is grounded in an expanding research literature on early literacy, bilingualism, and effective preschool practices for DLLs who began the process of acquiring English once acquisition of the home language was already in progress—the majority of under-5 DLLs in the United States (Genesee, 2010). The chapter begins with a review of some of the most relevant findings from this research base that undergird the instrument design. The CASEBA's application in a sample of 100 of New Jersey's Abbott preschool classrooms serving low-income Spanish-speaking children and the instrument's construct and concurrent validity based on that data are then examined. The chapter ends with a discussion of the instrument's potential applications and future directions for our research.

THE LITERATURE

Hundreds of studies in the United States and internationally have shown that high-quality preschool can result in short-term gains for children across all domains of development, and a large number of studies have shown that these results last throughout school and well into adulthood (see Barnett, 2008, for a recent review of the literature, and Deming, 2009, for recent adult results for Head Start). These beneficial outcomes include increases in language and literacy abilities, math gains, and better social development that lead to reduced special education placement, less grade retention, and greater high school graduation rates. Classrooms that provide high-quality language and literacy environments have shown particular promise for enhancing acquisition of many early literacy skills that reliably predict later reading achievement—oral language, phonological awareness, and print knowledge—with stronger effects observed for more economically disadvantaged and Hispanic children (Dickinson & Sprague, 2001; Gormley, 2007; Gormley, Gayer, Phillips, & Dawson, 2005; National Early Literacy Panel, 2008; Snow, Burns, & Griffin, 1998).

Emergent Bilingualism and Reading Achievement

Understanding of the complexities of English literacy acquisition in young bilingual children is certainly incomplete, but a growing body of research suggests that predictors of successful outcomes include language and literacy skills in both the primary language and English (see August & Shanahan, 2008, and Frede & Garcia, 2010, for comprehensive reviews). For example, in a study that followed 66 Spanish-speaking English language learners (ELLs) from kindergarten into middle school, Reese, Garnier, Gallimore, and Goldenberg (2000) used path analysis to determine that *both* emergent literacy skills in Spanish—oral story comprehension, print concepts, and letter knowledge—*and* oral English proficiency at kindergarten entry made strong and unique contributions to English reading performance in Grade 7. During the early stages of reading development, evidence is found in longitudinal studies of both within- and cross-language influences. Hammer, Lawrence, and Miccio (2007) found English and Spanish vocabulary in preschool to predict English and Spanish letter–word identification, respectively, at the end of kindergarten. Rinaldi and Paez (2006, 2008), on the other hand, found that preschool vocabulary in both languages as well as English vocabulary and Spanish word reading in kindergarten predicted English word reading in Grade 1.

Though the exact mechanisms by which these influences operate are not well understood, the transfer of skills across languages within specific language and literacy domains has been strongly implicated (Durgunoglu & Oney, 2000; Espinosa, 2010; Lopez & Greenfield, 2004). The practical implication of this research is that both home and school support for DLL children's language and literacy skills in their home language positively affect the development of English literacy. The importance of early acquisition of oral English should not be minimized, however. Limitations in depth and breadth of English vocabulary are implicated in many of the difficulties older ELLs experience with English text comprehension (August, Carlo, Dressler, & Snow, 2005; August & Shanahan, 2008), and a recent analysis of data from the Early Childhood Longitudinal Study–Kindergarten Cohort by Galindo (2010) suggests that children who fail to achieve a minimum threshold of oral English proficiency by kindergarten may never catch up to their native-English-speaking peers in English reading.

Language of Instruction in Preschool

The empirical literature on preschool practice and DLLs is exceptionally limited in comparison with the sizable body of research on effective practices for low-income English speakers. There is, nonetheless, emerging information about the effects of home language classroom supports on low-income Spanish-speaking children who represent the largest group of DLL preschoolers. In his evaluation of the universal pre-K program in Tulsa, Oklahoma, for example, Gormley (2007) found that children from Spanish-only homes in classrooms staffed by Spanish-speaking teachers made the greatest gains on both Spanish and English literacy measures. Barnett, Yarosz, Thomas, and Blanco (2007) conducted an experimental study in New Jersey's Abbott preschool program that compared Spanish-speaking children in two-way bilingual immersion classrooms with children in comparable English immersion classrooms. Researchers found that the two-way bilingual immersion program's support for language acquisition in both English and Spanish produced child gains on English literacy measures equivalent to those of DLL children in the English immersion setting, accompanied by greater gains on Spanish language and literacy measures. Similarly, in an experimental comparison of English-only and transitional bilingual small-group literacy instruction, Farver, Lonigan, and Eppe (2009) found that children in both conditions gained in English emergent literacy skills but the children who received the treatment in both languages also gained in Spanish. Studies that have quantified the amount of instructional talk devoted to Spanish versus English, as in Freedson's (2005) study of six Texas prekindergarten classrooms, have similarly found higher levels of Spanish language teacher talk to predict greater gains in Spanish at no cost to children's English acquisition. The positive effects of home language classroom supports extend beyond cognitive-academic skills to include enhanced social-emotional outcomes (Chang et al., 2007).

Specific Preschool Teaching Practices Linked to Enhanced Dual Language Learnering Outcomes

Several recent intervention studies have demonstrated that, as with native English speakers, explicit vocabulary discussions and direct comprehension instruction during English language read-alouds support English vocabulary acquisition in DLLs, even when children's oral proficiency in English is limited (Collins, 2005; Roberts & Neal, 2004). Parent read-alouds in the home language that parallel English read-alouds in the classroom can also support English vocabulary learning (Roberts, 2008). Children's access to culturally relevant, bilingual or native language literacy materials may also enhance emergent literacy growth (Bernhard, Cummins, Campoy, Ada, Winsler, & Bleiker, 2006), though it cannot be determined based on the available research if the observed learning benefits are derived from culturally relevant content, the language of instruction, or some combination of the two.

Qualitative studies offer further insight into classroom communication strategies that support English acquisition. Based on her year-long investigation of language interactions in a multilingual Boston-area preschool classroom, Tabors (1997) identified teachers' use of simplified language, extending and expanding of children's talk, and fine-tuning of communication to children's level of English proficiency as particularly facilitative of second language learning, among many other strategies. Freedson (2008) found similar scaffolds to be characteristic of Texas prekindergarten classrooms where large English vocabulary gains were documented among low-income Spanish-speaking DLLs but found additionally that use of the home language to support comprehension of lesson content, even by teachers with relatively limited knowledge of the language, may enhance child outcomes.

A number of variables that have yet to be investigated in classrooms serving DLL children are known to be predictive of emergent literacy skills among low-income English speakers. Of particular interest to this team, the lexical richness of preschool teachers' classroom talk is associated with children's vocabulary outcomes in kindergarten and with reading comprehension through Grade 7 (Dickinson & Tabors, 2001). One can reasonably hypothesize that lexical richness and other measures of high-quality teacher talk in preschool in both languages influence the trajectory of children's dual language learning.

CLASSROOM ASSESSMENT OF SUPPORTS FOR EMERGENT BILINGUAL ACQUISITION DESIGN

Using this best evidence of effective supports for DLLs in preschool, we developed the CASEBA (Freedson et al., 2009). Although some existing observation instruments measure some aspects of support for DLLs, when development of CASEBA began there was no instrument with adequate psychometric properties that provided comprehensive information on supports for both home language and English acquisition. For example, the NIEER (2005) developed the Supports for English Language Learners Classroom Assessment (SELLCA) for use in the Two-Way Immersion study described previously (Barnett et al., 2007), and the SELLCA has been used extensively in classrooms in New Jersey to inform program improvements. However, the eight items in the SELLCA focus almost exclusively on promoting home language development. In addition, the Support for Early Literacy Assessment (SELA; Smith, Davidson, & Weisenfeld, 2001) includes two items that measure strategies to promote native language and second language acquisition, but no studies have investigated the instrument's psychometric properties. Several well-validated observation instruments assess the quality of classroom language interactions, but either these instruments do not focus on instructional supports for literacy specifically (e.g., the Classroom Assessment Scoring System™ [CLASS™; Pianta, La Paro, & Hamre, 2007] and the Early Childhood Environment Rating Scale–Revised [ECERS-R; Harms, Clifford, & Cryer, 1998]) or they do not examine supports for DLLs in both languages (e.g., the Early Language and Literacy Classroom Observation [ELLCO; Smith & Dickinson, 2002] and the Observation Measure of Language and Literacy Instruction [OMLIT; Abt Associates, Inc., 2006]), although versions of the ELLCO and OMLIT that will do so are also under development (see, for example, the ELLCO Addendum for English language learners [Castro, 2005] and Chapter 6 of this volume).

The CASEBA was designed to assess the degree to which preschool teachers and classrooms provide support for the social, cognitive, and linguistic development of DLLs, with a focus on supports for language and literacy development in both the home language and English. The instrument consists of 26 distinct rating scale items clustered around six broad aspects of the early childhood curriculum: 1) collection of child background information, 2) supports for home language development, 3) supports for English acquisition, 4) social–emotional supports and classroom climate, 5) curriculum content, and 6) child assessment. Each of the 26 items (see Table 7.1 on pages 242 and 243) measures one component of a high-quality classroom environment and instruction based on what the research literature suggests about effective language and emergent literacy supports for 3- to 5-year-old children who speak a language other than English at home and who are in the process of acquiring English as a second language. Each item is rated on a seven-point Likert scale, where a score of 7 (*strong*) indicates that a specific form of support and accompanying practices are present in close to an ideal form, and a score of 1 (*poor*) represents the total absence of any such practices.

The purpose of the current study was to determine if the CASEBA is reliable and valid. In this chapter, the instrument's construct validity and its relationship to another widely used measure of preschool classroom quality—the ECERS-R—is examined, and preliminary findings on classroom quality based on the application of the CASEBA in a sample of New Jersey's Abbott preschool classrooms are reported. The guiding research questions were as follows: 1) What are the distinct underlying constructs of quality in classroom supports for DLLs measured by the CASEBA? 2) What strengths and weaknesses vis-à-vis DLL support does CASEBA identify in New Jersey classrooms serving low-income children from Spanish home language backgrounds? 3) Do CASEBA scores correlate with scores on the ECERS-R?

Method

The study was conducted in New Jersey's state-funded Abbott preschool program, which mandates preschool access for all 3- and 4-year-olds in the state's 31 lowest income districts. All Abbott classrooms possess several structural features of high-quality preschool: a class size of no more than 15 with a teacher and an aide, lead teachers with bachelor's degrees and certification in early childhood education, and use of a district-selected, developmentally appropriate, state-approved curriculum model (Barnett et al., 2009). In 2008–2009, the Abbott program served 40,439 children who were 3 and 4 years old at an average per-pupil rate of $12,530 for a full school day per year.

Participants

Classroom observation data were collected from 100 classrooms in 17 school districts with large Spanish–bilingual populations in the late winter through early spring of 2009. Within each district, classrooms were selected from the total randomly selected classroom sample of the state-funded Abbott Preschool Program Longitudinal Effects Study II (APPLES II) (Frede, Jung, Barnett, & Figueras, 2009), which included both in-district and contracted provider sites (i.e., local Head Start and child care programs), based on whether there were children in the classroom who required testing in both English and Spanish at the time of fall child assessments. Thirty-one percent of the overall APPLES II child sample reported Spanish as the home language.

Measures

Each classroom was observed concurrently using the CASEBA and the ECERS-R (Harms et al., 1998). The CASEBA design has been described previously. The ECERS-R provides a global measure of preschool classroom quality with 43 items that cover a broad range of quality considerations, from safety and hygiene to classroom materials and teacher–child interactions. This measure has been used extensively in the field and has well-established validity and reliability (Snow & Van Hemel, 2008). The validity of the ECERS-R is supported by high correlations between both the scale items and ratings of items as highly important and between scale scores and ratings of classroom quality by a panel of nationally recognized experts (Clifford, Rossbach, & Reszka, 2010). Internal consistency as measured by Cronbach's alpha is reported to be adequate, ranging from .81 to .91. Classroom quality is rated on a seven-point Likert scale, indicating a range of quality from *inadequate* (1) to *excellent* (7). Six of the seven ECERS-R subscales were administered: Space and Furnishings, Personal

Care Routines, Language-Reasoning, Activities, Interaction, and Program Structure. Average subscale scores were calculated, as was a total scale score averaged across all 37 items administered.

Procedures

Highly trained bilingual assessors with degrees in either early childhood education, psychology, or the equivalent completed the observations in each classroom. Each observation lasted from arrival time in the morning until children began their nap—a period lasting from 3 to 4 hours—affording observers the opportunity to capture the instructional dynamics and conversations during routine parts of the day, such as morning circle, small-group time, independent play, lunch, and preparation for nap. Teachers were asked at the beginning of each observation to identify the DLL children in the classroom, including the linguistic and cultural background of each child, and to specify present staff members' roles and languages spoken. Teachers and assistants were also asked to rate the level of their own proficiency in the other languages that they reported speaking as *good*, *fair*, or *poor*.

Assessor Training and Reliability

Observers underwent a rigorous training process involving both formal classroom and field training. Each observer was held to a high standard of reliability requiring at least three visits with previously trained and reliable ECERS-R observers and with CASEBA authors who had themselves trained to reliability during the instrument's pilot phase. To continue assessing classrooms, observers had to achieve an 80% agreement level based on consensus scoring within one rating point over three consecutive observations. Every observer also complied with a reliability check after every 10 observations.

RESULTS

Presented next is a descriptive overview of sample classrooms that includes teachers' self-reported bilingual proficiency and average classroom scores on the 26 CASEBA items and ECERS-R subscales. We then present results of the confirmatory factor analysis (CFA) used to identify the underlying constructs of quality in classroom supports for DLLs measured by the CASEBA, followed by analysis of the strengths and weaknesses of sample classrooms based on the newly identified factor structure. The results section concludes with an examination of correlations between CASEBA and ECERS-R factors.

Teacher Language Proficiency

When surveyed, 61% of the sample classroom teachers reported speaking a language other than English; 36% rated their proficiency in that language as good, 16% reported proficiency as *fair*, and 9% reported their proficiency as poor. In addition 73.3% of the sample classroom assistant teachers reported that they spoke another language. The vast majority of both teachers and assistant teachers who reported speaking another language spoke Spanish.

Preliminary Analyses

Descriptive statistics were computed for each of the 26 items on the CASEBA as well as for the six ECERS-R subscales and two ECERS-R factors. Table 7.1 lists the descriptive information by item for the CASEBA. Item means (M) ranged from 1.44 to 6.03, with the lowest being Item 13, "Teaching staff support print-related early literacy skills in the home language" ($M =$ 1.44), and Item 7, "Lead teacher uses high-quality talk in the home language" ($M = 1.96$). The highest mean scores were obtained for Item 24, "Teaching staff foster a calm and respectful learning environment" ($M = 6.03$) and Item 21 "Books, print, and literacy props are available in English." Only one item related to home language support rose above the level of 3 (indicating minimal quality)—Item 12, "Books, print, and literacy props are available in the home language," with a mean of 3.11. The mean of all item scores on the CASEBA was 3.75, with a standard deviation (SD) of 0.69.

For comparison, Table 7.2 provides the means and ranges for subscales and factors on the ECERS-R. The ECERS-R subscale scores ranged from 4.48 on the Personal Hygiene subscale to 5.74 on the Interactions subscale, with Language and Reasoning also among the lowest of the subscale scores. A mean ECERS-R score of 5.01 ($SD = 0.81$) indicated the quality in sample classrooms to be *good* on average. Mean scores for sample classrooms on the ECERS-R factors identified by Cassidy, Hestenes, Hegde, Hestenes, and Mims (2005) were 5.29 for Activities/Materials and 4.95 for Language/Interactions.

Confirmatory Factor Analysis

To identify the underlying dimensions of classroom quality being measured by the CASEBA, a CFA was conducted. CFA is a theory-testing procedure that allows researchers to hypothesize the underlying constructs a given measurement tool likely measures and then to test the fit of this theorized structure to the collected data (Thomson, 2004). Initially, the presence of four factors was hypothesized: 1) Supports for English Acquisition, 2) Supports for Home Language, 3) Culturally Responsive Environment,

Table 7.1. Sample sizes, mean, standard deviation (SD), and ranges for Classroom Assessment of Supports for Emergent Bilingual Acquisition (CASEBA; Freedson, Figueras-Daniel, & Frede, 2009) observations by item (N = 100)

Items	n	Mean	SD	Minimum	Maximum
1. Teacher/center collects information on child language/culture	97	4.96	1.31	1.00	7.00
2. Lead teacher knows child language and culture	100	4.98	1.09	2.00	7.00
3. Culture of dual language learners incorporated into classroom life	100	4.12	1.06	2.00	6.00
4. Lead teacher uses home language for instruction	100	2.23	1.42	1.00	7.00
5. Assistant teacher uses home language for instruction	100	2.76	1.95	1.00	7.00
6. Teacher attempts to learn and use home language	77[a]	2.45	1.30	1.00	7.00
7. Lead teacher uses high-quality talk in home language	100	1.96	1.66	1.00	7.00
8. Assistant teacher uses high-quality talk in home language	99	2.63	1.83	1.00	6.00
9. Teaching staff support home language during group instruction	100	2.59	1.60	1.00	7.00
10. Teaching staff support home language in one-on-one interactions	98	2.72	1.39	1.00	6.00
11. Teaching staff use strategies to expand vocabulary in home language	100	2.11	1.44	1.00	6.00
12. Books, print, and literacy props are available in home language	100	3.11	0.98	1.00	6.00
13. Teaching staff support print-related literacy skills in home language	100	1.44	0.91	1.00	6.00
14. Teaching staff encourage parents to maintain home language	100	2.35	1.76	1.00	7.00
15. Lead teacher uses high-quality talk in English	100	4.79	1.65	1.00	7.00
16. Assistant teacher uses high-quality talk in English	100	3.34	1.93	1.00	6.00
17. Teaching staff scaffold comprehension of English	100	4.92	1.53	1.00	7.00
18. Teaching staff support communication in English during group instruction	100	4.37	1.28	1.00	7.00
19. Teaching staff support communication in English during one-on-one interactions	100	4.60	1.43	1.00	7.00

	n				
20. Teaching staff use strategies to expand vocabulary in English	100	4.28	1.35	1.00	7.00
21. Books, print, and literacy props are available in English	100	5.19	1.18	3.00	7.00
22. Teaching staff support print-related literacy skills in English	100	4.72	1.29	2.00	7.00
23. Teaching staff provide emotionally supportive environment for DLLs	67[b]	4.88	1.32	2.00	7.00
24. Teaching staff foster calm and respectful learning environment	99	6.03	1.12	3.00	7.00
25. Teaching staff create a content-rich curriculum	99	4.87	1.51	1.00	7.00
26. Teaching staff use assessment to identify strengths and needs in both languages	99	5.08	1.16	1.00	7.00
Overall score	100	3.75	0.69	1.76	5.79
Valid N (listwise)	100				

Note: [a]A smaller n on this item reflects the allowable use of a "nonapplicable" code for those classrooms in which the lead teacher reported that he or she speaks the language spoken by the majority of the ELLs in the class. Observers neglected to score some items or had clearly scored incorrectly for some items, thus, the n on certain items is slightly lower than 100.
[b]The low n on item 23 was attributed to observer error.

Table 7.2. Sample sizes, mean, standard deviation, and ranges for Early Childhood Environment Rating Scale–Revised (ECERS-R; Harms, Clifford, & Cryer, 1998) observations by subscale and factor

	n	Mean	Standard deviation	Minimum	Maximum
Space and furnishings	100	4.93	0.96	2.25	7.00
Personal care routines	100	4.48	1.29	1.33	7.00
Language and reasoning	100	4.63	1.14	2.00	6.75
Activities	100	4.73	0.95	2.10	6.90
Interactions	100	5.74	1.18	1.40	7.00
Program structure	100	5.50	0.99	2.00	7.00
Overall ECERS-R score	100	5.01	0.81	2.42	6.88
ECERS-R Factor 1: Activities/materials	100	5.29	0.95	1.55	6.91
ECERS-R Factor 2: Language/interactions	100	4.95	0.88	2.50	7.00
Valid N (listwise)	100				

Note: The six items related to the ECERS-R Parents and Staff subscale were not administered as part of this study because they rely almost entirely on teacher self-report.

and 4) Knowledge of Child Background. Items that assess print-related literacy practices were assumed to be language specific and were thus hypothesized to fall within either the Supports for English Acquisition or Supports for Home Language factors. Each CASEBA item was included in only one factor, with the exception of Item 25, "Teaching staff create a content-rich curriculum," which we suspected would contribute to both the English Acquisition and the Home Language factors. The items initially hypothesized within each factor are presented in Table 7.3.

A series of CFA models were fit, beginning with a four-factor solution. Based on the results of this first analysis, a revised four-factor solution was tested, followed by five- and six-factor solutions. The models were fit using Mplus 5.1 (Muthén & Muthén, 2006). The model allowed for correlated factors among all of the variables. Variances of the factors were fixed at 1, allowing the factor loadings to be interpreted as correlation coefficients between the measurement variables and the factors.

Standard measures of overall model fit are presented in Table 7.4. Fit for the four-factor model was adequate. However, three items—Item 16, "Assistant teacher uses high-quality talk in English," on the Supports for English Acquisition factor; Item 25, "Teaching staff create a content-rich curriculum," on the Supports for Home Language factor; and Item 26, "Teaching staff assess strengths and needs in both languages," on the Knowledge of Child Background factor—showed only weak relationships to the latent variables. These paths were removed from the model and it was

Table 7.3. Classroom Assessment of Supports for Emergent Bilingual Acquisition (CASEBA; Freedson, Figueras-Daniel, & Frede, 2009) items in hypothesized four-factor solution

CASEBA items	Supports for English Acquisition	Supports for Home Language	Culturally Responsive Environment	Knowledge of Child Background
1. Teacher/center collects information on child language/culture				X
2. Teacher knows child language and culture				X
3. Culture of dual language learners (DDL) incorporated into classroom life			X	
4. Lead teacher uses home language for instruction		X		
5. Assistant teacher uses home language for instruction		X		
6. Teacher attempts to learn and use home language		X		
7. Lead teacher uses high-quality talk in home language		X		
8. Assistant teacher uses high-quality talk in home language		X		
9. Teaching staff support home language during group instruction		X		
10. Teaching staff support home language in one-on-one interactions		X		
11. Teaching staff use strategies to expand vocabulary in home language		X		
12. Books, print, and literacy props are available in home language		X		
13. Teaching staff support print-related literacy skills in home language		X		
14. Teaching staff encourage parents to maintain home language		X		
15. Lead teacher uses high-quality talk in English	X			
16. Assistant teacher uses high-quality talk in English	X			
17. Teaching staff scaffold comprehension of English	X			
18. Teaching staff support communication in English during group instruction	X			
19. Teaching staff support communication in English during one-on-one interactions	X			
20. Teaching staff use strategies to expand vocabulary in English	X			
21. Books, print, and literacy props are available in English	X			
22. Teaching staff support print-related literacy skills in English				
23. Teaching staff provide emotionally supportive environment for DLLs			X	
24. Teaching staff foster calm and respectful learning environment			X	
25. Teaching staff creates a content-rich curriculum	X	X		
26. Teaching staff assess strengths and needs in both languages				X

Table 7.4. Measures of fit for four-factor, four-factor reduced, five-factor, and ending six-factor models

Measures-of-fit information	Four-factor model	Four-factor model (reduced)	Five-factor model	Six-factor model
Number of items	26	24	24	24
Chi-square value[a] (*df*)	471.40 (246)	426.81 (245)	386.74 (245)	393.20 (240)
Ratio of chi-square/*df*	1.92	1.74	1.58	1.64
RMSEA	0.09	0.09	.08	.08
Comparative Fit Index (CFI)	0.81	0.83	.87	.86

[a]All chi-square $p < .001$.

Key: df, degrees of freedom; RMSEA, root mean square error of approximation.

refit. Although this adjustment did not have an appreciable impact on the overall fit, it did result in some notable changes in the magnitude of some of the factor loadings (see Table 7.5). With regard to the Supports for English Acquisition factor, the weights on Items 17, 22, and 25 decreased notably, and the weight for Item 21 increased. The loadings for two of the Culturally Responsive Environment items changed, with 23 decreasing and 24 increasing. These changes indicated possible model misspecification, including the possibility of additional factors.

Upon review of the measurement variables, we speculated on the possible presence of a new factor, Supports for English Print Literacy. We tested a new five-factor solution that included this factor, as measured by Item 21, "Books, print, and literacy props are available in English," and Item 22, "Teaching staff support print-related literacy skills in English," which resulted in some evidence of improvement in model fit. Factor loadings for the final five-factor model are presented in Table 7.6. The improved overall goodness of fit, combined with the strong factor loadings on the new factor, supported the addition. Note also that the Supports for English Acquisition factor was improved by this change. Most of the loading remained about the same, but the loading for Item 17 increased dramatically. We assert that the removal of Items 21 and 22 stabilized the estimation of this factor.

Next, we attempted a six-factor solution, adding Supports for Home Language Print Literacy to the model, with parallel items 12, "Books, print, and literacy props are available in home language," and 13, "Teaching staff support print-related literacy skills in home language," removed from the Supports for Home Language factor as the measurement variables. This change was not supported by tests of model fit, which actually decreased slightly. As such, this specification was rejected and the five-factor solution was retained.

Table 7.5. Factor loadings for four-factor and four-factor reduced models

	Four-factor				Four-factor reduced			
	Supports for English Acquisition	Supports for Home Language	Culturally Responsive Environment	Knowledge of Child Background	Supports for English Acquisition	Supports for Home Language	Culturally Responsive Environment	Knowledge of Child Background
Item 1				0.72 (0.04)				0.73 (0.04)
Item 2				0.54 (0.11)				0.54 (0.11)
Item 3			0.74 (0.03)				0.73 (0.03)	
Item 4		0.83 (0.04)				0.83 (0.04)		
Item 5		0.77 (0.05)				0.76 (0.05)		
Item 6		0.69 (0.08)				0.69 (0.08)		
Item 7		0.69 (0.06)				0.69 (0.06)		
Item 8		0.59 (0.08)				0.59 (0.08)		
Item 9		0.82 (0.04)				0.82 (0.04)		
Item 10		0.89 (0.03)				0.89 (0.03)		
Item 11		0.82 (0.04)				0.82 (0.04)		
Item 12		0.64 (0.07)				0.64 (0.07)		
Item 13		0.59 (0.08)				0.59 (0.08)		
Item 14		0.37 (0.10)				0.37 (0.10)		
Item 15	0.58 (0.03)				0.58 (0.03)			
Item 16	0.10 (0.12)							
Item 17	0.84 (0.04)				0.17 (0.11)			
Item 18	0.80 (0.04)				0.83 (0.04)			
Item 19	0.74 (0.05)				0.80 (0.05)			
Item 20	0.89 (0.03)				0.77 (0.05)			
Item 21	0.31 (0.11)				0.89 (0.03)			
Item 22	0.54 (0.08)				0.32 (0.11)			
Item 23			0.83 (0.07)				0.51 (0.10)	
Item 24			0.54 (0.10)				0.78 (0.07)	
Item 25	0.67 (0.08)	−0.10 (0.10)			0.41 (0.10)			
Item 26				0.14 (0.13)				

247

Table 7.6. Factor loadings for final five-factor model

	Supports for English Acquisition	Supports for English Print Literacy	Supports for Home Language	Culturally Responsive Environment	Knowledge of Child Background
Item 1					0.74 (0.04)
Item 2					0.49 (0.10)
Item 3				0.74 (0.03)	
Item 4			0.76 (0.03)		
Item 5			0.73 (0.05)		
Item 6			0.65 (0.08)		
Item 7			0.61 (0.06)		
Item 8			0.56 (0.07)		
Item 9			0.80 (0.04)		
Item 10			0.87 (0.03)		
Item 11			0.70 (0.04)		
Item 12			0.60 (0.07)		
Item 13			0.56 (0.07)		
Item 14			0.34 (0.10)		
Item 15	0.58 (0.03)				
Item 17	0.83 (0.04)				
Item 18	0.81 (0.04)				
Item 19	0.75 (0.05)				
Item 20	0.91 (0.03)				
Item 21		0.70 (0.03)			
Item 22		0.82 (0.07)			
Item 23				0.80 (0.08)	
Item 24				0.58 (0.10)	
Item 25	0.64 (0.07)				

Factor Correlations

Correlations between the five-factor-based scales are presented in Table 7.7. The analysis revealed moderate to strong relationships among all scales with the exception of the correlation between Supports for English Print Literacy and Knowledge of Child Background, which was quite low ($r = .12$). The Supports for English Acquisition and Supports for English Print Literacy scales were strongly correlated ($r = .72$), as would be expected, whereas the two English language support scales were only minimally associated with Supports for Home Language (.34 and .25, respectively).

Table 7.7. Correlations between the five Classroom Assessment of Supports for Emergent Bilingual Acquisition (CASEBA; Freedson, Figueras-Daniel, & Frede, 2009) factors ($N = 100$)

	Supports for English Acquisition	Supports for English Print Literacy	Supports for Home Language	Culturally Responsive Environment	Knowledge of Child Background
Supports for English Acquisition	1.00				
Supports for English Print Literacy	.72	1.00			
Supports for Home Language	.34	.25	1.00		
Culturally Responsive Environment	.78	.74	.66	1.00	
Knowledge of Child Background	.66	.12	.39	.52	1.00

Key: SD, standard deviation.

Table 7.8.   Rescaled mean factor scores for sample classrooms ($N = 100$)

Factors	Mean (SD)
Supports for English Acquisition	4.79 (1.34)
Supports for English Print Literacy	5.16 (0.81)
Supports for Home Language	2.23 (1.56)
Culturally Responsive Environment	4.12 (0.48)
Knowledge of Child Background	4.95 (1.02)

Key: SD, standard deviation; N, Sample size.

Descriptive Statistics for Factors

The metric of factor scores is arbitrary, and they are typically estimated with a mean of zero. As noted previously, factor variances were fixed to 1. To gain insight about the location of this sample on the factors, the factor scores were rescaled. First, the five-factor model was rerun with the factor loadings for the first item of each factor fixed to 1, setting the scale for the latent variables. These factor scores were exported for analysis. Next, the factors were rescaled to have the same mean and standard deviations as their scaling measurement variable. Results of this analysis are presented in Table 7.8. On average, sample classrooms scored highest on Supports for English Print Literacy ($M = 5.16$, $SD = 0.81$) and Knowledge of Child Background ($M = 4.95$, $SD = 1.02$). They scored lowest by far on Supports for Home Language ($M = 2.23$, $SD = 1.56$).

Relationship Between Classroom Assessment of Supports for Emergent Bilingual Acquisition and Early Childhood Environment Rating Scale–Revised Factors

One of the most common means of establishing concurrent validity is to examine the correlations of scores on the new measure with scores obtained using a previously validated instrument that was designed to measure the same construct (Clifford et al., 2010). Although the CASEBA was designed with a narrower focus than the ECERS-R, as the most widely used and extensively researched measure of preschool classroom quality, and given the fact that no other instruments with the same focus as the CASEBA have established validity, the ECERS-R was the obvious choice for this purpose, and it afforded the opportunity to examine the structure of the relationships among factors with similar conceptual intent across instruments.

Correlations between the five CASEBA factors and the two ECERS-R factors identified by Cassidy et al. (2005) are presented in Table 7.9. Correlations ranged from moderate to strong; the strongest relationship was found between the CASEBA's Culturally Responsive Environment factor and the ECERS-R Activities and Materials factor ($r = .70$). The weakest

Table 7.9. Correlations between CASEBA and ECERS-R factors

CASEBA factors	ECERS-R factors	
	Activities/ materials	Language/ interactions
Supports for English Acquisition	.63	.60
Supports for English Print Literacy	.57	.54
Supports for Home Language	.44	.29
Culturally Responsive Environment	.70	.56
Teacher Knowledge of Child Background	.44	.42

Key: CASEBA, Classroom Assessment of Supports for Emergent Bilingual Acquisition (Freedson, Figueras-Daniel, & Frede, 2009); ECERS-R, Early Childhood Environment Rating Scale–Revised (Harms, Clifford, & Cryer, 1998).

association was found between the CASEBA's Supports for Home Language factor, and the ECERS-R Language/Interactions factor ($r = .29$). The only moderate associations between some of the CASEBA and ECERS-R factors may be viewed as evidence of CASEBA's ability to capture important variation in instructional quality that is not captured by ECERS-R.

DISCUSSION

Results of this study suggest that the CASEBA is a promising new measure of classroom quality for preschool DLLs, one that can be used to assess several key dimensions of classroom support for a rapidly growing population of young bilingual children whose needs must be considered as part of any more general assessment of preschool program quality. The instrument can be administered reliably, shows good construct validity, and has acceptable concurrent validity with the ECERS-R when factor scores are used as the basis of analysis.

Results of the confirmatory factor analysis indicate that the CASEBA measures five related but distinct dimensions in the quality of classroom supports for DLLs: 1) Supports for English Acquisition, 2) Supports for English Print Literacy, 3) Supports for Home Language, 4) Culturally Responsive Environment, and 5) Knowledge of Child Background. The Supports for English Acquisition factor includes Items 15–20, which collectively measure teachers' use of strategies to scaffold acquisition of oral English as a second language, as well as the lead teacher's use of lexically rich and grammatically correct English-language instructional talk. Of note, Item 16, measuring the quality of paraprofessionals' English-language classroom talk, did not load on this or any other factor and thus was dropped from the analysis. This finding may reflect the relatively low quality of English spoken in sample classrooms by paraprofessionals, who are typically less educated and far more likely to speak English as a second language themselves than the lead teacher, and whose contribution to the overall quality of supports for English language acquisition may therefore be relatively limited. Also notable was the contribution of an item assessing the content richness of the enacted classroom curriculum to the Supports for English Acquisition factor, suggesting that teachers are either more likely or better able to foster second language acquisition when their daily activities are organized around exploration of rich and meaningful content. Calls for a stronger curricular emphasis on building content knowledge at both the preschool (Neuman, Roskos, Wright, & Lenhart, 2007) and elementary (Hirsh, 2003) levels figure prominently in recent proposals to help narrow the language disparities that contribute significantly to the achievement gap.

Two items we expected to find included in the Supports for English Acquisition factor were shown instead to perform best in a separate factor identified as Supports for English Print Literacy. Examination of the specific indicators for Items 21 and 22 reveals that unlike Items 15–20, which focus primarily on teachers' English language verbalizations and interactions with children, these two items measure the presence of books and functional print in the environment, alphabet and print concepts instruction, and children's literacy products. One can easily imagine a preschool classroom rich in meaningful labels, books, and developmental writing supports in English, in which teachers nonetheless have relatively few well-scaffolded or extended language interactions with children. Such a scenario is all the more likely in classrooms in which teachers are familiar with the expectation for visible literacy supports dictated by the ECERS-R and the SELA—both used widely for accountability purposes in New Jersey's Abbott preschool program—but are not sufficiently trained to provide rich language experiences for all children. In fact, rescaled mean scores showed classrooms in this sample to perform better, on average, on Supports for English Print Literacy than on Supports for English Acquisition—the latter score of 4.79 indicating less than *good* quality on this critically important dimension of DLL support.

The Supports for Home Language factor consists of 11 items measuring various teaching practices and features of the classroom environment that foster children's home language development in both oral and written forms. The factor includes items that measure both the quantity and quality of native language support and separately assesses the practices of the teacher and paraprofessional. Of relevance for programs and policies that recognize the merit of a truly bilingual approach in preschool, the analysis revealed that the Supports for Home Language factor captures a dimension of classroom quality largely distinct from any supports for English that teachers may provide, as indicated by the low correlations between these factors. A classroom could, in theory, receive a moderate to high rating on both the Supports for English Acquisition and Supports for English Print Literacy factors by providing well-scaffolded, language- and literacy-rich learning experiences in English but nonetheless provide very limited native language support. This was the case in the Abbott preschool classrooms in the sample, which showed moderate to good quality support for English language and literacy development on average—rescaled mean scores were 4.79 and 5.16 on the English Acquisition and English Print Literacy factors, respectively—but a mean score of only 2.23 on Supports for Home Language. Given the known contributions of both native and English language proficiencies to bilingual children's long-term English reading outcomes (Espinosa, 2010; Reese et al., 2000; Rinaldi & Paez, 2006, 2008), this finding is troubling though not unexpected. Native language support remains the domain of bilingual paraprofessionals rather than fully certified lead teachers in most Abbott preschool classrooms, so there is often little relationship between the types and quality of support provided in English and Spanish. Furthermore, numerous factors may prevent even teaching staff who self-report as proficient speakers of Spanish from adequately supporting children's home language, including lack of training in bilingual development and teaching methods, lack of clear district and state language policies, ambivalence about the value of native language maintenance, and limited academic language proficiency in Spanish (Freedson, 2010).

Examination of specific item means provided further insight into particular areas of strength and need within New Jersey's Abbott classrooms. Classrooms obtained the highest scores on Item 24, "Teaching staff foster a calm and respectful learning environment" ($M = 6.03$), suggesting a general order and calm that is certainly a necessary precondition to all learning but may be especially important for children who must be able to hear and make sense of teacher and peer language input in a second language. Encouragingly, classrooms also scored highly on Item 21, "Books, print, and literacy props are available in English" ($M = 5.19$). The presence of book- and print-rich environments in Abbott classrooms is not accidental but rather the result of years of statewide emphasis on literacy enhancements, supported by the systematic use of the SELA as both a program evaluation and professional development tool. It must be noted, however, that classrooms were not equally rich in books and print in Spanish, as indicated by a mean score of just 3.11 on Item 12.

In fact, the 10 lowest mean item scores were all part of the Supports for Home Language factor, the very lowest being Item 13, "Teaching staff support print-related early literacy skills in the home language" ($M = 1.44$); Item 7, "Lead teacher uses high-quality talk in the home language" ($M = 1.96$); and Item 11, "Teaching staff use strategies to expand vocabulary in the home language." Many CASEBA items—these lowest-scoring items among them—include indicators that necessitate teachers' use of extended discourse in children's home language, making it nearly impossible for classrooms with lead or assistant teachers who did not speak Spanish to obtain high scores. However, the lack of support for print-related literacy skills in Spanish, even where staff speak the language, may also reflect a classic diglossia whereby speakers use the minority language to support communication in certain circumstances but reserve English for the privileged sociolinguistic role as the medium of literacy instruction.

Perhaps the greatest reflection of the prevailing negative attitudes toward Spanish in sample classrooms was the mean score on Item 6, "Teaching staff attempt to learn and use the home language." A high score on this item requires only that teachers who do not speak the language show some interest in learning it or otherwise demonstrate the valuing they assign the language as children's first and most culturally significant resource. It is, in essence, a measure of teacher dispositions rather than language proficiencies. The sample mean on this item was just 2.45, falling between the rating categories of *minimal* and *poor*. Clearly, far better preservice and in-service training of preschool teachers will be required before even adequate classroom supports for children's home language development are found.

Of final note regarding the factor structure of the instrument, none of the five underlying factors was strongly correlated with an overall CASEBA score, nor did analyses exploring the possibility of a single overall factor bear fruit. This finding suggests that for the purpose of assessing the quality of DLL supports and guiding interventions to improve preschool classroom quality, individual factor scores are likely to be of greater conceptual value than an overall CASEBA score, although an overall score will facilitate comparison across classrooms and programs and allow for tracking general program improvement over time.

New Jersey's Abbott program ranks as one of the highest quality state preschool programs in the nation (Barnett et al., 2009). The program is well funded and accessible to both 3- and 4-year-old children. Large-scale evaluations of the program have shown incremental improvements each year over the last 8 years in general classroom quality—average scores on the ECERS-R increased from 3.9 in 2000 to 5.2 in 2008 (Frede, Jung, Barnett, & Figueras, 2009)—as well as in the quality of the classroom language and literacy environment and practices as measured by the SELA, which rose from an initial statewide score that showed mediocre support to the average classroom scoring very close to *good*. These substantial increases in classroom quality are in part due to the implementation of a continuous improvement cycle that uses classroom observation and other data to inform program improvement at the classroom, program, and state level (Frede & Barnett, in press; Frede, Gilliam, & Schweinhart, in press).

The CASEBA, with its targeted and nuanced examination of instructional supports for DLLs, has enhanced our understanding of how this generally high-quality program may or may not address the needs of the nearly 30% of the state's 3- and 4-year-old preschoolers whose home language is not English. For the purposes of ongoing program evaluation and improvement that is central to the Abbott preschool program mission, the information gathered by the CASEBA should prove invaluable to improving services for DLLs and help guide the state's early childhood teacher preparation and professional development initiatives in the coming years.

The findings reported in this chapter represent only the first stage of our work on the psychometric properties of the CASEBA. Forthcoming reports on the instrument's predictive validity will draw on beginning and end-of-year child assessment data collected as part of the APPLES II evaluation study, including measures of children's language and emergent literacy and math skills in both English and Spanish. These analyses will establish if and how the various dimensions of classroom quality captured by CASEBA contribute to child learning across developmental domains and languages. NIEER is also currently beginning the second year of a 2-year research study in a large urban New Jersey school district that uses CASEBA to examine variation in preschool classroom quality and to enhance classroom supports for DLLs through ongoing professional development. This research will allow us to reexamine the CASEBA's factor structure and to investigate the instruments' predictive validity over the entire 2-year period that children typically attend New Jersey's Abbott program.

REFERENCES

Abt Associates, Inc. (2006). *Observation training manual: OMLIT early childhood.* Cambridge, MA: Author.

August, D., Carlo, M., Dressler, C., & Snow, C. (2005). The critical role of vocabulary development for English language learners. *Learning Disabilities Research & Practice, 20*(1), 50–57.

August, D., & Shanahan, T. (Eds.). (2008). *Developing reading and writing in second language learners.* New York: Routledge

Barnett, W.S. (2008). *Preschool education and its lasting effects: Research and policy implications.* Boulder, CO, and Tempe, AZ: Education and Public Interest Center & Education Policy Research Unit. Retrieved December 20, 2010, from http://epicpolicy.org/publication/preschool-education.

Barnett, W.S., Epstein, D., Freidman, A., Sansanelli, R., & Hustedt, J. (2009). *The state of preschool 2009.* New Brunswick, NJ: National Institute for Early Education Research.

Barnett, W.S., Yarosz, D.J., Thomas, J., & Blanco, D. (2007). Two-way and monolingual English immersion in preschool education: An experimental comparison. *Early Childhood Research Quarterly, 22,* 277–293.

Bernhard, J., Cummins, J., Campoy, F., Ada, A.F., Winsler, A., & Bleiker, C. (2006). Identity texts and literacy development among preschool English language learners: Enhancing learning opportunities for children at risk for learning disabilities. *Teachers College Record, 108*(11), 2380–2405.

Cassidy, D., Hestenes, L., Hedge, A., Hestenes, S., & Mims, S. (2005). Measurement of quality in preschool child care classrooms: The Early Childhood Environment Rating Scale–Revised and its psychometric properties. *Early Childhood Research Quarterly, 20*(3), 345–360.

Castro, D.C. (2005). *Early language and literacy classroom observation. Addendum for English language learners.* Chapel Hill: The University of North Carolina, FGP Child Development Institute.

Chang, F., Crawford, G., Early, D., Bryant, D., Howes, C., Burchinal, M., et al. (2007). Spanish-speaking children's social and language development in pre-kindergarten classrooms. *Early Education and Development, 18*(2), 243–269.

Clifford, R.M., Rossbach, H.-G., Reszka, S.S. (2009, May). *Reliability and validity of the ECERS-R: An update* (Conference proceedings). ECERS International Workgroup Meeting, Porto, Portugal.

Collins, M. (2005). ESL preschoolers' English vocabulary acquisition from story-book reading. *Reading Research Quarterly, 40*(4), 406–408.

Deming, D. (2009). Early childhood intervention and life-cycle skill development: Evidence from Head Start, *American Economics Journal of Applied Economics, 1*(3), 111–134.

Dickinson, D., & Sprague, K. (2001). The nature and impact of early childhood care environments on the language and early literacy development of children from low-income families. In S. Neuman & D. Dickinson (Eds.), *Handbook of early literacy research* (pp. 263–280). New York: Guilford Press.

Dickinson, D.K., & Tabors, P.O. (Eds.). (2001). *Beginning literacy with language: Young children learning at home and at school.* Baltimore: Paul H. Brookes Publishing Co.

Durgunoglu, A., & Oney, B. (2000). *Literacy development in two languages: Cognitive and sociocultural dimensions of cross-language transfer.* Paper presented at the Research Symposium on High Standards in Reading for Students from Diverse Language Groups: Research, Practice & Policy, April 19–20, 2000. Washington, DC: U.S. Department of Education.

Espinosa, L. (2010). Classroom teaching and instruction "best practices" for young English language learners. In E. Garcia & E. Frede (Eds.), *Young English language learners* (pp. 143–164). New York: Teachers College Press.

Farver, J.M., Lonigan, C.J., & Eppe, S. (2009). Effective early literacy skill development for young Spanish-speaking English language learners: An experimental study of two methods. *Child Development, 80*(3), 703–719.

Frede, E., & Barnett, W.S. (in press). New Jersey's Abbott Pre-K program: A model for the nation. In E. Zigler, W. Gilliam, & W.S. Barnett (Eds.), *Current debates and issues in prekindergarten education.* Baltimore: Paul H. Brookes Publishing Co.

Frede, E., & Garcia, E. (2010). *Young English language learners.* New York: Teachers College Press.

Frede, E., Gilliam, W., & Schweinhart, L. (in press). Assessing accountability and ensuring continuous program improvement: Why, how, and who. In E. Zigler, W. Gilliam, & W.S. Barnett (Eds.), *Current debates and issues in prekindergarten education.* Baltimore: Paul H. Brookes Publishing Co.

Frede, E., Jung, K., Barnett, S. & Figueras, A. (2009). The APPLES blossom: Abbott preschool program longitudinal effects study. New Brunswick, NJ: National Institute for Early Education Research.

Frede, E., Jung, K., Barnett, W.S., Lamy, C.E., & Figueras, A. (2007). *The Abbott preschool program longitudinal effects study: Interim report.* New Brunswick, NJ: National Institute for Early Education Research.

Freedson, M. (2005). *Language of instruction and literacy talk in bilingual and English immersion prekindergarten classrooms: Contributions to the early literacy development of Spanish-speaking children.* Unpublished doctoral dissertation. Harvard Graduate School of Education.

Freedson, M. (2008). Supports for dual language vocabulary development in bilingual and English immersion prekindergarten classrooms. *Journal of School Connections, 1*(1), 25–63.

Freedson, M. (2010). Educating preschool teachers to support English language learners. In E. Garcia & E. Frede (Eds.), *Young English language learners* (pp. 165–183). New York: Teachers College Press.

Freedson, M., Figueras-Daniel, A., & Frede, E. (2009). *The Classroom Assessment of Supports for Emergent Bilingual Acquisition.* New Brunswick, NJ: National Institute for Early Education Research.

Galindo, C. (2010). English language learners' math and reading trajectories in the elementary grades. In E. Garcia & E. Frede (Eds.), *Young English language learners* (pp. 42–58). New York: Teachers College Press.

Genesee, F. (2010). Dual language development in preschool children. In E. Garcia & E. Frede (Eds.), *Young English language learners* (pp. 59–79). New York: Teachers College Press.

Gormley, W. (2007, August 31). *The effects of Oklahoma's pre-K program on Hispanic children.* Paper presented at the annual meeting of the American Political Science Association, Chicago. Retrieved October 9, 2009, from http://www.crocus.georgetown.edu/reports/CROCUSworkingpaper11.pdf.

Gormley, W.T., Gayer, T., Phillips, D., & Dawson, B. (2005). The effects of universal pre-K on cognitive development. *Developmental Psychology, 41*(6), 867–884.

Hammer, C.S., Davison, M.D., Lawrence, F.R., & Miccio, A.W. (2009). The effect of home language on bilingual children's vocabulary and emergent literacy development during Head Start and kindergarten. *Scientific Studies of Reading* [Special issue], *13*(2), 99–121.

Harms, T., Clifford, R.M., & Cryer, D. (1998). *Early Childhood Environment Rating Scale–Revised.* New York: Teachers College Press.

Hernandez, D. (2010). A demographic portrait of young English language learners. In E. Garcia & E. Frede (Eds.), *Young English language learners* (pp. 10–41). New York: Teachers College Press.

Hirsh, E. (2003, Spring). Reading comprehension requires knowledge—of words and of the world. *American Educator*, 10–30.

Lopez, L., & Greenfield, D. (2004). Cross-language transfer of phonological skills of Hispanic Head Start children. *Bilingual Research Journal, 28*(1), 1–18.

Muthén, L.K., & Muthén, B.O. (2006). *Mplus*, Los Angeles: Author.

National Early Literacy Panel. (2007). *Findings from the National Early Literacy Panel.* Paper presented at the annual National Conference on Family Literacy, Orlando, Florida.

Neuman, S., Roskos, K., Wright, T., & Lenhart, L. (2007). *Nurturing knowledge.* New York: Scholastic.

National Institute for Early Education Research. (2005). *Support for English Language Learners Classroom Assessment.* New Brunswick, NJ: Author.

Pianta, R., La Paro, K., & Hamre, B. (2008). *Classroom Scoring Assessment System^{TM} (CLASS^{TM}): K–3.* Baltimore: Paul H. Brookes Publishing Co.

Rinaldi, C., & Paez., M. (2006). Predicting English word reading skills for Spanish-speaking students in first grade. *Topics in Language Disorders, 26*(4), 338–350.

Rinaldi, C., & Paez, M. (2008). Preschool matters: Predicting reading difficulties for Spanish-speaking bilingual students in first grade. *Learning Disabilities: A Contemporary Journal, 6*(1), 71–86.

Reese, L., Garnier, H., Gallimore, R., & Goldenberg, C. (2000). Longitudinal analysis of the antecedents of emergent Spanish literacy and middle-school English reading achievement of Spanish-speaking students. *American Educational Research Journal, 37*(3), 633–662.

Roberts, T. (2008). Home storybook reading in primary or secondary language with preschool children: Evidence of equal effectiveness for second-language vocabulary acquisition. *Reading Research Quarterly, 43*(2), 103–130.

Roberts, T., & Neal, H. (2004). Relationships among preschool English language learner's oral proficiency in English, instructional experiences and literacy development. *Contemporary Educational Psychology, 29*, 283–311.

Smith, Davidson, & Weisenfeld. (2001). *Supports for Early Literacy Assessment (SELA).* Unpublished instrument.

Smith, M.W., & Dickinson, D.K. (2002). *Early Language and Literacy Classroom Observation (ELLCO) Toolkit.* Baltimore: Paul H. Brookes Publishing Co.

Snow, C., Burns, S., & Griffin, P. (1998). *Preventing reading difficulties in young children.* Washington, DC: National Academies Press.

Snow, C., & Van Hemel, S. (2008). *Early childhood assessment: Why, what and how.* Washington, DC: National Academies Press.

Tabors, P.O. (1997). *One child, two languages: A guide for preschool educators of children learning English as a second language.* Baltimore: Paul H. Brookes Publishing Co.

Thomson, B. (2004). *Exploratory and confirmatory factor analysis: Understanding concepts and applications.* Washington, DC: American Psychological Association.

Early Childhood Classrooms Serving English/Spanish Dual Language Learning Children

An Afterword

Carollee Howes

There are increasing numbers of very young children whose home language is not English in early childhood education (ECE) classrooms. These children, called dual language learners (DLLs), are particularly interesting for researchers because they are simultaneously developing spoken and written language in at least two language systems. Theories of how children develop language and how language development is tied to literacy development are challenged and enriched by understanding the experiences of DLL children. Accepted notions of effective classroom practice in ECE are also challenged and enriched as a greater percentage of the children that arrive in ECE classrooms are DLL. Furthermore, in some parts of the country (e.g., California, Texas) many classrooms are predominantly filled with DLL children, whereas in other parts (e.g., North Carolina, Pennsylvania) only a few children are DLL. This variation raises another set of questions about how best to organize a classroom to serve all of the children, DLLs and single language learners, well.

Note: The research reported here was supported by the Institute of Education Sciences, U.S. Department of Education, through Grant R305A060021 to the University of Virginia. The opinions expressed are those of the author and do not represent views of the U.S. Department of Education.

The largest proportion of DLL children currently enrolled in ECE classrooms are children whose home language is Spanish (see the Introduction to this volume). Not only is this the largest group of DLL children, but the convergence of poverty, lack of documentation, and relatively poorly educated mothers from impoverished rural areas of Mexico and Central America as well as the ideological debate in the United States over immigration require a sophisticated multidimensional research approach toward examining practices within classrooms serving Spanish–English DLL children. For these reasons, the majority of the chapters in this book have focused on Spanish–English DLL children.

Domains of influence on variations in ECE classroom experiences of Spanish–English DLL children include the home cultural community of the children, the language competence of the individual child, the characteristics of the teacher, the characteristics of the classroom, and the institutional practices of the system or systems. The ECE classroom may be a feeder school for a school district or within a school district. For example, Head Start classrooms feed into kindergartens within a school district. Policies around classification of children as English speakers and the languages used in the Head Start and school district classrooms may or may not be compatible. In other cases, the ECE classroom is within a school district.

The chapters in this book have provided some insights into the influences of variation within each of these domains and interactions between domains on DLL children's experiences in ECE classrooms. As well, the research reported in this book suggests future directions in terms of research and evaluation of interventions into processes within ECE classrooms that enhance the experiences of DLL children, particularly Spanish–English DLL children.

VARIATIONS WITHIN HOME CULTURAL COMMUNITIES AND BETWEEN SCHOOL AND HOME CULTURAL COMMUNITIES

Perhaps because home language and ethnicity are such salient identifiers of Spanish–English DLL children, it is easy for researchers and practitioners to consider these children as belonging to one category. However, as pointed out by Garcia in the Introduction to this volume, variations within Spanish–English DLL children are extensive. A useful construct for understanding these variations and their contributions to children's experiences is the cultural community. Rather than simply ethnicity or home language, participants in a cultural community share goals, beliefs, and everyday practices (Rogoff, 2003). Within the grouping of Spanish-speaking Latino families there are numerous cultural communities that differ in their relations with their heritage country and their host country, in social networks, in beliefs about children's schooling, and in language practices within the home (Howes, Wishard Guerra, & Zucker, 2007). All children experience the practices within a family cultural community. ECE classrooms construct their own cultural communities with goals, beliefs, and practices about how children learn (Howes, 2010). Practices within the ECE classroom cultural community may be similar to practices within the family or very different. The authors have highlighted several practices relevant to classroom practices that vary within Latino Spanish-speaking families. These include practices of what language to use in what cultural community, variations in parental English proficiency, types of talk within home and classroom cultural communities, variations in poverty and parental education, and variations in parental experiences with, beliefs about, and hopes for school.

PRACTICES OF WHAT LANGUAGE TO USE IN WHAT CULTURAL COMMUNITY

Garcia reminds us in the Introduction that practices vary widely within Latino families who speak Spanish. Parents may insist that children speak Spanish within the home and encourage the use of formal English outside of the home, encourage children to speak English as part of a belief system that privileges English as the American language, or only speak Spanish. These variations mean that Spanish–English DLL children come into ECE classrooms with varying degrees of comfort and competence in using either English or Spanish.

VARIATIONS IN PARENTAL ENGLISH PROFICIENCY

Within Latino families, parents themselves have varying relations with the English language, from no English to using English outside the home while preserving Spanish within the home. In Jung et al.'s work (Chapter 4) all of the parents were non-English speakers enrolled in English as a second language (ESL) classes. Children were enrolled in ECE classrooms associated with the adult classes. A goal of both the adult and the ECE program was to teach the English language. Not surprising, the children in this study entered the ECE classrooms with almost no English proficiency. A point of interest is that, the Latina teachers in this program reported more conflict in their relationships with these children than did the non-Latino teachers. Children's literacy engagement within the program had a less positive impact on them when the quality of teacher–child relationships wasmore conflicted, perhaps indicating a lack of match between teacher and children's experiences with and expectations for English language learning. This highlights the need for including information on home language practices as part of professional development for ECE teachers.

TYPES OF TALK WITHIN HOME AND CLASSROOM CULTURAL COMMUNITIES

Language experiences within all families' homes vary in practices regarding the type of talk in the home. Family talk can include conversation and story-telling or simply social directions, and these variations influence children's familiarity and comfort with literacy activities in ECE classrooms (see the Introduction to this volume). DLL children in ECE classrooms may have to learn language practices that are different from those at home as well as learning a new language (see Chapter 1).

VARIATION IN POVERTY AND PARENT EDUCATION

Some of these family language practices may vary more by parental edu-cation or poverty level than by ethnic heritage. Although some of the par-ents of English–Spanish DLL children in classrooms may have gone to school in the United States, a significant number were schooled within the rural Mexican school system. These variations in parental experiences with school and beliefs about school influence family language practices, which in turn influence the children's expectations and beliefs about school (see the Introduction to this volume).

PARENTAL EXPERIENCES WITH, BELIEFS ABOUT, AND HOPES FOR SCHOOL

Parental experiences and beliefs about school as well as their hopes for their children as they enter American schools may also influence children's behav-iors and approaches to learning in ECE classrooms (see the Introduction to this volume). This is particularly true for the children of immigrant families, where hopes for a new life are often centered on education. In many Latino Spanish-speaking immigrant families, moral education is emphasized more than literacy education. It may be more important to the parents that the child engages in proper respectful behaviors than to develop academic skills (see Chapter 1). This lack of congruence between the practices and expecta-tions of teachers and the parents may create variations in children's behav-iors and performances in ECE classrooms.

LANGUAGE COMPETENCE OF THE CHILD ENTERING EARLY CHILDHOOD EDUCATION CLASSROOMS

The participants in cultural communities, including children in home cul-tural communities, are actively constructing practices. Children's practices vary not only as they develop but also due to their individual temperaments, attributes, and interests. Of particular importance to the topic of classroom experiences of Spanish–English DLL children are variations in language competence as children enter the classrooms. Two types of language competence are relevant: vocabulary knowledge in either English or Spanish and English language knowledge and fluency.

Vocabulary Knowledge

Several authors in this book who assessed children's preacademic knowledge using the Spanish or English versions of the Peabody Picture Vocabulary Test (PPVT; Dunn & Dunn, 1997) or its Spanish equivalent, Test de Vocabulario en Imágenes Peabody (TVIP) (Dunn, Padilla, Lugo, & Dunn, 1986). Across all chapters, standardized vocabulary scores in both languages tended to be low with a wide range. This suggests that one challenge for teachers in ECE classrooms serving Spanish–English DLL children is that, in general, children do not have large enough vocabularies to make fluent conversational talk in either language. The wide range of vocabulary scores suggest that teacher–child talk in whole groups—for example, circle time—could easily be dominated by the more expressive children. Teachers would need to be particularly attentive to the silent children in these situations. The low scores and wide range further suggest that teachers need to emphasize individual child–teacher conversations rather than whole-group responses. The descriptive data proved in this volume paint an opposite picture of current classrooms. Instead, classrooms provide relatively infrequent opportunities for teacher–child conversation (see Chapters 1, 2, and 5–7).

English Language Knowledge and Fluency

Spanish–English DLL children have widely varying scores on the Pre-Las instrument used to assess English language knowledge and fluency (Duncan & De Avila, 1998). As pointed out by Freedson et al. (Chapter 7), children who fail to achieve a minimum threshold of oral English proficiency by kindergarten may never catch up to their native-English-speaking peers in English reading. Moreover, many formal schools are English only, and there is a perception by many parents and teachers that children will fare better if they learn English earlier. This means that ECE classrooms often have as a goal English proficiency and a huge variation in English proficiency and knowledge within their children. This variation, along with other related belief systems, influences the language of instruction in ECE classrooms. Vitello et al. (Chapter 3) report that for children who enter ECE classrooms with very low English proficiency have the lowest likelihood of becoming English proficient. For these children, less instruction provided in Spanish may be better for their ability to attain proficiency in English, but only within the classrooms that have instructional climates characterized by rich, elaborate instruction be-tween children and teachers. This finding illustrates the delicate balance in ECE classrooms between the individual dual language competence of the children, the instructional and emotional climate of the classroom, and the language(s) the teachers use in engaging children in vocabulary-rich interactions.

CHARACTERISTICS OF THE TEACHER

It has long been known that variations in teacher beliefs, knowledge, and teaching expertise are important influences on children's experiences in ECE classrooms. These variations are, of course, important for Spanish–English DLL children. The chapters in this volume have highlighted some additional characteristics of teachers that are particularly important for these classrooms. These characteristics include teachers' beliefs about and knowledge of children's home cultural community, language and liter-acy development, language use in the classroom, and the issue of ethnic and language match between teachers and children.

Beliefs About and Knowledge of Children's Home Cultural Community

Teachers in ECE may be challenged by disparities between their own home and professional cultural communities and those of the children they teach (Howes, 2010). Despite ECE professional organizations' rather strong stands against bias and for recognizing the strengths of different families, particularly families who are poor and not from the dominant culture, professional development for ECE teachers traditionally has been mixed both with regard to helping teachers recognize their own beliefs and biases regarding children and families unlike their own and with the need to combat bias. Many teachers have few skills for working with dif-ferent and often challenged and challenging families. Garcia (see the Introduction to this volume) suggests that teachers can start by recogniz-ing and using the home resources of Spanish–English dual language chil-dren in their classrooms.

Beliefs About and Knowledge of Language and Literacy Development

Teachers in ECE classrooms are more effective when they have a deep knowledge of children's development of language and literacy (Mashburn, Downer, Hamre, Justice, & Pianta, 2010). However, as pointed out by Solari et al. (Chapter 2), instructional methods for DLL children may dif-fer from teachers' general knowledge. For example, teachers of DLLs need to understand when using children's home language is more effective for literacy development than using English and when building on home language knowledge either facilitates or challenges the learning of English. Freedson et al. (Chapter 7) also describes a variety of instructional strategies that support English acquisition in Spanish–English DLL that may be used by teachers with only limited knowledge of the children's home language. As is discussed subsequently, observations within ECE classrooms with DLL children report very low frequencies of these instructional supports and strategies, raising concerns about their focus in ECE teacher preparation.

Beliefs and Knowledge About Language Use in the Classroom

Few issues in the field of education are as emotionally and politically salient as the use of English in classrooms for DLL children. Freedson et al. (Chapter 7) provide a historical view of this debate and a review of the research literature relevant for young DLLs. On the basis of this review, the authors suggest that children benefit from language and literacy skills in both their home language and in English. In contrast to this conclusion, Freedson et al. observed high levels of teacher negative attitudes toward using Spanish ECE classrooms for Spanish–English DLL children. Not only did teachers not speak the language, but they also did not value the children's home language. The implications of this work suggest that teachers require more professional development in respecting and using children's home language.

Issue of Ethnic and Language Match

A second somewhat contentious issue in ECE classrooms is the issue of ethnic and language match between children and teachers. Jung et al. (Chapter 4) argue that this match may be particularly important for Spanish–English DLL children both for facilitating home language development and teacher–child relationships. However, Latino teachers in ECE home literacy programs for very low income Spanish–English DLL reported more conflict in their relationships with children than did non-Latino teachers. The authors argue that Latino teachers' cultural knowledge of children's expected behaviors in school might make teachers more sensitive to and upset by children's speaking Spanish rather than English in a classroom intended to increase English proficiency. Using Spanish may have been seen as disrespectful to teachers.

Certainly ECE professional organizations have emphasized the importance of providing some instruction in home language for children who have limited English proficiency. This is often interpreted as having native-language-speaking teachers in the classroom. Atkins-Burnett et al. (Chapter 5) report that this policy often results in having low-status native-language adults serving as assistants or aides in the classroom with higher status English-only teachers, a policy that could be interpreted as children learning Spanish as a second-class language. These findings highlight the problems of using language and ethnic categories as markers rather than examining the behaviors and interactions of teachers and children. A more complex analysis of the roles of race, ethnicity, and home language within ECE classrooms suggests that the presence of a respectful appreciation of children's home cultural communities is a better predictor of teacher–child relationships than ethnic and language match (Howes, 2010).

CHARACTERISTICS OF THE CLASSROOM

Central to this volume is the classroom domain. All of the chapters have described classroom experiences of DLL children. All seven chapters have described detailed observational coding schemes for classrooms for DLL children. In each case, demographic characteristics of the children in the classroom—for example, proportion of DLL children—are also collected. Table 8.1 provides a schematic of observed categories within each instrument. Five instruments are rated at the classroom level, and all observe the quality of language and literacy instruction. The Classroom Assessment of Supports for Emergent Bilingual Acquisition (CASEBA; Freedson, Figueras-Daniel, & Frede, 2009) and the Bilingual-Teacher Behavior Rating Scale (B-TBRS; Solari, Landry, Crawford, Gunnewig, & Swank, 2009) rate the quality of instruction specific to DLL children, whereas the Classroom Assessment Scoring System (CLASS; La Paro, Pianta, Hamre, & Stuhlman, 2001) and the Early Childhood Environment Rating Scale–Revised (ECERS-R; Harms, Clifford, & Cryer, 1998) are more general ratings of classroom process quality. Four instruments record behaviors at the child level and one at the teacher level. In all cases, rating at the child level involves recording the language of the interaction. The Language Interaction Snapshot (LISn; Atkins-Burnett, Sprachman, & Caspe, 2010) also includes the person (teacher or aide) who is engaged with the child. The type of talk and the activity settings are recorded in each instrument at the teacher or child level. The coding categories within the type of talk or instructional strategies are consistent across instruments and map onto research literature on language and literacy learning of DLL children.

Although all of these instruments have impressive reliability and validity data, the descriptions that emerge from these observational measures paint a relatively dismal picture of the contemporary classroom environments provided for DLL children. In terms of classroom rating schemes, Fuligni and Howes (Chapter 1) report very low average CLASS instructional climate scores in classrooms serving predominantly Spanish–English DLL children.

Table 8.1. Classroom observational measures

Measure	Chapter	Unit observed	Language of instruction	Spanish with whom	Type of talk	Activity setting	Quality of instruction
CLASS	1, 3, 4, 5	Classroom					X
ECERS-R	1, 7	Classroom					X
CASEBA	7	Classroom	X				X
B-TBRS	2	Classroom	X		X	X	X
OMLIT	6	Teacher Classroom Child	X		X	X	X
EAS	1, 3, 4	Child	X		X	X	
LISn	5	Child	X	X	X	X	

Key: B-TBRS, Bilingual-Teacher Behavior Rating Scale (Solari, Landry, Crawford, Gunnewig, & Swank, 2009); CASEBA, Classroom Assessment of Supports for Emergent Bilingual Acquisition (Freedson, Figueras-Daniel, & Frede, 2009); CLASS™, Classroom Assessment Scoring System™ (La Paro, Pianta, Hamre, & Stuhlman, 2001); EAS, Emerging Academics Snapshot (Ritchie, Howes, Kraft-Sayre, & Weiser, 2001); ECERS-R, Early Childhood Environment Rating Scale–Revised (Harms, Clifford, & Cryer, 1998); OMLIT, Observation Measures of Language and Literacy Instruction (Goodson, Layzer, Smith, & Rimdzius, 2004); LISn, Language Interaction Snapshot (Atkins-Burnett, Sprachman, & Caspe, 2010).

Freedson et al. (Chapter 7) report ECERS-R scores in the good range but very low scores on the CASEBA for items particularly related to teacher encouragement of language and literacy development in children's home language. Turning to child ratings, Fuligni and Howes (Chapter 1) report that children spend low proportions of time engaged in literacy activities. Atkins-Burnett et al. (Chapter 5) report few decontextualized adult–child talk in any language and very low incidence of sustained conversation.

Vitello et al. (Chapter 3) provide evidence that CLASS factor structures are similar in classrooms serving the general population and classrooms serving differential proportions of DLL children. Likewise, both Fuligni and Howes (Chapter 1) and Layzer and Maree (Chapter 6) report that although the linguistic composition of the classroom seems to be strongly associated with the language use in the classrooms, the instructional strategies and children's preacademic outcomes are not. These findings are consistent with prior research that finds that common measures of classroom quality and instructional strategies tend to be valid for DLL children. Solari et al. (Chapter 2) and Freedson et al. (Chapter 7) modify this general conclusion by suggesting that more complex descriptions of classrooms for DLL children require additional measures sensitive to the learning experiences of bilingual children.

The work reported in this volume has begun the task of developing observational instruments to capture the language and literacy experiences of DLL children in preschool classrooms. The next step in this program of research is to examine associations between features of classrooms, instructional strategies, and children's preacademic outcomes. There are promising preliminary results in this area, where theoretically expected associations are emerging. (See Chapters 1–4 and 6.)

INSTITUTIONAL PRACTICES OF EDUCATIONAL SYSTEMS

The final domain influencing classroom experiences of DLL children is institutional practices. Language use in classrooms, particularly English only or home language, is increasingly dictated at the school district or even state level (see the Introduction to this volume). The chapters in this volume suggest that the use of home language in the classroom does make a positive difference in children's experiences (see the Introduction and Chapters 3, 6, and 7).

Whereas these chapters have focused on languages spoken by children and teachers during instructional activities, in the Introduction, Garcia suggests that future directions in observational research could include identifying the language use of teachers, DLL children, and their peers to study two-way immersion programs. With minor modifications, all of the child-based observational systems could accommodate this change.

Assessment of DLL children's language and literary skills is important for placement of children within an educational system (see the Introduction to this volume). Assessment becomes particularly important as children make the transition between preschool or prekindergarten and kindergarten and in monitoring children's development in both language systems (see Chapters 1 and 2). The goal is for children to have language and literacy skills in both their home language and English, not to lose the home language and only retain English.

FINAL THOUGHTS

This third National Center for Research on Early Childhood Education volume focuses on preschool-age children who are simultaneously learning two languages, English and their home language—usually Spanish. Each of the seven studies reported in this volume collected observational data in the early education classrooms of children identified as DLLs. Taken together, these chapters describe contemporary educational practices within ECE classrooms of DLL children and examine how best to measure the experiences of these children. These classroom experiences interact with children's own characteristics and home cultural communities, the attributes of their teachers, and the institutional practices of their school systems to predict preacademic readiness for school.

REFERENCES

Atkins-Burnett, S., Sprachman, S., & Caspe, M. (2010). *Language Interaction Snapshot End of Visit Ratings (LISn EVR)*. Princeton, NJ: Mathematica Policy Research.

Duncan, S., & De Avila, E. (1998). *Pre-LAS*. Montgomery, CA: McGraw-Hill.

Dunn, L.M., & Dunn, L.M. (1997). *Peabody Picture Vocabulary Test (PPVT)*. Circle Pines, MN: American Guidance Service.

Dunn, L.M., Lugo, D.E., Padilla, E.R., & Dunn, L.M. (1986). *Test de Vocabulario en Imágenes Peabody: Adaptacion Hispanoamericana (TVIP)*. Circle Pines, MN: American Guidance Service.

Freedson, M., Figueras-Daniel, A., & Frede, E. (2009). *The Classroom Assessment of Supports for Emergent Bilingual Acquisition (CASEBA)*. New Brunswick, NJ: National Institute for Early Education Research.

Goodson, B.D., Layzer, C., Smith, W.C., & Rimdzius, T. (2004). *Observation Measures of Language and Literacy Instruction (OMLIT)*. Developed under contract ED-01-CO-0120, as administered by the Institute of Education Sciences, U.S. Department of Education, with Westat as the prime contractor.

Harms, T., Clifford, R.M., & Cryer, D. (1998). *Early Childhood Environment Rating Scale–Revised (ECERS-R)*. New York: Teachers College Press.

Howes, C. (2010). *Culture and child development in early childhood education: Practices for quality education and care*. New York: Teachers College Press.

Howes, C., Wishard Guerra, A.G., & Zucker, E. (2007). Cultural communities and parenting in Mexican-heritage families. *Parenting: Science and Practice*, 7, 1–36.

Landry, S.H., Crawford, A., Gunnewig, S., & Swank, P.R. (2002). *Teacher Behavior Rating Scale (TBRS)*. Unpublished research instrument, Center for Improving the Readiness of Children for Learning and Education, University of Texas Health Science Center at Houston.

La Paro, K., Pianta, R.C., Hamre, B., & Stuhlman, M. (2001). *Early Elementary Classroom Quality Observation System.* Charlottesville: University of Virginia.

Mashburn, A., Downer, J., Hamre, B., Justice, L., & Pianta, R.C. (2010). Consultation for teachers and children's language and literacy development during pre-kindergarten. *Applied Developmental Science, 14,* 179–196.

Ritchie, S., Howes, C.H., Kraft-Sayre, M., & Weiser, B. (2001). *Emergent Academics Snapshot Scale (EAS).* Unpublished measure, University of California, Los Angeles.

Rogoff, B. (2003). *The cultural nature of human development.* New York: Oxford University Press.

Solari, E.J., Landry, S.H., Crawford, A., Gunnewig, S., & Swank, P.R. (2009). *Bilingual-Teacher Behavior Rating Scale (B-TBRS).* Unpublished research instrument. Children's Learning Institute, University of Texas Health Science Center at Houston.

Index

Tables, figures, and exhibits are indicated by *t*, *f*, and *e* respectively

271